Safe Enough?
Managing Risk and Regulation

1

Safe Enough?

Managing Risk and Regulation

EDITED BY LAURA JONES

The Fraser Institute

Vancouver   British Columbia   Canada

2000

Printed in Canada.

Canadian Cataloguing in Publication Data

Main entry under title:

Safe enough?

Includes bibliographical references.
ISBN 0-88975-208-7

1. Health risk assessment. 2. Environmental risk assessment. 3. Risk management. 4. Safety regulations. I. Jones, Laura, 1970- II. Fraser Institute (Vancouver, B.C.)

HM1101.S33 2000   363.1   C00-910918-8

Contents

3   Too Safe?

About the Authors

H. STERLING BURNETT is the Senior Policy Analyst with the National Center for Policy Analysis, a non-partisan, non-profit, research and education institute in Dallas, Texas. Mr. Burnett has an M.A. in Applied Philosophy from Bowling Green State University and expects to receive his Ph.D. in Applied Philosophy in 2000. He specializes in environmental ethics. He has been published in *Ethics, Environmental Ethics, International Studies in Philosophy, The World and I,* and the *USA Today.*

LAURA JONES is the Director of Environment and Regulatory Studies at The Fraser Institute. She joined The Fraser Institute in 1996 to develop the Institute's policy on the environment. During 1997, she edited *Fish or Cut Bait! The Case for Individual Transferable Quotas in the Salmon Fishery of British Columbia* and *Global Warming: The Science and the Politics.* Ms Jones has also published articles in *Fraser Forum, The Vancouver Sun,* the *Ottawa Citizen,* and the *Financial Post.* She is the author of *Crying Wolf? Public Policy on Endangered Species in Canada* and was a co-author of the first and second editions of *Environmental Indicators for Canada and the United States,* a Fraser Institute Critical Issues Bulletin. She received her B.A. in Economics from Mount Holyoke College in Massachusetts, and her M.A. in Economics from Simon Fraser University in British Columbia. Prior to joining the Institute, she taught economics at Coquitlam College and is currently teaching Economic Issues at the British Columbia Institute of Technology.

JOHN C. LUIK has taught philosophy and management studies at a number of universities, has been Senior Associate of the Niagara Institute with responsibility for its work in public policy and leadership and organizational change, and has worked as a consultant for governmental institutions, professional organizations, and corporations in the United States, Europe, Asia, Africa, the Middle East and Latin America.

He was educated on a Rhodes Scholarship at the University of Oxford where he obtained his B.A., M.A. and D.Phil. degrees. His academic interests include public policy, particularly the use of science in policy and the question of government intervention to change risky behaviours, the ethics of advertising and business, and philosophy. He is a frequent media commentator and conference speaker and the author of numerous articles and several books. His most recent publications include: The Assault on Pleasure: Health Promotion and Engineering the Human Soul, Pandora's Box: The Dangers of Corrupted Science for Democratic Public Policy, *Smokescreen: Passive Smoking and Public Policy*, I Can't Help Myself: Addiction as Ideology, *Advertising and Markets*, Humanism, and The Problem of Permission for Pleasure in a Democratic Society. Most recently, he is the co-author with Gio Gori of the book, *Passive Smoke: The EPA's Betrayal of Science and Policy*, published by The Fraser Institute

LYDIA MILJAN is the Director for the Alberta Initiative of The Fraser Institute. She holds a Ph.D. in political science specializing in politics and the media from the University of Calgary. Her dissertation, which will be published in fall, 2000, is a survey of Canadian journalists and will provide the first publicly available survey of French and English journalists compared with how the news is reported.

Dr Miljan is also the Director of the National Media Archive at the Fraser Institute. She has been at the Fraser Institute since 1988. One of her first studies at the Institute was a controversial content analysis of CBC television and the *Globe and Mail*'s coverage of the free-trade agreement. Since that initial study, Dr Miljan has conducted over 80 content analyses on television, radio, and newspaper coverage of public-policy issues. Her analysis of issues ranging from free trade to privatization, from health care to women's issues and from elections to referendum campaigns has made her a most sought after media critic. This body of work has been printed in almost every newspaper in the country and she has been a guest on many open-line talk shows and television programs in Canada and the United States.

Dr Miljan's tenure at the National Media Archive has received international recognition as well. She is a member of an international organization, members of which assess media coverage in their own countries. In 1994, Dr Miljan was invited by the British Commonwealth Secretariat to travel to South Africa to help establish a methodology for their monitoring of the South African Election campaign. Her work in that capacity helped to ensure a free and fair electoral process. In 1996, she was awarded the H.B. Earhart Fellowship.

MARK NEAL is Lecturer at Zayed University in the United Arab Emirates. He is currently researching the hidden costs of health, safety, and environmental regulations, particularly those concerning the pharmaceutical, chemical, food, and biotechnology industries. In 1995, he wrote *Keeping Cures from Patients: The Perverse Effects of Pharmaceutical Regulations*, London, Social Affairs Unit. Dr. Neal has further research interests in comparative and international management; he has a Ph.D. in International Management and is the author of *The Culture Factor:*

Cross-Cultural Management and the Foreign Venture (Macmillan Business). Most recently, he was co-author of the book, *The Corporation under Siege: Exposing the Devices Used by Activists and Regulators in the Non-Risk Society* (Social Affairs Unit 1998). He has also carried out extensive research on the gambling industry.

PETER J. NEUMANN is an Assistant Professor of Policy and Decision Sciences in the Department of Health Policy and Management and the Deputy Director of the Program on the Economic Evaluation of Medical Technology at the Harvard School of Public Health. His research focuses on economic evaluations of medical technologies, including ongoing evaluations of pharmacological treatments for Alzheimer's Disease, asthma, lung cancer, and schizophrenia. He has also contributed to the literature on the use of willingness to pay and quality-adjusted life years (QUALYs) in valuing health benefits.

His other research has focused on the Food and Drug Administration's regulation of health-economic information, government uses of cost-effectiveness analysis, and the impact of medical technology on health costs. His articles have appeared in the *New England Journal of Medicine, Health Affairs, Medical Care*, the *Health Care Financing Review*, and many other journals. From 1990 to 1992, Dr. Neumann served as Special Assistant to the Administrator at the Health Care Financing Administration. He received his doctorate in health policy and management from the Harvard School of Public Health.

DOUGLAS POWELL completed a B.Sc. (honors) in molecular biology and genetics at the University of Guelph in 1985 and a doctoral degree in the department of Food Science at the University of Guelph in May 1996, applying risk-communication theory to issues of food safety and agricultural biotechnology. In August 1996, he began an appointment as Director of the Science and Society project at the Universities of Guelph and Waterloo and is currently an assistant professor in the Department of Plant Agriculture at the University of Guelph. Dr Powell is currently director of the five-year Agri-Food Risk Management and Communication project at Guelph, where he leads a diverse research team that integrates scientific knowledge with public perceptions to garner the benefits of a particular agricultural technology or product while managing and mitigating identified risks.

WILLIAM T. STANBURY recently retired from his position as UPS Foundation Professor of Regulation and Competition Policy, Faculty of Commerce and Business Administration, University of British Columbia. He obtained his Ph.D. in economics from the University of California at Berkeley in 1972. Dr. Stanbury has published studies on many areas of government regulation, including airlines, telecommunications, rent control, financing of political parties, forestry, marketing boards, and occupations. In 1989, he won the Jacob Biely and Killam prizes for his research in university-wide competitions.

TAMMY O. TENGS is an Assistant Professor in the departments of Urban and Regional Planning and Environmental Analysis and Design in the School of Social Ecology at the University of California, Irvine, and has been an Assistant Research Professor in the Center for Health Policy at Duke University. She completed her doctorate in Health Policy and Management at the Harvard School of Public Health in 1994. Before entering Harvard, she earned an M.A. in Industrial Engineering and Operations Research at the University of Massachusetts, Amherst, and studied in the Engineering-Economic Systems Department at Stanford University. Dr. Tengs directed the four-year Life-Saving Priorities Project at the Harvard Center for Risk Analysis, supervising a team of 20 that amassed cost-effectiveness data for hundreds of lifesaving interventions. She is the principal author of the papers, Five-hundred Life-Saving Interventions and Their Cost-effectiveness and The Opportunity Costs of Haphazard Societal Investments in Life-saving. When the *Wall Street Journal* published an article based on the Life-Saving project in 1994, about 20 other newspapers followed suit, and since then she has received approximately 1,500 requests for these publications. Dr. Tengs is a "decision scientist." Her research interests include the rational allocation of societal resources devoted to averting premature death and the economic efficiency of investments in science.

WILLIAM G. WATERS, II, is Professor and Chair, Transportation and Logistics, in the Faculty of Commerce and Business Administration at the University of British Columbia. He is also Editor-in-Chief of *Transportation Research E (Logistics and Transportation Review)*, a highly respected international academic journal. Dr. Waters has published extensively, over 100 publications including demand, cost, and productivity analysis in transportation, ocean shipping and bulk logistics systems, railway costing and performance measurement, project evaluation methods and the analysis of public policies.

He has taught 20 different university courses in economics, transportation, public utilities, project evaluation, and relations between government and business. He has held visiting appointments at the Universities of Oxford, Sydney, Tasmania, and Wisconsin. He has served as a consultant to companies large and small, to various governments and other agencies including the World Bank and the Association of American Railroads.

Safe Enough?
Managing Risk and Regulation

Introduction

LAURA JONES

Risks all around us?

Citizens of wealthy countries such as Canada and the United States have become preoccupied with health, safety, and environmental concerns. Even as we go about such ordinary activities as applying deodorant, driving to work, and eating, we worry. "Didn't I read somewhere that deodorants can clog pores and cause cancer?" "Is my car contributing to the global-warming crisis?" "Is there any pesticide residue on these carrots?" "Are they genetically modified?" "Will that second-hand smoke that I was exposed to at lunch make me sick?"

In the first chapter, **Risk Aversion: The Rise of an Ideology,** Mark Neal reminds us that it is a luxury to be concerned about such risks. Until relatively recently people feared death from influenza, tuberculosis, starvation, or, before penicillin, even a simple cut. According to Neal:

> It is ironic that the obsession with health and safety over the last 20 years should come at a time in our history when we are living longer and healthier lives than ever before. If we consider standard indicators of general welfare—maternal death in childbirth, infant mortality, income per capita, death from infectious diseases, average life-span—it is plain that we have never had it so good. (Neal: 16).

But, it is hard to remember that we have never had it so good when it seems that we hear another story about how everything from baby toys to cell phones cause cancer every time we turn on the television. We rely heavily on the media for our information about health, safety, and environmental issues. As Lydia Miljan explains in **Unknown Causes, Unknown Risks**: "About half of the 1500 respondents in a survey by Health Canada said they receive 'a lot' of information on risk from the media and about 35 percent said they receive a 'fair' amount. Physicians, the next most popular source, give only about a quarter of the respondents 'a lot' of information" (Miljan: 32). Dr Miljan goes on to explain how media coverage systematically distorts our perception of risk by focusing on unusual occurrences, alleging consensus among scientists where none exists, and relying heavily on interest groups for information.

Case studies in risk management

As we have become more affluent our demand for safety has increased. We no longer tolerate risks that were accepted as unavoidable as recently as 50 years ago. Of course, this decreased tolerance for risk is not in and of itself undesirable. But, it has made us susceptible to scares based on junk science. These scares can be costly and counterproductive. The next four chapters of the book explore specific examples of how risks associated with transportation, second-hand smoke, toys, and food have been handled. The studies illustrate how the media, interest groups, and government departments can affect our perceptions of risk and influence regulatory decision making.

In **Science and Policy in the Economic Assessment of Transport Regulations**, William G. Waters examines risk regulation in the transportation sector including the American regulations on fuel economy for automobiles, the 55-mph speed limit, and automotive airbags. His conclusion applies broadly to all policy debates:

> Policies, however good their intention, will set changes in motion as people respond to the new environment and its signals. In some cases, the behavourial response might thwart the policy intention completely. More typically, it will reduce but not eliminate the desired policy outcomes. In almost every case, this means that policies cannot be as effective as we desired, unless the behavourial responses are anticipated in the design and coordination of policy packages. (Waters: 68)

In some of Waters' examples, policy makers have considered the unintended consequences of their proposals. A proposal requiring infants traveling on airplanes to have their own seat rather than sit on a par-

ent's lap was abandoned after policy makers realized that it would require that parents purchase an additional ticket, which would make
them more likely, at least on short routes, to drive. Since driving is not
as safe as flying, the regulation would have been counterproductive.
Waters shows that in other cases, however, the unintended consequences of regulations affecting the transportation sector were not adequately considered. Following the fuel crises in the 1970s, Americans
tried to increase the fuel economy of automobiles through regulations
by introducing Corporate Average Fuel Economy (CAFE) standards.
What was the consequence of these new rules?

> The goal of increasing fuel economy (whether by regulation or
> price mechanisms) sets forces into motion that alter the design of
> vehicles. In this case, increased fuel economy led to smaller and
> lighter vehicles. But, there is a significant correlation between the
> size of a vehicle and personal safety in crashes. Crandall and Gra-
> ham (1989) estimate that the down-sizing of cars to meet fuel-
> economy standards resulted in a 14 percent to 27 percent reduc-
> tion in safety. (Waters: 60–61)

By introducing regulations to address one policy concern (using
too much gasoline) risks in another area (safety) were excacerbated.
While economists are trained to recognize these risk-for-risk trade-
offs, decision makers in policy often are not. The unfortunate and unintended result of introducing policies without considering these
trade-offs can be an overall increase in risk.

In **Second-hand Smoke and Cancer: The Research Evidence**,
John Luik examines on how science and policy can be distorted by the
actions of interest groups and a regulatory agency. Despite the lack of
scientific evidence linking second-hand smoke with lung cancer in non-
smokers, the majority of the public now believe that such a risk exists
and many governments are regulating smoking as if it poses such a risk.
Dr Luik looks at two cases, the court case against the United States Environmental Protection Agency (EPA), where the EPA's classification
of second-hand smoke as a human carcinogen was overturned, and the
1998 study by the International Agency for Research on Cancer (IARC)
that did not find a statistically significant link between lung cancer and
second-hand smoke. "In the first instance, the public-health community and the anti-smoking movement manufactured a health risk and, in
the second instance, they attempted to discredit their own scientific
study when it failed to support their manufactured risk" (Luik: 74).
Dr Luik shows in detail how these cases "reveal the same key characteristics of junk science—the misrepresentation of scientific findings,

the misrepresentation of scientific procedure, and the desire, at all costs, to suppress dissent in the service of junk policy" (Luik: 74).

The next chapter, **Much Ado about (Almost) Nothing: Greenpeace and the Allegedly Toxic Teethers and Toys,** by William T. Stanbury focuses more specifically on the tactics of interest groups. Stanbury's study of Greenpeace's "Play Safe" campaign, which tried to eliminate polyvinylchloride (PVC) from children's toys, illustrates how sophisticated some anti-risk activists have become. He notes that Greenpeace's tactics to gain media visibility during the campaign, which began in the fall of 1997, included hanging banners at toy stores, removing toys from shelves, confronting store managers, and interrupting the annual meeting of the International Council of Toy Industries in Toronto to demand the withdrawal of PVC toys from shelves. Greenpeace also pressured leading retailers such as Toys 'R' Us, Walmart and Zellers by sending them letters demanding they stop selling all soft PVC infant toys. Professor Stanbury points out that many of these tactics were copied from similar campaigns against PVC toys in Europe and that the Campaign waged in Canada was only part of a well-orchestrated international campaign: "The multinational approach gives the appearance of international or even worldwide concern. It also increases the odds that one government will 'crack' under pressure and take action along the lines proposed by Greenpeace. Greenpeace then treats this as a 'precedent' or example for other countries" (Stanbury: 124).

By attracting media attention through its stunts in Canada, Greenpeace pressured the regulatory agency, in this case Health Canada, into action. Stanbury explains how the dynamic in this and other risk controversies works.

> Greenpeace's skill in initiating and advancing risk controversies is able to create enormous pressures on governments and other established organizations. They must respond in some fashion, no matter how ridiculous the claim by an interest group, particularly if that group can claim some scientific support for its position. (Stanbury: 126)

Stanbury concludes that from Greenpeace's perspective the campaign was successful in terms of attracting sufficient media attention to convince many parents to stop buying PVC toys and convincing many toy sellers worldwide to "voluntarily" stop selling PVC toys. Supporters of rational public policy lost this battle:

> [G]overnments in a number of nations, by banning phthalates in toys and teethers, over-reacted to a minute risk of a modest harm.

This was another example of weak risk management in the face of a skilled and determined interest group. Fear of harm to children created sufficient fear of political repercussions in a number of countries to result in over-regulation. Thus, rationality in policy-making took another beating. (Stanbury: 129).

Finally in this section, Douglas Powell, in **Genetically Engineered Angst: From Frankenstein to Frankenfoods**, describes how a "combination of scientific *naïveté*, media hyperbole, and allegations of corporate conspiracy" have come to characterize public discussions of genetically engineered foods. Powell explains how the evidence that genetically engineered foods are often better for the environment, contain lower levels of natural toxins, and are rigorously tested has been eclipsed by irrational rhetoric about "frankenfoods." He concludes: "Appropriate levels of risk management coupled with sound science and excellent communication about the nature of risk are required to garner further benefits of any technology, including agricultural biotechnology" (Powell: 149).

Too Safe?

The last four chapters in the book look more generally at regulatory decision-making designed to reduce risk. In **Progress at Risk: Using the Precautionary Principle as a Standard for Regulatory Policy**, H. Sterling Burnett takes a critical look at using the precautionary principle as a guide to regulatory decision making. The principle has been interpreted to mean that no new technology or product should be used until it is proven that it poses no threat to human health or the environment. It has the familiar appeal of an adage we all know well: "better safe than sorry." Although it is increasingly being used in legislation and international treaties, Mr Burnett warns:

> While the precautionary principle may sound reasonable in theory, it would be disastrous if practised. One cannot prove a negative. Every food (including organic foods), product, and tool poses some risk of harm. Without the use of fire, automobiles, antibiotics, coffee, water, salt, and chlorine—to name just a few natural and human-created foods, application, and tools—human life, in the words of the philosopher Thomas Hobbes, "would be nasty, poor, brutish, and short." (Burnett: 156)

Our quest for a risk-free society, if carried too far, could lead us back to a miserable existence.

The next two papers look at the use of cost-effectiveness in regulatory decision-making. First, in **Dying Too Soon: How Cost-**

Effectiveness Analysis Can Save Lives, Tammy O. Tengs looks at how making better use of cost-effectiveness information in public-policy decision-making could increase the number of life-years that are saved. Not surprisingly, she finds that currently the cost-effectiveness of regulation varies dramatically among government departments. For example, she shows that the median regulation proposed by the US Environmental Protection Agency costs 100 times more per year of life saved than the median proposed safety standard for highway safety or consumer products. "Because of this haphazard pattern of investment, government regulations save fewer lives than they might, given the resources consumed, and consume more resources than necessary, given the survival benefits offered" (Tengs: 184). Tengs evaluates the cost-effectiveness of 139 government regulations that consumed $4.11 billion annually and saved 94,000 years of life. She shows that the same $4.11 billion invested in the most cost-effective regulations could save more than twice as many years of life—211,000 rather than 94,000 annually. She concludes: "Because we fail to base public health decisions on cost-effectiveness, we sacrifice many lives every year. Allowing cost-effectiveness to inform those decisions will improve the allocation of scarce life-saving resources" (Tengs: 185).

Given the almost incredible increases in the number of years of life that could be saved if resources were allocated according to cost-effectiveness criteria, the obvious question is why it is not used more? In **The Reluctance to Use Cost-Effectiveness Analysis in Regulatory Decision-Making**, Peter J. Neumann addresses this question. He identifies a number of barriers to the explicit use of cost-effectiveness analysis including lack of training for decision-makers on how to use cost-effectiveness analysis and skepticism on the part of decision-makers about the information coming from cost-effectiveness studies sponsored by industry. Decision-makers also identify lack of timely and relevant information as a barrier to using cost-effectiveness information. Neumann reminds us, however, that "[c]onsiderations of cost will always play an important role in health-care decisions, whether they lurk in the shadows or are appraised openly" (Neumann: 192). He suggests that some of the barriers to using cost-effectiveness analysis as a tool in decision-making can be overcome by increasing research activity in the field, ensuring that research adheres to high standards recommended by experts in the field, and establishing mechanisms for independent, third-party review of cost-effectiveness claims.

The book concludes with **Reforming Risk Regulation in Canada: The Next Policy Frontier?** by William T. Stanbury, who outlines an agenda for reforming risk regulation in Canada. Stanbury argues that government management of risk regulation is subject to a number of "routine pathologies." These pathologies include lack of economic analysis, haphazard selection of risks for government action, lack of collaboration between government departments, one-size-fits-all types of government action to deal with risks, and poor risk communication to the public. His specific recommendations to remedy these problems include establishing a government-wide risk-management policy, applying to risk management the same oversight as the Treasury Board now applies to expenditures, increasing the amount of information routinely disclosed about risk-management activities, mandating better analysis of risk, and making a systematic effort to rank risks in terms of their importance and establish priorities for government action.

How safe is safe enough?

As Professor Stanbury points out in the last chapter of this book, risk regulation—that is regulation that attempts to protect human health—has increased dramatically since the 1980s. This book helps us understand why. Attitudes to risk have changed as advances in medicine, sanitation, and agriculture contributed to dramatic improvements in life expectancy throughout the last century. Risks that were once seen as unavoidable are now considered intolerable. Zealous anti-risk activists have heightened our intolerance for small risks and their campaigns often promote product bans or new regulation to reduce the "hazards" that they have identified.

But, risk regulation as it is currently implemented has many pitfalls. In some cases, regulations to address one risk can introduce other risks. In many cases, expenditure to reduce a risk could save many more years of life if spent reducing another risk. These issues are not currently considered by many of the interest groups calling for more risk regulation, the public supporting those calls, or the governments who respond by introducing more regulation. Instead, risk activists and regulators focus on the potential benefits of risk regulation while ignoring the costs.

The chapters in this book help us to understand the importance of considering the costs of regulation and basing decisions about regulation on sound science and economics. They help us to struggle with the difficult question: how safe is safe enough?

1 Risks All around Us

Risk Aversion
The Rise of an Ideology

MARK NEAL

In recent years, there has been a huge increase in concerns about the risks involved in industrial products and processes (see Beck 1992). Over the past three years alone, there have been controversies about biotechnology, pharmaceuticals, nuclear power, overhead power lines, alcohol, tobacco, food additives, silicone breast implants, computer games, toys, fireworks, contraceptive pills, mobile phones, automobiles, sugar, salt, soft drinks, and water purity. The list is seemingly endless. In recent years, we have also witnessed a huge expansion in the number and influence of anti-risk watchdogs, lobby groups, and activists. The exposure, discussion, and elimination of real or potential risks has become a primary political concern. Any risk of disease or death, no matter how small, is newsworthy and the need to eliminate even minor risks goes unquestioned, contributing to a widespread fatalism in the face of ever-tightening health and safety regulations.

Some say we are now living in a "risk society" (Beck 1992), a new era in human history in which industrial development is producing risks that are global in scale and threaten to undermine or even destroy ongoing economic progress. There is much in this line of argument. Certainly, the environmental impact of industry is higher than ever before and there is widespread concern about the risks involved in developments such as biotechnology.

We prefer, however, to talk of the "non-risk society" (Neal and Davies 1998), a combination of cultural, economic, and political developments that has resulted in a widespread obsession with, and intolerance of, any risks, great or small. This ideology of extreme risk aversion is not restricted to industrial products and processes: lighting a cigarette in public is now a risky business in itself as is trying to defend the present regulations for drinking and driving. The culture of risk-aversion is now so strong and so pervasive in western societies that heavy-handed and irrational responses to risk do not concern or surprise us. Risk-aversion has become the both the norm and the key *fin-de-siecle* cultural value.

Aversion to risk now affects all areas of our lives. Most children are now driven to and from school, even though the rate of child homicide is at an all-time low. Smokers are abused and discriminated against for the smoke in the air near others, even though there is little convincing evidence of a link between "passive," environmental tobacco smoke and lung cancer (Nilsson 1997; Johnson and Ulyatt 1991). Genetically engineered foodstuffs are banned from the British Parliament, although there is no evidence that they are at all harmful.

From an historical point of view, we can see just how radical the cultural and political changes have been. Human existence has always been a risky affair and high levels of risk used to be reflected in, and integrated with, the activities and cultures of bygone societies. Even in the early part of this century, the incidence of death in childbirth was high; infant mortality was high; the risk of death in war was high; the risks of death from influenza and tuberculosis were correspondingly high. Before penicillin, a grazed knee or a cut from a dirty knife could mean death and surgery of any kind, even dental surgery, was much more dangerous than it is today. These kinds of "class A" risks have now all but disappeared. The kinds of risks that concern us today would once have been seen as unimportant.

Medicines and risk

The pharmaceutical sector is a good example of an innovative industry where risk assessment, management, and perception are prime concerns. In order to put the current ultra-vigilant climate in its context, consider that the first regulations concerning the development of new medicines were introduced in the United Kingdom only 30 years ago, in the 1968 Medicines Act. Before this, the development of drugs was almost completely unregulated (Neal 1995). Consider as well that adverse drug reactions (ADRs) at this time were more common and more serious than they are today but were understood to be just one among many serious risks to life. Risk was thus an integrated aspect of life—

not one to be eliminated at all costs. Indeed, so strong was the tolerance of risk by recent standards that it took the 1961 Thalidomide tragedy, which resulted in 4,500 deformed children (Burnstall and Reuben 1990; Deutsch, Sjostrom, and Nilsson 1972), to effect a widespread demand for safety regulation.

Even then, the government of the United Kingdom was reluctant to act. In 1964, it set up the Committee on the Safety of Drugs (sometimes called the "Dunlop Committee" after its chairman, Sir Derek Dunlop) to administer and oversee the testing of new medicines but, tellingly, the Committee was given no statutory power to inspect or demand comprehensive testing procedures (Maynard and Hartley 1984). At that period in the history of British society, the establishment of such a committee would usually have been sufficient to assuage public and professional fears about risk. However, the Thalidomide disaster was not a discrete event but an ongoing and highly visible tragedy, as every neighbourhood was forced to witness one or two children growing up with severe disabilities. Eventually, ongoing public disquiet and political agitation led to the more stringent regulations of the 1968 Act (Neal 1995).

The situation in the mid-1960s, therefore, differed markedly from that today, when the Medicines Control Agency, the Committee on the Safety of Medicines, and the European Medicines Evaluation Agency constitute a powerful anti-risk establishment and public anxieties about drug safety are hypersensitive. As was the case with Opren (benoxaprofen) in the early 1980s, the mere whiff of concern about drug safety now leads to sensationalization by the media, public outcry, and political pressure to impose a ban or further regulation. The Opren case was particularly instructive, as the panic resulted in the withdrawal in August 1982 of a highly effective medicine from the market (Inman 1993). Indeed, residual public anxieties about the drug have remained so strong that it has been impossible for the authorities to reintroduce it, regardless of the fact that research has established its safety and efficacy.

The comparison between Thalidomide and Opren demonstrates how far-reaching the changes have been in British society. The Thalidomide tragedy happened in a culture of risk tolerance, wherein anxieties about medicines were largely restricted to expert and political lobby groups. Even after 4,500 children had been damaged, it was very difficult to secure comprehensive safety regulation and the initial response to the tragedy was the establishment of a voluntary scheme friendly to industry. The tragedy thus happened when there was no safety infrastructure and no "culture of fear" (Furedi 1997). Today, the pharmaceutical industry has to cope with a comprehensive safety establishment and infrastructure, a large number of highly motivated lobby groups and industry critics, and a cynical and entrepreneurial army of lawyers who exploit the safety imperative that has developed over the last 30 years. During this period, society has moved from one extreme to another: in the 1960s, it took a real human tragedy to change the system; now it takes only the rumour of harm.

Most industries now have a safety bureaucracy that has the power to test their products, oversee their manufacturing processes and, in the end, ban a product or shut down operations. In addition, most industries have one or more highly organized lobby groups who make it their business to monitor the industry, to demand ever-increasing regulation, and to report any breaches of existing ones. Many industries now also contend with less organized but more energetic activist groups whose primary concern is to ban a specific product, to increase the regulations imposed upon particular industries, or even to shut down a whole industry. An important feature of the modern corporate environment thus consists of existing or potential safety regulations and the influence of lobby groups and activists upon these regulations and upon demand for products.

The rise of the non-risk society

It is ironic that the obsession with health and safety of the last 20 years should come at a time in our history when we are living longer and healthier lives than ever before. If we consider standard indicators of general welfare—maternal death in childbirth, infant mortality, income per capita, death from infectious diseases, average life-span—it is plain that we have never had it so good. It is puzzling, then, that the anti-risk society should have arisen just when we were making the most spectacular progress in all of these areas.

In the old high-risk societies, people were confronted on a daily basis with real and immediate risks to their lives and those of their children. Reading through accounts of the Victorian working classes, one sees that the attitude towards risk was stoic and realistic and an assessment of risks to life and of the strategies for dealing with them were integrated into everyday life. Expectations from life were modest. They had to be, as an accurate assessment of circumstances and prospects was essential for survival. With no welfare state and scarce resources, impractical dreamers were liable to perish.

In western industrial democracies, huge advances have been made in general health and welfare: there have been obvious advances in the effectiveness and availability of medicine; most western countries have welfare states of one form or another, which protect people from absolute poverty; scarcity of food is a thing of the past. Other technological and social changes have contributed to new forms of culture: western societies have become more "open"; television exposes people to a daily dose of beauty, wealth, and physical perfection; and the certainties and restrictions of religious belief have disappeared for most people.

The interrelationship of these changes has meant a shift in the way people understand the relationship between themselves, their circumstances, and their place in society (Neal 1998). An important feature of this has been the on-going expansion of expectations. Every day we are exposed to accounts of instant wealth, instant beauty, instant perfection. People are brought up to seek individual growth, to express themselves with no regard to self-control or restrictions—in other words, to expect health and happiness. It is no coincidence that the rise in aversion to risk should coincide with the rise of "healthism," for the two are related. Everybody, no matter how ugly or physically repulsive, now believes in physical perfectability (Charlton 1998): if only one worked-out twice a week, if only one replaced chips with grated carrots, if only one stuck to a regime of 30 sit-ups a day, one could attain one's birthright, physical attractiveness, health, and longevity.

A related contributory factor in the rise in aversion to risk has been the denial of death (Walter 1994). In the high-risk societies of old, death was integrated into everyday life. People of all ages, mothers, children, and the aged ailed at home and died surrounded by family and friends. Death was a sad business but it was understood and treated realistically. People did not expect to live to a ripe old age nor did they expect their family and friends to do so. When the time came, both caring and dying was integrated into the practicalities and ethos of domestic life, where children were fully exposed to the sights and sounds of expiring relatives and learned not to expect too much of their own lives.

In the twentieth century, due largely to medical advances and the growth of wealth, death has become less common among the young and middle-aged. Most people who die do so now in old age. The threat of death at any age from infection has retreated from most groups in society and people thus expect to live healthy and fulfilling lives and to die when they are old. Death has become segregated as a feature of old age. Furthermore, with the expansion of the health services and the welfare state, dying has become separated from the home. More people now die in hospital rooms that are spatially and symbolically separate from their everyday lives. As a result, the twentieth century has seen the denial of death and dying. From being something expected and integrated within the domestic sphere, death has become increasingly segregated and hidden from view.

This trend has contributed to the development of healthism and aversion to risk in two ways. First, health now resembles a pension-fund as people seek to accumulate "health-credits" during youth and middle-age by doing regular exercise, eating the right foods, and avoiding risk-factors. When they think of it at all, people view their deaths as a function of how virtuous they have been in terms of body maintenance and how vigilant they have been in terms of avoiding "body-attack." Although most prefer not to think of their deaths at all, they are concerned to push the dreadful moment back in time and out of sight.

Second, whereas premature deaths were once commonplace and accepted, such deaths are now seen to be singular atrocities. In the culture that denies death, premature deaths are now so shocking that they make potent media stories and can become the focus of angry campaigns. One such case involved Leah Betts, who died in 1995 as a result of taking a tablet of Ecstasy (Methylenedioxymethamphetamine or MDMA). Whereas death at this age through infection or accident would once have been commonplace, in the 1990s it was shocking. As Douglas (1992) and Douglas and Wildavsky (1982) have observed, when risky events happen, blame tends to follow. In the early days of the Leah Betts tragedy, everybody concerned with her death—her parents, their lawyers, and the media—pinned the blame on the tablet of Ecstasy and, thus, on the person who had supplied her with the drug. Very soon, however, the blame shifted to a problem with the system of educating young people about drugs. Within a week of her funeral, Leah Betts became the mascot of an anti-drugs campaign that used her premature death to shock those who might be tempted to take drugs. One particularly tasteless campaign used a poster showing Leah Betts and the slogan "Sorted," drug-culture jargon for having been supplied with drugs for the night (Saunders 1997).

The shock value of premature deaths is now such that blame is not restricted to immediate circumstances but becomes a resource for wider campaigning. If a child dies from leukaemia or a woman of middle age dies from a thrombosis, those related to the victims are unlikely to face these singular tragedies with the stoicism of old. The first question on the lips of the bereaved is still "Why?" but the second question is now "Who or what is to blame for this?" In the death-denying, anti-risk culture that exists today, the answer to these questions is invariably that there is a problem with the "system."

A child runs out in front of a fast-moving truck. In the 1930s, such an event may have been met with grim stoicism. Child mortality was higher and there was much more of a sense that "these things happen." Today, however, grief is met with the conviction that no child should ever be run over, that such an event is avoidable and, indeed, immoral. The stoic acceptance that such things happen will have been replaced with a conviction that the child has been let down by "the system":

trucks are allowed to drive too fast through the town centre; there is absence of speed bumps on that particular stretch of road; there should be a crossing-guard on that corner in school hours. The next question, "Who is to blame for this?" leads the bereaved to point the finger at those responsible for flaws in the traffic-control system.

Likewise, if a woman dies from a thrombosis—something that has happened to generations of women—the bereaved are unlikely to accept that such things can happen spontaneously. Because premature death is unexpected nowadays, there is the feeling that something must have caused this to happen. The system let the woman down. If no active cause can be found, then the question becomes "what allowed this to happen?" The reason for death can thus be cast in terms of neglect—too few check-ups or blood checks, for example—and the blame can be attributed to a lack of vigilance on the part of the medical authorities. This can lead to a lawsuit or a campaign against the negligent bodies. If a possible active cause can be identified, however, then blame can be assigned directly both to the suppliers and to the regulators. If the woman had been taking an oral contraceptive, for instance, then blame can be assigned both to the manufacturers for providing the product and to the regulatory authorities for allowing it to be sold. The possibility that the contraceptive was either unrelated to the death or contributed only partially to it is neither here nor there. Increasingly there is no such thing as a blame-free premature death.

The rise of the health and safety establishment

Along with the rise of healthism, aversion to risk, and denial of death, there has been an explosion in healthist and anti-risk bureaucracies, anti-industry lobby groups, and industry-specific activists. These bodies are important features of non-risk society and culture and sustain the widespread cultural values of avoiding risk and denying death. In turn, they themselves are validated and sustained by these values.

The blueprint for intervention by large-scale health-and-safety bureaucracies was established in the municipal works of the mid-nineteenth century (Davies 1995). Throughout the late nineteenth and early twentieth centuries, however, the power and influence of such bodies was limited: the *laissez-faire* attitude towards commerce and risk and regulation remained strong so that Britain remained a high-risk culture up until 1945. During the same period, expectations concerning health and death remained low until the establishment of the welfare state and the National Health Service, which enshrined the principle that the state should be responsible for ensuring the health and welfare of its people. At first, the health bureaucracies controlled by the state were overwhelmingly concerned with treating injury and illness and overseeing death. Over the years of expansion, however, the institutions have increasingly developed a secondary concern, prevention.

The public-service sector has always attracted people whose political views are left of centre. This is understandable as the notion of community and public service is at the heart of socialist and communitarian ideologies. The growth of the new bureaucracies overseeing health, welfare, and safety and the increase in the number of regulators thus provided attractive employment opportunities for those with altruistic philosophies concerned with "equalizing," "helping," "empowering," or "saving" people. The "Long March" to the regulatory health, welfare, and safety bureaucracies thus began as soon as they were established and has continued to this day.

Partly due to their political constituency and partly because their primary concern was to ensure public health and safety, such organizations have traditionally been unsympathetic to industry. As we have seen in the case of the Dunlop Committee, until the mid-1960s the influence of most regulatory bodies was modest compared to the power they wield today. In the wake of scandals such as the Thalidomide tragedy, the asbestos controversy, and the establishment of the link between tobacco and lung cancer, however, the view grew that industry was taking unnecessary risks with workers and consumers and should be more tightly regulated. Since the 1970s, industrial processes and products in Britain have been ever more tightly controlled by domestic and European regulators. The health-and-safety bureaucracies and regulators have proved to be largely unsympathetic both to the need to sustain consumer demand for particular products and to the costs that increased regulations impose upon industry. Ironically, perhaps, the time of the greatest expansion of health-and-safety bureaucracies and regulatory bodies was in the 1980s, when Chicago-School style economics seemed to be winning the day and there was a true collapse in the egalitarian ideologies that had sustained many in the trade unions and the public sector for so long. Over the 1980s and into the 1990s, there has been a huge expansion in bureaucratic power. In an era when conservative politicians espoused deregulation, the health-and-safety bureaucracies and regulators quietly issued regulation after regulation, increasingly responding not just to established risks but also to "potential risks." From 1979 to 1989, the main threat to economic liberalism shifted quite clearly from the Soviet Union and the resistance of organized workers to the systematic regulation and bureaucratization of industry in the name of health and safety.

The "bureaucratic ratchet"

Once a critical mass of bureaucracy was established, a regulatory dynamic—which we term the "bureaucratic ratchet"—set in. The first feature of this concerns blame in the event of injury. When somebody is damaged by an industrial product or process, people look around for someone or something to blame. As we have seen, in the non-risk society blame is typically two-pronged. The first kind of blame—*blame for commission*—is directed at the manufacturers of the harmful process or product. The regulatory authorities do not mind this kind of blame. Indeed, through fingering companies or through general campaigning, they often actually encourage it. The second kind of blame—*blame for omission*—however, is more often directed at the regulators. If an industrial product or process is found to be harmful, then people blame not only the provider but the regulator as well. Those concerned with the victim or victims berate and even sue the regulators for not having regulated this particular risk out of existence.

As a result, there is an incentive for regulators to "play safe." It is their job to keep the public from harm from a particular industrial process or product. If they fail to do so, it is not only the industry but they who are in the firing line. Another feature of the bureaucratic ratchet that leads to greater and greater regulation concerns the job of the regulators. Health-and-safety regulators are employed to ensure health and safety. They have a mission. If they are to progress in their chosen career, they have to be seen to have achieved something. Leaving existing regulations intact achieves nothing. Understandably, as regulators are paid to regulate particular industries, this is precisely what they do. For them to do nothing might well be the best thing for the industry, its workers, and its consumers. Because of their brief, however, the regulators simply cannot do this. So, they have meetings; they "liaise" with other health-and-safety executives; they fly to Brussels to discuss harmonization and pan-European directives; they commission research to find undiscovered risk factors; if such are revealed, they publicize them and seek a mandate for ever more stringent regulations. This is not to criticize such professionals; they are doing what society pays them to do and that is to regulate.

Although there is a tendency among regulators to "play safe" so that they cannot be blamed for the sin of omission, they may nevertheless benefit from harm being done to people by industrial products and processes. Should one or a number of people be harmed or killed by an industrial product, it invariably ensures a popular mandate for a further tightening-up of the existing regulations.

A minor disaster may also have structural implications for the regulatory body itself. Regulatory organizations are not homogeneous and within them there will always be those who support the status quo and those who want more regulation. An industrial disaster or widespread harm from a product strengthens the hand of those who want enhanced regulations. The "I told you so" factor is extremely powerful in times of crisis and can result in a shifts of power within the regulatory body, usually in favour of further regulation.

Power without responsibility—lobby groups and anti-risk activists

Another significant force in the non-risk society consists of those pressure groups whose primary concern is to see further regulation or a complete ban on a particular process or product. Such groups are well known for their attention to the generation of nuclear power and the reprocessing of nuclear waste, the biotechnology industries, road-building, tobacco, alcohol, the meat industries, and the fur industry. And, the list goes on. Such groups campaign by publicizing as much bad news about an industry as possible. As well as generating a constant stream of anti-industry propaganda, some of the larger and wealthier groups are able to commission or carry out their own research aimed at identifying breaches in regulations, demonstrating the inadequacies of the present regime, or identifying further hazards and risks. They have a vested interest in establishing harm or damage done by the industry so that they can point out the inadequacies of the status quo, "name and shame" particular individuals and institutions, and put pressure on the regulatory bodies to regulate or to ban. They are thus the masters of two-pronged blame—of commission by industry and of omission by regulators.

The position of such groups differs from that of the regulators in that they do not have to be circumspect in their approach. They do not have to "listen" to industry. They can, in other words, be one-sided and more reckless in their claims. One of the main weapons of such groups is the press-release. Activists and academics are often masters at putting "spin" on particular opinions, developments, or research findings. Bad news for industry is good news for them. Every death or injury caused by a product or process is followed by a detailed and carefully crafted press-release, which is despatched with immediate effect to selected news-sources and journalists. The aim of such releases and statements is to produce a full-blown public panic by sensationalizing negative news about a particular product or process.

Such attacks are easy to make but difficult to refute so that anti-risk lobby groups, activists, and academics can make wild claims with impunity. Alarmist claims of risk can be made and disseminated without adequate scientific research into the actual probabilities of harm. If, as often happens in the non-risk society, their claims are widely accepted, then the targeted industry is forced either to ignore the claims and face a sharp drop in demand, increased lobbying, and increased regulation or to attempt to refute them. As many industries have discovered to their cost, refuting such claims is a long, tedious, and expensive process that can involve commissioning expensive consultancy and research. Scare-mongering is easy; countering such claims is expensive and difficult. For those wishing to harass and discredit an industry, a drip-feed of sensationalist stories of unanticipated risks or environmental damage is a sure-fire winner.

Activists are also drawn to exaggerate because risk is news while safety is not. A well-crafted scare story is almost guaranteed media coverage by journalists who are themselves prone to sensationalize in order to make the front page. Industries thus face the problem of having to counter risk-stories, often with as little research on the issue as their accusers. Even if the industry responds immediately to the resultant public outcry by commissioning scientific research into the alleged risks, it has to wait for many months or even years for the results. When the research finds the allegations of risk to have been inaccurate, companies commonly find that the media are simply not interested. Risk stories are in tune with our "culture of fear" (Furedi, 1997); stories about safety have little appeal. Journalists and editors know this and so scientific refutations of wild and one-sided allegations usually remain enclosed within the covers of scientific journals. Anyway, by this time, the allegations will have usually changed.

A typology of anti-industry devices

Through the study of attacks on industrial products and processes, and subsequent public alarms about them, it is possible to identify patterns in the methods used in scare-mongering. Through an analysis of over 50 such scares, our on-going study has found that activists routinely use a combination of one or more devices or stratagems in order to exploit public anxieties and exert pressure for regulation or bans. Our categorization of these devices has been confirmed by journalists, who themselves are experts in "spin," and by those in industry who have to deal with such devices on a regular basis (Neal and Davies 1998: 38–41).

(1) Initial exaggeration of hazard

Exaggeration gets headlines. Even when claims are later reduced or abandoned, the original impression will remain. Later evidence that challenges or disproves exaggerated and alarmist claims tends to get less media coverage than the original irresponsible allegation. Some examples are:

- the alleged dangers of infant's formula baby milk
- Greenpeace's assessment of the oil in Shell's Brent Spar rig
- the risk of diet-related disease
- the risk from drinking alcohol
- the scare about Alar (a growth hormone) sprayed on apples
- the presence of asbestos in schools
- the controversies over calcium channel blockers.

(2) *The cluster controversy*

When cases of a disease or problem are found "clustered" in one particular place, this is identified as abnormal or suspicious. In reality, distributions are nearly always irregular for clusters occur naturally and spontaneously. They are not in themselves evidence of a health or environmental "problem." Two examples are:

- leukaemia and other cancer clusters around nuclear plants or military installations
- scares over electrical transmission wires and cancer.

(3) *Coincidence equals causality*

The coincidence of a particular "risk" factor with a negative health or environmental outcome is often treated as hard evidence of a causal relationship. Two examples are:

- scares over drugs like Opren, Nifedipine and other calcium channel blockers
- scares over Prozac.

(4) *Stressing relative risks while ignoring absolute risks*

The absolute chance of suffering harm from many hazards is very low. This awkward fact can be concealed by playing up the relative risk and showing that those who use a product are x times more likely to suffer harm that those who do not. This sounds impressive and makes good headlines. The actual absolute chances of harm remain very low, but that is rarely mentioned, for low absolute risks do not make good headlines. Some examples are:

- environmental tobacco smoke

- various scares about contraceptive pills

- toxic-shock syndrome and tampons

- calcium channel blockers.

(5) *Denial of dosage*

It is often argued that because large amounts of x are dangerous, small amounts must also be harmful, though on a smaller scale. In fact, large amounts of anything tend to be dangerous and small amounts of a substance that is toxic in large doses can often be safe and even beneficial. Some examples:

- agrochemicals

- residues from pesticides and weedicides

- water quality

- artificial sweeteners

- asbestos

- food additives

- radiation.

(6) *Devices with words and images.*

Such devices include the use of the familiar "Up to as many as 20 million people may be at risk of . . ."; the use of doctored photographs to shock; the cutting out of the "ifs" and "buts" normally associated with science; the portrayal of consumers as naive innocents, companies as malign conspiracies, and health and environmental activists as selfless heroes; and the artful suggestion that all things new are risky and the old and familiar are safe. Some examples are:

- anti-biotechnology scares

- Brent Spar drilling rig

- assorted anti-pharmaceutical scares

- anti-meat campaigns

- campaigns against hunting

- campaigns against nuclear power.

(7) Harm minimization that ignores pleasure, benefit and convenience

Many products can be harmful for some consumers or even third parties. It is not however, legitimate to add up these costs as part of an indictment while ignoring the pleasure and benefits for which they are purchased and used. A low-risk world is not necessarily an optimal one and harm minimization can lead to tedium and misery. Some examples are:

- alcohol

- tobacco

- automobiles

- fireworks

- "unhealthy" foods

- irradiated foods

- T-bone steaks

- campaigns against roads.

(8) Claiming a false consensus

Scientists often disagree. This is inconvenient for activists. The device used to get around this is to cite sources selectively so as to suggest that a consensus of scientific opinion exists. Alternatively, a collection of old studies can be added together to create a new collective "meta-study." Sometimes, the statistics from the individual studies are illicitly added together to create a big and impressive pseudo-sample. Some examples are:

- passive smoking

- the extent to which man's activity is responsible for global warming and for the hole in the ozone layer, and what the consequences are likely to be

- the severity of acid rain and the degree of harm it causes

- what the "healthy diet" is.

(9) Appeal to nature and purity

Nature is portrayed as being benign even though untamed nature has been the greatest threat to the human race. Environmentalists and healthists alike use the sentimental appeal of the natural as good and the artificial as bad. Some examples are:

- infant's formula baby milk
- campaigns against agro-chemicals
- food irraditation
- silicone breast implants
- nuclear power
- pharmaceuticals
- artificial sweeteners
- protests against roads and runways
- Brent Spar drilling rig
- biotechnology
- food additives.

(10) Sentimentalizing the victims: protecting innocent children.
Activists divide the world into innocent consumers and bystanders, on the one hand, and greedy corporations, on the other. The most innocent of all are children and the most powerful rhetoric asks that they be protected. In real life, children need to learn incrementally to take risks and exercise judgement as they grow older. Some examples are:

- environmental tobacco smoke
- infant's formula baby milk
- hand guns
- computer games
- snack foods
- toys
- fireworks
- food additives.

(11) Omitting the costs and dangers of regulation
Those who want products regulated stress the dangers of the product but are rarely able to show that the regulation will work as intended. Nor do they investigate or measure any costs the regulation may have, such as their impact on employment. The costs and dangers of regulation are simply ignored. Some examples are:

- alcohol

- pharmaceuticals

- meat industry

- eggs

- biotechnology.

(12) Demanding the impossible

After a product has been shown not to be unsafe, the activist demands that it be proven to be safe. In reality, the best that can be proved is a low level of risk. Activists, however, demand a perfect solution when, in the real world, of necessity we have to choose between solutions offering different patterns of costs and benefits, none of which is perfect. Activists may even rule out the least costly and least harmful of these because they insist that it is necessary to adhere to some irrational absolute criterion. Some examples are:

- silicone breast implants

- pharmaceuticals

- Brent Spar drilling rig

- biotechnology

- nuclear power stations.

These kinds of devices can be spotted in the media most weeks of the year. One would think, perhaps, that alerting journalists and broadcasters to these devices would encourage them to be more critical in their coverage of stories about risk. When talking to such journalists, however, it becomes obvious that they are fully aware of the "spin" put on statements and press-releases. Journalists operate in a story market. The current risk-averse, death-denying culture means that there is strong demand for scare stories, particularly about mundane household products.

The stories are also widely believed. In the non-risk society, identifying and eliminating dangers are self-evidently noble acts in the moral crusade to eliminate premature illness and death. The activists, the press, and the public are all much more interested in harm than in benefits; thus, the overriding fact that the effects of industrial activity on general welfare are overwhelmingly beneficial is rarely reported.

On the contrary, industry is almost always cast in the role of the villain. This is not surprising as the reputation of industry as a whole continues to suffer from the legacy of Thalidomide, asbestos, and tobacco. Likewise, it has suffered greatly at the hands of anti-industry groups like Greenpeace, and of public-service television programs like *Watchdog*. Many people do not trust industry to tell the truth, whereas they continue to trust and support anti-risk and anti-industry activists.

This pattern of trust and mistrust is one of the most bizarre and damaging features of the modern industrial scene. On the one hand, people continue to trust anti-risk activists regardless of their poor record and their reckless behaviour. People continue to believe anti-industry scares though the majority have been proved to be groundless or exaggerated. On the other hand, they continue to mistrust industry, particularly when it responds to activist attacks. The vision is still of brave, principled, little people taking on the might of the greedy multinationals.

There is a strong argument that, if one is pursuing the truth about risk, the pattern of trust should be reversed. Unconstrained by responsibilities or hard science, activists are able to make wild statements. For sure, they often couch them in sober language and use one or many of the devices outlined above to conceal the flimsiness of their arguments. Their claims should, however, be met with extreme scepticism.

Of course, the same is true of industry rebuttals to such claims although, in practice, industry statements are more likely to be true because their every word is put on record, monitored, and criticized by their enemies. If a company produces data on risk or damage to the environment that is patently wrong or mendacious, it would be quickly spotted by the expert regulators or scientifically trained activists and used to discredit them. The risks industry runs by lying or by pushing junk science are prohibitively high.

The corresponding risks for activists are low: many of their claims are pseudo-scientific in the sense that they are untestable and, therefore, cannot be refuted. If a company does decide to sue over a risk claim, public credence and sympathy lie automatically with the health and safety bravados. Finally, if an industry does spend the time and money to research its claims, the activists can continue to push the lie for a while—then, they can change the accusation.

The attractions of anti-industry activism are obvious. Unlike most of us who have to muddle along in a world of compromise, actvists live in a world of black and white, good and evil, safe and unsafe, eco-friendly and environmentally damaging. They have dragons to slay—industrial monsters that threaten the world. Saving people's lives and saving the planet are impressive crusades that confer a sense of self-worth. The self-evident nobility of their cause means that they do not have to consider trivial details like the costs of regulations, the shutdown of industries and the families that rely upon them for their livelihood. They do not have to consider people of modest means who have to pay more for altered or alternative products. These are prices worth paying for a natural world where premature death is banished, a pure world, unsullied by the compromises of cost-benefit analyses.

In addition, the activists themselves are safe. The development of non-risk culture means that anti-industry activism will continue to attract recruits.

References

Beck, U. (1992). *Risk Society: Towards a New Modernity.* London: Sage.

Burnstall, M., and G. Reuben (1990) Critics of the Pharmaceutical Industry. London: Remit Consultants.

Charlton, B. (1998) Life before Health: Against the Sentimentalisation of Medicine. In D. Anderson and P. Mullen (eds.), *Faking It: The Sentimentalisation of Modern Society* (London: SAU): 19–39.

Deutsch, A., H. Sjostrom, and R. Nilsson (1972). *Thalidomide and the Power of Drug Companies.* Harmondsworth: Penguin.

Douglas, M. (1992). *Risk and Blame: Essays in Cultural Theory.* London: Routledge.

Douglas, M., and A. Wildavsky (1982). *Risk and Culture: An Essay on the Selections of Technological and Environmental Dangers.* Berkeley, CA: University of California Press.

Furedi, F. (1997). *Culture of Fear: Risk-Taking and the Morality of Low Expectation.* London: Cassell.

Inman, B. (1993). 30 Years in Post-Marketing Surveillance. *PEM News* (Southampton: Drug Safety Research Unit): 19–58.

Johnson, J.R., and C. Ullyatt (1991). *Health Scare: The Misuse of Science in Public Health Policy.* Critical Issues 14. Perth: Institute for Policy Study.

Maynard, A., and K. Hartley (1984). The Regulation of the Pharmaceutical Industry. In M. Lingren (ed.), *Arne Ryde Symposium on Pharmaceutical Economics* (Swedish Institute for Health Economic / Liber Forlag): 123–37.

Neal, M. (1995) *Keeping Cures from Patients: The Perverse Effects of Pharmaceutical Regulations.* London: SAU.

―――― (1998). *The Culture Factor: Cross-National Management and the Foreign Venture.* London: Macmillan Business.

Neal, M., and J.C.H. Davies (1998). *The Corporation under Siege: Exposing the Devices used by Activists and Regulators in the Non-Risk Society.* London: SAU.

Nilsson, R. (1997) Is Environmental Tobacco Smoke a Risk Factor for Lung Cancer? In R. Bate (ed.), *What Risk?* (Oxford: Butterworth-Heinemann): 96–151.

Saunders, N. (1997). *Ecstasy Reconsidered.* Exeter: BPC Wheatons.

Walter, T. (1994). *The Revival of Death.* London : Routledge.

Unknown Causes, Unknown Risks

LYDIA MILJAN
with Kate Morrison and Kelly Torrance

Canadians are living longer than ever. Increased longevity has been attributed to declines in mortality rates for most leading causes of death, such as cancer and heart disease (Statistics Canada 1999b). Not only are deaths from diseases declining but fewer people are dying from plane accidents, car crashes, or even by their own hand. Most likely because of these cheery statistics, Canadians believe that a risk-free lifestyle is attainable (Health Canada 1993). At the same time, however, Canadians are bombarded with news stories that link pesticides, nuclear power, and even electro-magnetic impulses to cancer. These headlines and stories make any death, any cancer diagnosis, appear an aberration and starkly contrast the desire for a risk-free life to a life that is desperately trying to avoid unknown, dangerous risks from everyday events.

A sampling of some headlines from across the country, in print, on television and on the web, illustrate the media's focus on risks outside our control. On July 29, 1999, the *Globe and Mail* reported, PESTICIDES AT ROOT OF CANCER, VICTIM SAYS. On June 20, 1999, columnist Michele Landsberg's headline in the *Toronto Star* encouraged LET'S ACT NOW TO CURTAIL CANCER EPIDEMIC. A few months earlier on May 22, 1999, the same paper printed this sensational headline: STUDY SUGGESTS LINK BETWEEN CELLULAR PHONE USE, CANCER. And, a year earlier on September 21, 1998, the *Toronto Star* reported: FEAR OF CANCEROUS CELL PHONES AND MURDEROUS MICROWAVES IS FUELING A WORLDWIDE EPIDEMIC OF LAWSUITS. Similarly, on March 23, 1993, the *Winnipeg Free Press* gave this headline: DIALING FOR DISASTER? Alison MacGregor's article on cell-phones in March, 1999 was printed in several Southam newspapers across the country with the headline: GROUP WANTS FEDS TO USE CELLULAR-PHONE WARNINGS: SOME EVIDENCE SAYS FREQUENT USERS MAY HAVE INCREASED HEALTH RISKS. The *National Post* on January 16, 1999, warned, HOTLINE TO AN EARLY GRAVE: GET OFF YOUR CELL-PHONES! EVIDENCE SUGGESTS THEY ARE A DANGER TO YOUR HEALTH. The most provocative headlines came from the Canadian Broadcasting Corporation's web site, funded by taxpayers: BREAST CANCER EXPERTS TARGET POLLUTION, STUDY CONFIRMS LINK BETWEEN PCBS AND BREAST CANCER, RESEARCHERS FIND RISE IN RADIATION IN CHILDREN'S TEETH.

Just as people are living longer, the environment is getting cleaner (see, for example, Hayward and Jones 1999). However, it would be difficult for people to know this if they relied on the media for their main diet of information. But, that is exactly where the majority of Canadians receive their information about health issues and risk. About half of the 1500 respondents in a survey by Health Canada said they receive "a lot" of information on risk from the media and about 35 percent said they receive a "fair" amount. Physicians, the next most popular source, give only about a quarter of respondents "a lot" of information (Health Canada 1993). Media reports are extremely influential. One study found that "media coverage of a toxic exposure may lead people to report symptoms, even though their actual exposure was very slight" (Lees-Haley and Brown 1992).

The National Media Archive (NMA) conducted several media studies on risk, which show how the media portray risk to the public. In all cases, the NMA found that the media overemphasize minute risks about which little can be done and ignore those that their readers can do something about. Much of this phenomena can be explained by examining the way in which journalists come to think about a story as newsworthy. For a story to make the news, it should have one or more of the following components: simplification, dramatization, personalization, themes and continuity, consonance, and the unexpected (Ericson, Baranek and Chan 1987: 140–49).

Most stories on risk fill many, if not all, of these criteria. Take, for example, this headline from *CBC Online*: RESEARCHERS FIND RISE IN RADIATION IN CHILDREN'S TEETH. The headline itself meets four of the six criteria for newsworthiness. What could be more simplistic than the link between children's teeth and radiation? There is considerable drama in the statement. Whenever children are evoked in a news story, it becomes a personal story. Clearly the public did not expect to find radiation in children's teeth, fulfilling the unexpected component.

While stories on risk make good headlines for journalists, those who promote these stories manipulate journalists into committing several errors of omission or commission. The criteria for newsworthiness tends to blind journalists to the bigger picture and consequently they misinform their audiences and perpetuate myths and misunderstanding. There are generally five errors that journalists fall into when they pursue this type of reporting.

(1) *Mistaken emphasis on unavoidable risk*   Here the media overemphasize things that we have no control over or they report on the bizarre story while ignoring common place occurrences.

(2) *Unanimity alleged*   When there is a suspected causal agent that is dramatic or adheres to a conspiratorial conclusion, journalists fail to represent the information as such. Dissension from the original premise or any mention of disagreement among experts is downplayed.

(3) *Use of dubious sources*   In order to achieve unanimity in these stories requires two things: avoiding reputable scientific sources and elevating interest groups.

(4) *Calls for increased government involvement*   Having declared a crisis using extremist sources and reporting unanimity, the agenda moves towards calls for increased government involvement to solve the problem.

(5) *Contrary evidence is ignored or downplayed*   Considering the way in which journalists give little room for alternative explanations, it is not surprising that when evidence comes in to refute the original assumptions that new evidence is either ignored completely or downplayed in subsequent reports.

The remainder of this chapter gives examples and instances of these errors in the media's coverage of risk.

Mistaken emphasis on unavoidable risk

News tends to emphasize bizarre or unusual occurrences over the mundane. Journalists often defend their reporting practices by saying that the news consists of the unusual; otherwise, it would not be news. However, it is this quest for the unusual that distorts the public's sense of real risk. One example of how the news media emphasize unavoidable though small or negligible risk at the expense of mundane but real risk is found in its coverage of cancer.

Cancer is the term for a process of abnormal cell division that spreads throughout the body, invading and destroying normal tissue. While scientists do not understand why this process occurs, decades of research have determined the principal causes of cancer. Dr. Robert Scheuplein, head of the United States Food and Drug Administration's Office of Toxicology, states: "There are essentially three causes of cancer—to the extent that they can be separated ... tobacco or cigarettes would account for one-third of all cancers; diet would be one-third; and everything else would be the other third" (Scheuplein 1991: 30–33).

This too, is a simplification of the factors that have been linked to cancer but is useful for analytical purposes. In our analysis of television's coverage of cancer in 1993, the NMA found that the risks associated with diet and smoking were practically ignored by the national television networks. Instead, the Canadian Broadcasting Corporation (CBC) and CTV Television (CTV) focused on the environmental causes of cancer. In 1993, two-thirds of coverage by CBC and over one-half of coverage by CTV of cancer focused on environmental factors (Morrison 1993: 2).

The environmental factors being blamed for cancer were pesticides, man-made chemicals, man-made radiation, asbestos, general pollution, ozone depletion as a result of CFCs and magnetic fields—all by-products of the modern industrial world. In contrast, in a widely-cited paper, Oxford researchers R. Doll and R. Peto found that the best estimate for pollution and industrial products as a cause of cancer deaths was less than 3 percent (Doll and Peto 1981).

The Alberta Cancer Board agreed with this analysis. In its book on the subject, in a chapter entitled Can Cancer Deaths Be Avoided? the Board stated: "There is no current evidence to suggest that environmental factors play a major role in cancer causation" (Birdsell et al. 1990: 48). Yet, with the greatest portion of television coverage focusing on the environment as a cause of cancer, the public is being led to believe that these factors pose a serious health risk. More important, these reports on risk of environmental causes of cancer occurred at the same time pollution levels and uses of pesticides were on the decline (Hayward and Jones 1999).

Television reports consistently ignored the causes of cancer that were within the control of the individual. Diet, alcohol, tobacco, and sun tanning were given only 15 percent of total attention to the causes of cancer by CBC and only 25 percent, by CTV (Morrison 1993: 3). It is estimated that these factors cause almost three-quarters of cancer deaths.

Bruce Ames, a professor of biochemistry and molecular biology at the University of California, is concerned that there is "a public misconception that pollution is a significant contributor to cancer and that cancer rates are soaring" He points out: "Cancer is fundamentally a degenerative disease of old age, although external factors can increase cancer rates (cigarette smoking) or decrease them (fruits and vegetables)" (Ames 1993b: 38).

The fact that Canadians believe that the causes of cancer are beyond the control of the individual supports Dr. Ames' belief. Instead of focusing on decisions about one's lifestyle that can significantly reduce one's risk of getting cancer, Canadian television networks focused on the environmental causes of cancer, which pose a relatively small risk but are not within the control of the individual. This attention to the causes of cancer may have been a factor in the finding that Canadians think that cancer is "a powerful disease with a mysterious course of its own, controlled by fate and not by its victim" (Morrison 1993: 3).

Ozone depletion was the cause of cancer most often cited by the national television networks. Twenty-five percent of the CBC's attention to the environmental causes of cancer, and over 40 percent of CTV's attention, focused on ozone depletion (Morrison 1993: 4). A similar trend is shown by the attention given on television to the type of cancer. Forty-seven percent of the CBC's attention to the various cancer sites, and 44 percent of CTV's attention, focused on skin cancer (Morrison 1993: 6).

The risks posed by excessive exposure to sunlight and ozone depletion are, in fact, relatively small. While sun-tanning is the cause of approximately one-quarter of cancer incidence, the vast majority of these cases are curable. Only one form of skin cancer, melanoma, is considered deadly and, as melanoma is relatively rare, skin cancer accounts for only 1 percent of cancer deaths (Roach 1992: 42). This fact was not mentioned, however, by either CBC or CTV. For example, on the March 30, 1992, CTV News reporter Michael O'Byrne stated: "Melanoma is the deadliest form of skin cancer and Dr. Abarca predicts he'll treat a massive outbreak in the next few years." Following this statement, Dr. Bedric Magas who studies ozone predicted a 20 percent to 40 percent increase in the incidence over the next ten years.

Similar alarmist reports were given on CBC. On the July 21, 1992, *Journal* by Dr. Robin Marks said:

> There's no doubt in my mind that in order to get a sun tan, is enough sunlight to lead to the epidemic of skin cancer that we're seeing in Australia, you're seeing in Canada, they're seeing in the United States, Britain, Europe, South America, throughout the western world. Melanoma is rising at a rate that no other cancer is rising. It's becoming the cancer of the late twentieth century.

On the April 4, 1991, on *The National,* CBC reporter Eve Savory reported that there had been a "1,250 percent increase in the most lethal skin cancer, melanoma" over the past 55 years. Following this statement, environmentalist Robert Hornung stated: "Every one percent decline in the ozone layer leads to a three-to-four percent increase in the rate of skin cancer. And in Canada we're already near an epidemic level of skin cancers." However, according to Mary Roach, an editor of *Health* magazine, "there's more to the story than ozone. This is especially true of melanoma. Melanoma risk is a complicated conspiracy of genes and moles and childhood sunburns. The hole in the sky plays a role but not the lead" (Roach 1992: 42).

Just as the ozone layer was linked to the increase in skin cancer, television linked pesticides to cancer. The CBC focused over 20 percent of its attention to the environmental causes of cancer upon pesticides. In contrast, on CTV, pesticides accounted for only 7 percent of the coverage (Morrison 1993: 8). Yet Doll and Peto estimate that pesticides in pollution causes only 2 percent of all cancer deaths Doll and Peto 1981).

One difference between the networks is the manner in which these studies were reported. Of the coverage devoted to pesticides, more than 60 percent of CBC's statements presented these substances as a definite cause of cancer. In contrast, on CTV less than 10 percent of the statements linked pesticides with cancer in a definitive manner. Instead, the vast majority of CTV's coverage stated that pesticides were a suspected cause of cancer (Morrison 1993: 8)

The significance of these findings is even more apparent when one considers how substances are determined to be carcinogenic. Most product testing is conducted on laboratory rats. Using a process called maximum tolerated dose (MTD) researchers determine the level of a chemical that will kill the animal and then give it a little less than that every day. According to Dr. Ames: "Animal cancer tests are being misinterpreted to mean that low doses of synthetic chemicals and industrial pollutants are relevant to human cancers . . . testing at the MTD frequently can cause chronic cell killing and consequent cell replacement, a risk factor for cancer that can be limited to high doses" (Ames 1993a).

One of the reasons that pesticides received more attention on CBC than on CTV is that an entire edition of *The Journal* was dedicated to the issue (Morrison 1993: 8). On May 2, 1989 Barbara Frum asked a panel of experts whether consumers should be concerned about the fresh produce being sold in Canada. While the other two panelists agreed that Canadians had no cause to be worried, environmentalist Julia Langer, Executive Director of Friends of the Earth replied:

Well, frankly, Barbara, I don't think we know enough about the kinds of chemicals that are on the food, what the effects are on ourselves and on the environment to really be able to say with confidence that the food is safe ... There are carcinogenic substances in the food—and no safe level of those is conceivable—so I think it's a bit presumptuous to be taking the approach that it's all safe.

According to Dr. Ames, however: "Approximately half of all chemicals—whether natural or synthetic—that have been tested in standard animal cancer tests have turned out to be carcinogenic" (Ames 1993a). Further, Ronald Hart of the National Center for Toxicological Research has pointed out that the cancerous tumors found in rodents are likely unrelated to the carcinogen that is being tested.

We feed rodents "all-you-can-eat" buffets every day, yet we know that calorie intake is the single greatest contributing cause of cancer. In fact, we found that you can modify the cancer-causing impact of one of the most potent carcinogens from 90 percent down to less than 3 percent, just be cutting calorie intake 20 percent. (Brookes 1990: 161–70)

In the same edition of the *Journal*, Ms. Langer called for complete withdrawal of pesticide use. She stated: "These are chemicals which are put deliberately into the environment, which have health effects, environmental effects, effects on wildlife, and—if we can grow fruits and vegetables, and we can, without pesticides—then we should, for public health and for environmental health."

In contrast, Dr. Ames believes "all this business of organic food is nonsense basically. We should be eating more fruits and vegetables, so the main way to do that is to make them cheaper. Anything that may make fruits and vegetables more expensive may increase cancer." However, this view was never presented in national television reports.

The media's overemphasis on environmental cancer is not an isolated reporting practice. In a study by the NMA on transportation, we found that high-risk but rare accidents dominated headlines while mundane but relatively frequent car accidents were underplayed (Torrance 1998). Accidents account for a significant proportion of media coverage—around 4 percent to 5 percent of the national news on CTV and CBC, more than coverage of health and disease (Miljan 1998). Yet health and disease far out-pace accidents as a cause of death. Of all deaths reported in Canada in 1996, only 6 percent were external causes (Torrance 1998). This includes all accidental deaths, as well as suicides, murders and unknown causes.

Most transport accidents involve motor vehicles. Of the 3,488 people who died in transport-related accidents in Canada in 1996, 89 percent were killed in automobile collisions. Water-transport accidents accounted for 4 percent of transport-related deaths; air accidents, 2 percent; and railway accidents, one percent (Statistics Canada 1999a).

The world according to national television news is rather different. On CBC and CTV in 1997, motor-vehicle accidents accounted for less than half of collision reports (49 percent). Air accidents were greatly over-represented as they were the subject of 35 percent of accident stories. Railway and water-transport accidents were also overemphasized, accounting for 11 percent and 5 percent of accident reports respectively (Torrance 1998). Motor vehicle accidents only received as much coverage as they did because of stories involving celebrities; the death of HRH Diana, Princess of Wales, in a car accident was one of the most reported events of the year (Miljan 1998: 8).

Unanimity alleged

Just as the media emphasize the unusual or dramatic they too misrepresent the degree of scientific acceptance. In our study of environmental causes of cancer (Morrison 1993), not only did television news overstate the link between ozone depletion and melanoma but it consistently blamed chloroflurocarbons (CFCs) for the reduction in the ozone layer without acknowledging that scientists are still debating the issue. For example, on the April 5, 1992 edition of *The Journal* Barbara Frum stated: "The depletion of the ozone layer is something scientists have been wrestling with for years. They know chemicals like CFCs . . . eat away at the layer once they're released into the atmosphere."

However, neither CBC nor CTV reported that ozone readings have always experienced great fluctuations. James Hogan, a writer for *Omni* magazine points out:

> The ominous term "ozone hole" was coined by a media machine well rehearsed in environmental politics and anything the scientific community had to say has been drowned out. Missing from the press and TV accounts, for instance, is that an unexpectedly low value in the Antarctic winter-spring ozone level was reported by the British scientist Gordon Dobson in 1956—when CFCs were barely in use. (Hogan 1993: 34)

Some scientists go so far as to say that there is no relationship between the depletion of the ozone layer and the increased incidence of skin cancer. According to Martin Weinstock of the Rhode Island Moles and Melanoma Unit, "What's been happening with melanoma rates is in no

way related to ozone . . . It's the emphasis on having a tan." John Hast-
ings of the American Cancer Society points out: "Skin cancer rates have
been climbing ever since French designer Coco Chanel came back from
a cruise sporting a tan in the 1920s and sent everyone scrambling for a
place in the sun" (Roach 1992: 42).

While sunlight is the primary cause of skin cancer, the television
reports have downplayed this cause. On CBC, statements linking ozone
depletion with cancer were twice as frequent as statements that simply
focused on sunlight. On CTV, ozone depletion received four times
more coverage than sunlight (Morrison 1993). Although both networks focused on the increased incidence of melanoma, neither CBC
nor CTV reported the good news that the odds of being alive five years
after being diagnosed with melanoma had increased significantly. In
the early 1970s, the five year survival rate for melanoma was 65 percent
for men and 85 percent for women. By the early 1980s, this probability
had increased to 82 percent for men, and 88 percent for women. One's
risk of either developing or dying from melanoma is relatively small
(Morrison 1993).

Use of dubious sources

One reason why the media has failed to provide simple, factual information regarding risk is that, in setting their news agenda, they have
acquiesced to the environmental lobby. Journalists have elevated to an
honoured status activists who have taken up breast cancer as their
cause. Journalists applaud their rejection of the medical community
and traditional care. A report posted on *CBC Online* on July 31, 1999
told of the lengths to which the activists went to get their message
across. "These women are also trying to shake up what they refer to as
the 'cancer establishment'—governments, drug companies and the research bodies that decide where cancer money will be spent. To do that,
they challenge the status quo and they provoke controversy. They've
certainly done that during this conference." Later in the story it was revealed that the headlines had some effect on the direction of the Canadian Cancer Society; the effect was "certainly not revolutionary change,
but those comments are enough to make conference organizers feel
they've done their job. They've said over and over that they just want
to put the concerns of women on the agenda. It seems they have—at
least for this week. But what about next week and beyond?"

On July 29, 1999, Sasa Petricic, in a CBC television story about the
conference on *The National*, contrasted the conventional medical opinion with fear from a cancer victims: "For years Canadian women have
been told how to avoid the ravages of breast cancer, what to do—like
having regular X-rays—what not to do—like smoking—and what to

watch for—like a family history of the disease. And yet for more than half of Canadian women with breast cancer like Carol Dunn none of these factors apply." Carol Dunn, a cancer victim then presented her views on cancer, "It must still be something in the air, in the atmosphere, something that I can't control, and that's what I think scares most people with cancer." Petricic then introduced a study presented at the conference that he said, "seems to back up some of Dunn's unease of widespread chemical use." The study found that there was a higher risk of breast cancer when there were higher concentrations of PCBs. However, the study could not link pesticides to breast cancer. Petricic, referred to other studies that examined pesticides as well as PCBs, which found PDBs in the food chain but no evidence of pesticides. However, following researcher Kristan Aronson stating "We found increased risk of breast cancer associated with three specific PCBs," the Sierra Club's Elizabeth May was presented on camera to denounce all use of pesticides: "Pesticides should not be considered innocent until proven guilty. We should be sure that they don't pose a risk to public health before they are in use." The resulting picture of breast cancer and pesticides was confusing, contradictory, and scary but had nothing to do with the new study introduced at the cancer conference. In this instance, the journalist used scientific opinion to provide some of the information about breast cancer concerns but went to an environmentalist to provide the solution. All of this was buttressed by the image of a cancer victim fearful of the air and atmosphere around her. Nowhere in the story was age, diet, or other common factors associated with breast cancer discussed.

A similar trend occurred in the reports suggesting a connection between brain cancer and the use of cellular telephones. Stories were initiated by the news of a Florida man who wanted to sue the cellular-telephone industry for the wrongful death of his wife. He claimed that his wife developed brain cancer as a result of excessive use of her cellular telephone. To back up the claims, journalists used medical sources that said that there might be a chance of the antenna of a cellular telephone heating up brain cells, which, in turn, might cause cancer. Dr. Stephen Cleary conducted experiments on rats using wattage that far exceeded the amounts used in cell phones. His conclusion was that cancer cells were accelerated and he argued that more study was needed. In an article of March 23, 1993 in the *Winnipeg Free Press* he was quoted as saying "I don't think cellular phones cause cancer but, if the results at cellular phone frequencies and wattages are consistent, there is a possibility they could promote brain cancer."

Thirty-eight percent of the comments on cell phones and brain cancer sided with the claimants that there was a link. Added to that were the pointed demands that because cell-phone companies could not prove their product was safe that it must be treated with caution.

In the case of the scare over a link between cellular telephones and cancer, opinions coming from the anti-cell-phone groups, victims' families, and technology writers were given considerable credibility. These groups and individuals spoke in conspiratorial terms saying that the cellular telephone companies were waging a public-relations campaign similar to that of the tobacco industry. David Reynard, who launched the lawsuit against the cellular-telephone industry, remarked: "Are they carrying the how-to tobacco handbook in their back pocket? Yeah. It's almost directly in line with the tobacco industry and all the things that they did to try to keep information from the public, to try to suppress science, to try to only allow us to have the information that they want us to have" (Malarek 1999). Any statements by representatives of cellular telephone companies that studies could not show a link between brain tumours and the use of cellular telephones were treated with suspicion. In this story, aired on February 9, 1999 on the CBC's *Fifth Estate*, Victor Malarek remarked,

> Were the concerns raised by the Reynard lawsuit a real danger or a false alarm? The truth was no one knew for sure. The industry had been telling the pubic that cell phones were proven to be safe, but then had to admit that the science was at best incomplete. The cell phone industry needed to find a way to reassure their customers everything was fine, so they came up with a strategy that would be a textbook case for crisis management.

Calls for increased government involvement

Lacking evidence of the true nature of the risk or even the conventional scientific evidence of the cause of the problem, the news media quickly prescribes quick-fix solutions, such as government regulation. What is ironic about these prescriptions is that the news media often blames the problem on faulty government regulation or the government's not enforcing existing codes. In the case of environmental causes of cancer, either government was blamed for inadequate regulations or industry was blamed as the principal pollutant. Similarly a 1988 study on the environment identified ineffective governments who did not enforce existing legislation and big corporations only concerned with big profits as the cause of environmental damage (see Miljan 1989: 5). CBC blamed governments in 35 percent, and corporations in 36 percent, of the coverage of the causes.

The government was criticized for a number of reasons, one of which was not adequately enforcing existing legislation. For example, the government was held responsible for the entry into Canada of toxic chemicals hidden in gas and oil. Their inability to stop the practice was outlined by Paul Griffin in a report on May 10, 1989 on the *Journal*: "Government officials say they've known about the scam for several months but their spot checks seem fruitless. There's simply too much tanker traffic crossing the border for inspectors to handle."

Consistent with blaming government and corporations for environmental problems, 61 percent of the solutions to environmental problems offered by CBC, and 60 percent of those offered by CTV, called for increased government control via legislation and clean-up. At the same time, stories on companies cleaning up without government interference were reported but were accompanied by criticisms of past performance and dubious of efforts to improve. One comment from Linda Sims' report on July 24, 1988 on CBC's *Venture* is illustrative: "Once waste becomes a business issue, business solutions emerge ... Many companies may not want to shoulder more of the burden of garbage but they may not have a choice very much longer."

Another story on CBC's *The National* seemed to have difficulty showing a business as the antagonist and as a result provided a negative spin to the story. Peter Mansbridge introduced a story on February 27, 1989 on the greenhouse effect with: "The greenhouse effect—the gradual warming of the earth's atmosphere—is an international cause for concern and one US company thought it should make a contribution to help ... It's all because a company with the potential to be part of the problem wanted to be part of the solution."

Sheryl Sturges, a company spokesperson, identified why, on their own initiative, the corporation decided to spend thousands of dollars to negate their contribution to global warming: "We decided that the most effective way for AES to deal with our particular part of the problem was to plant trees." In assessing this effort, Eve Savory concluded the story by saying: "Trees are not the answer to global warming but they could buy time until the political and scientific problem of cutting emissions and developing alternative energy sources can be solved."

Corporate solutions were also met with distrust. Claude Adams, in a story published on February 19, 1989 reported that Britain's privatization efforts would have a negative effect on the environment: "Critics say private companies would have to make a profit and, for something as important as water, that could be dangerous." He then provided a clip from Andrew Lewis, a spokesperson for Friends of the Earth: "There's no profit in pollution prevention. There's little profit, little prospect of profit in environmental protection but there's every incentive to cut corners, to dodge the regulations."

The calls for increased regulation on the basis of small or indeterminate risk are not unique to environmental issues. In our study on transportation accidents (Torrance 1998), we found that both CTV and CBC reported the Ontario government's introduction of legislation to deal with flying truck wheels. Commercial truck drivers or fleet owners would pay from $2,000 to $50,000 if their trucks lost a wheel, regardless of the reason. "Flying truck wheels have been a horrifying and all-too-familiar sight lately on Canada's roads and highways," Lloyd Robertson began his report of February 21, 1997 on *CTV News*. The network noted that four people had been killed due to flying truck wheels in Ontario since 1995. Reporter George Wolff began with an account of an accident two months before, in which two people died after a flying tire hit their car. He then detailed the Ontario bill, the "toughest law in Canada," and provided comments from politicians calling for a federal truck-safety program.

The report was favourable to the new regulation, with interviews from politicians and a friend and relative of the accident victims. The only voice presented in opposition was that of the federal transport minister, who said the problem was a provincial responsibility and the provinces should ensure trucks meet existing standards. No one from the industry was quoted. The reporter concluded: "It's a danger that only tough laws can control and already tonight the Ontario Trucking Association was warning that [Minister Al] Palladini's new law could run head on into a constitutional challenge."

CBC, in its report the same day on *The National* saw the problem in a similar way: "an all-too-common sight on the highways around Toronto." The network granted more time to opposition voices than did CTV, however. A spokesman for the Ontario Trucking Association argued: "It's often not the truckers' fault themselves—maybe a third-party tire service company or whoever's doing work on the wheel is just as much at fault." An anonymous trucker voiced concern that the fines would put companies out of business. "Don't tell that to the family of Angela Worona," reporter Jeffrey Kofman responded. He recounted a fatal accident caused by a flying wheel two year before, which was used to dismiss the industry's concerns. The victim's sister called for the government to take away licenses. The story concluded with the Ontario government's suggestion of national standards and, in contrast to CTV, CBC reported that a spokesman for the federal transport minister agreed and called for continent-wide regulations.

National news networks apparently believe that flying truck wheels are a major problem that only government can fix. This, after CTV itself observed that only 4 people had died in Ontario in such accidents in two years. In 1995, trucks 5 tons or over accounted for 162 fatal accidents in all of Canada (Statistics Canada 1999a), not all of which, of course, involved flying wheels, that "all-too-familiar" sight.

Rarely does the media shy away from promoting regulation, even in the midst of freak accidents. On July 12, 1997, two small Quebec children were killed when a personal watercraft (more commonly known as a "jetski") collided with their inflatable boat. CTV's first report on the accident (*CTV News*, July 13, 1997), the next day, focused on safety concerns, quoting two sources. A marina operator said that almost anyone can rent a jetski and an owner defended himself against the charge of noise, claiming boats are just as noisy. Reporter Scott Laurie then concluded, "the accident might intensify demands for stricter regulations and licensing of jetski riders to control something that's made for fun but has caused so much grief." There was no mention of what caused the accident or how regulation could have prevented it and no sources other than the reporter made any arguments for regulation.

CTV network ran another report on *CTV News* on July 19, 1997 after the children's funeral. Reporter Cindy Sherwin translated a mourner's brief comments and a policeman was quoted discussing how to determine the speed of the crafts. No mention of regulation was made by any source but the reporter ended the story by saying: "[police] findings will likely lead to a municipal law controlling the speed of *Jetskis*. However, many here hope the federal government will pass broader legislation regulating the age and experience of the drivers as well."

The CBC also promoted regulation in a July 14 report on the accident on *The National*. Reporter Mark Kelley interviewed a boater who said simply that accidents should be prevented. As to how that should be done, the head of the federal Boating Law Task Force declared that "the sentiment of opinion was there should be mandatory training for everyone who operates a recreational boat in Canada." A spokesman for Bombardier, which makes *Sea-Doos*, (a brand of jetski), pointed out that his company gives a training video to its customers. "But critics say the federal government, not the boating industry, should be setting the rules and regulations," the reporter stated, quoting the Quebec transport minister. The story ended with the suggestion that the accident would result in the end of the jetski craze: "Even the [rental shop] owner says he doesn't think they're so much fun any more."

There were only 12 fatalities related to personal watercraft in 1997. In 1995, there were only four. Still, the government responded to media calls for regulation. In 1998 the federal government ruled that those under the age of 16 could not operate personal watercraft and, after April 1, 2002, craft operators must meet mandatory training requirements (Torrance 1998).

It seems that whenever there is an aircraft disaster, the stock response from journalists is to call for greater regulation. For example, *CTV News* examined safety concerns after Air Canada flight 646 crashed in Fredericton, New Brunswick on December 16, 1997 causing injuries but no fatalities. Though the cause of the crash was still unknown, Lloyd Robertson stated: "Critics say Liberal government cutbacks are putting the travelling public at risk—cuts like the ones that left Fredericton airport without an air traffic controller." No mention was made of how the crash related to an unmanned control tower. Still, the crash is evidence, insisted Harry Gow, a spokesman for the lobby group Transport 2000, that "the air traffic safety system in Canada is coming apart at the seams" and a spokesman for the Aircraft Operators Group agreed. The network did report opposing voices from the federal transport minister and a spokesman from NAVCAN, the private company that took control of the air navigation system in 1996. The insinuation, however, was that the unmanned control tower was responsible for the accident: reporter Craig Oliver observed that the company was still planning to remove controllers in other airports, "despite the Fredericton experience."

CBC's *The National* (December 17, 1997) also looked at cutbacks to air traffic control services "and whether they may have contributed to the accident." Again, there was no explanation of how cutbacks might have led to the accident, the cause of which was still unknown. A spokesman for the Transportation Safety Board admitted that having no control tower in Fredericton probably caused delays in helping the injured. Quoted next was Transport 2000's Harry Gow, who again argued that cutbacks were causing safety problems and warned "if they don't watch it, they'll have a 747 coming down in a Montreal suburb next." David Collenette, the federal Transport Minister, pointed out that the accident rate for aircraft has dropped steadily over the last decade. Reporter Sasa Petricic ended the story, however, by recounting three recent accidents and questioning whether cutbacks "have resulted in either savings or safety." A federal auditor's report concluded, said the reporter, that "the government didn't include measures to ensure that Transport Canada could continue to monitor safety" after privatization of air traffic control services.

CTV devoted a report on the edition of *CTV News* for Christmas Eve, 1997, to the safety concerns of fire chiefs arising from the crash of flight 646. "Now, no one died in last week's crash but the fire chiefs say that is no thanks to Ottawa," anchor Dana Lewis said. The fire-fighters complained that they are required to hose down a plane but not to rescue survivors. A Canadian Association of Fire Chiefs spokesman noted that he has been lobbying for tougher standards. He argued that there would not have been enough emergency workers at the Fredericton airport to handle a fire had one broken out after the accident, a situation that could have led to fatalities. The chief was the only person quoted in the story and his opinion went unquestioned. The report ended with the information that the government "now promises to clean up a planned review in the new year."

CTV's account of the fire-fighters' safety concerns gives the impression that the chiefs' opinions are irrefutable—no opposition was provided. A report commissioned by Transport Canada and reported in the *Vancouver Province* for June 16, 1998, however, provides another point of view. The report concluded that media reporting on the Fredericton crash caused a "distorted public perception" of emergency response measures. "No reasonable argument, moral or economic," supports full-time rescue and fire-fighting systems at all airports, the report found. "Using the Fredericton accident as a cause célèbre, fire-fighters have unnecessarily alarmed the Canadian public" (Canadian Press, *Vancouver Sun* 1998: A19). This may not be the entire story either but this perspective was not even considered by CTV.

The federal government responded to the media pressure in February, making fire-fighting services available for every flight in the country's busiest 28 airports. The Fredericton accident "renewed pressure on the government to review its rescue and fire-fighting standards at airports," the *Halifax Daily News* reported (Canadian Press 1998). Air travel, however, is already extremely safe: there were only 96 air-related fatalities in Canada in 1995. In 1996, that number dropped to 56 and only 14 deaths were attributed to accidents involving commercial aircraft (Statistics Canada 1996a: 252).

Other studies have also found cases in which the media, first, misrepresented risks and, then, called for government regulation. In Canada in 1996, the federal government wanted to ban cheese made from unpasteurized milk. Worldwide since 1971, there had been 4,228 illnesses and 57 deaths attributed to raw-milk cheese (D'Aoust 1996). The National Media Archive examined reports on the proposed regulation by CBC and CTV and in the *Globe and Mail* (Morrison 1996).

The CBC strongly supported the government's plan. Over 70 percent of the network's assessment agreed that government intervention was needed to protect the public from the risk. Coverage by CTV and the *Globe and Mail* was more balanced: 56 percent of CTV's coverage and 39 percent of coverage by the *Globe and Mail* argued that regulation was unnecessary. CBC also lagged behind the other outlets in presenting public reaction, including that of consumers, industry representatives, and the Quebec government—6 percent of their coverage gave public reaction compared to 25 percent in the *Globe and Mail* and 41 percent on CTV.

Contrary evidence is ignored or downplayed

One might be able to excuse the media for emphasizing the unusual and therefore providing a distorted picture of reality. What is inexcusable, however, is their failure to set the record straight when new evidence is provided that refutes the original claims. What this does is perpetuate the misinformation and make it appear more common and natural. Almost 25 percent of the CBC's attention to the environmental causes of cancer, and 30 percent of the CTV's attention, focused upon man-made chemicals—primarily dioxins, furans and polychlorinated biphenyls (PCBs). However, the Doll and Peto found that industrial products caused less than 1 percent of cancer deaths (Doll and Peto 1981).

For example, when well-water was banned in the town of Newcastle, New Brunswick, due to excessive levels of polyaromatic hydrocarbons (PAH), CBC and CTV both followed the story. However, the "facts" were presented differently.

On CBC's *The National* for April 19, 1989 reporter Bob Merzerol stated that Newcastle's main well had been shut down "when it tested positive for cancer-causing polyaromatic hydrocarbons." While the well contained three and one-half times the acceptable level, this report gave the false impression that any trace of the chemical will cause cancer. In contrast, on CTV *News* for April 23, 1989 Jonathan Gravener reported that the well had "excessive levels." Gravener also reported that these same chemicals are part of everyday life: "It's a chemical that's been linked to cancer ... PAH is a residue of combustion. Levels can be found in barbecued meats and cigarettes." By including this additional information, the CTV report gave the viewer perspective on the relative danger of PAH.

This incident prompted the New Brunswick government to conduct a study to determine whether or not the people of that region had a higher risk of getting cancer than people elsewhere in the province. The study, based on 500 families and conducted over two years, found that the people of Newcastle were in no greater danger than people elsewhere in the country. The report found that cancer rates were higher in New Brunswick than elsewhere in Canada due to diets too high in salt, fat, and alcohol and due to too much smoking.

CBC reported the findings of this study on the *The National* for July 23, 1990. Instead of using the findings of the study to highlight the dangers of consuming excessive fat, salt, alcohol, and tobacco, however, CBC questioned the validity of the government study. Reporter Susan Bonner began the story with the statement: "Marg Gorbert is one of hundreds of people in Newcastle who live in fear of cancer. Within six years she lost her mother, her sister, and her husband to the disease.

She thinks pollution, probably in the water, causes it. She calls the latest study a 'government cover-up'." This statement was made before the viewer was even told the results of the study. In the entire report, 11 statements were made that questioned the findings while only 4 statements reported the results of the study. Bonner concluded the story: "Marg Gorbert says she has lost too much. It will take more than one new government study to change her mind."

While the study found that it was the lifestyle of the inhabitants of Newcastle that had resulted in the higher cancer rates, CBC's report placed the blame on the government and, indirectly, on local industry. Bonner stated: "Newcastle is an industry town in New Brunswick's Miramichi area. There's a pulp mill here and a chemical plant. Two years ago cancer-causing chemicals were discovered in the town's water."

In fact, few studies have proven a link between industrial waste products and increased cancer rates. The British Columbia Cancer Agency analyzed cancer rates for 15 regions throughout British Columbia that have had pulp mills since 1970. While the initial analysis showed higher rates of lung cancer, when the data was adjusted for a greater incidence of cigarette smoking the findings "ceased to be significantly high" (Wigod 1992: A1, A3).

Conclusion

The media's misrepresentation of certain risks and the ensuing calls for government regulation have serious implications. Canadians get most of their information on risk from the media; the government, in turn, responds. In 1993/1994, the burden of federal, provincial, and local regulations was $85.7 billion, 12 percent of GDP. This translates into a hidden tax of about $12,000 annually per family of four (Mihlar 1997).

Attempts to eliminate or reduce risk often do not accomplish their goals. One example is government-mandated automobile safety and pollution standards. The estimated cost of an airbag is between $1,300 and $2,200. If airbags are mandatory, some people will be unable to afford a new car. They may keep their old cars or buy used cars that may be less safe than new cars without air bags (Mihlar 1996).

Pollution standards may produce similar results. Money may be spent on making cars that pollute less, with diminishing returns. But again, people may continue to use older cars that pollute more than newer cars, made before the new standards. Regulations can also carry unintended consequences. In the 1970s, for example, child-resistant caps on some medicines were made mandatory but the numbers of child poisonings actually increased. Parents, it seems, felt safer with the new caps and thus were not as attentive to their children's safety as they had been before the caps were introduced (Lott 1997).

Reports of risk is often taken out of context. If the media provided more information on the relative risks of activities on which they report, Canadians could judge meaningfully the various risks they face. Our resources are not unlimited. If risks are not assessed comparatively, resources will be wasted on attempting to decrease or eliminate minute risks that, paradoxically, could put more lives in danger. Many people object to the idea of putting a dollar value on life but with limited resources, money should be allocated where it can do the most good. Air travel, for example, has become extremely safe and there are diminishing returns to spending any more money on airline safety.

The Harvard Center for Risk Analysis examined 185 life-saving interventions. It found the regulations cost $21.4 billion and saved 56,700 lives annually. Tammy O. Tengs and John D. Graham estimated that those resources could be reallocated to save a total of 117,000 lives. As an example, they compared money spent on regulating fire retardant clothing with the cost of smoke detectors: "We regulate the flammability of children's clothing, spending $1.5 million per year of life saved, while some 30 percent of those children live in homes without smoke alarms, an investment that costs about $200,000 per year of life saved" (Tengs and Graham 1996).

Still, after many tragedies that have received media attention, the government, with media approval, is quick to introduce new regulations, regardless of their cost or potential effectiveness. Governments rarely seem to consider options outside of regulation. More often, it appears they respond to media-charged safety concerns, whether resources are best deployed there or not.

References

On Balance (1998). 1997 Year in Review. *On Balance* 11 (3): 1–8.

Ames, Bruce N. (1993a). Current Cancer Risk Assessment May Harm Health: Linear Extrapolation from High Doses in Animal Experiments to Low Doses in Human is Scientifically Invalid. Draft Statement, International Center for a Scientific Ecology.

Ames, Bruce N. (1993b). The Topic of Cancer: Sierra Magazine vs. Bruce Ames. *The American Spectator* (June).

Birdsell, J.M., et al. (1990). *Preventing Cancer in Alberta: Challenges and Opportunities*. Alberta Cancer Board, Epidemiology and Preventive Oncology.

Brookes, Warren T. (1990). The Wasteful Pursuit of Zero Risk. *Forbes* (April 30): 161–70.

Candian Press (1998). Feds Plan to Upgrade Firefighting at Busiest Canadian Airports. *Halifax Daily News* (February 4): 9.

D'Aoust, J.-Y (1996). Work in progress. Bureau of Microbial Hazards: Health Canada.

Doll, R., and R. Peto (1981). Quantitative Estimates of Avoidable Risks of Cancer in the United States Today. In R. Doll and R. Peto, *The Causes of Cancer* (Oxford: Oxford University Press).

Ericson, Richard, Patricia Baranek, and Janet Chan (1987). *Visualizing Deviance: A Study of News Organization*. Toronto: University of Toronto Press.

Foster, Kenneth R., David E. Bernstein, and Peter W. Huber, eds. (1993). *Phantom Risk: Scientific Inference and the Law*. Cambridge, MA: MIT Press.

Hayward, Steven, and Laura Jones (1999). *Environmental Indicators for North America and the United Kingdom*. Critical Issues Bulletin. Vancouver, BC: The Fraser Institute.

Health Canada (1993). *Health-Risk Perception in Canada*. Ottawa: Minister of Supply and Services Canada.

Hogan, James (1993). Ozone Politics: They Call This Science? *Omni* 15: 34.

Lees-Haley, P., and R.S. Brown (1992). Biases in Perception and Reporting Following a Perceived Toxic Exposure. *Percept. Motor Skills* 75: 531–44.

Lott, John R. (1997). Gun Locks: Bound to Misfire. *Wall Street Journal* (July 16).

Malarek, Victor (1999). Cone of Silence. *Fifth Estate* (February 9), CBC Television.

Mihlar, Fazil (1996). *Regulatory Overkill: The Cost of Regulation in Canada*. Critical Issues Bulletin. Vancouver, BC: The Fraser Institute.

——— (1997). *Federal Regulatory Reform: Rhetoric or Reality?* Public Policy Sources 6. Vancouver, BC: The Fraser Institute.

Miljan, Lydia (1989). Network Coverage of the Environment? *On Balance* 2, 9.

——— (1998). 1997 Year in Review. *On Balance* 11, 3.

Morrison, Kathleen (1993). Cancer and Health: TV Attention to the Environmental Causes of Cancer. *On Balance* 6, 7.

——— (1996). Cheese, Politics and Human Health. *On Balance* 9, 5.

Roach, Mary (1992). Here's the Hole Story about the Ozone and Your Chance of Getting Skin Cancer: Sun Struck. *Health* (May/June): 42.

Scheuplein, Robert (1991). Do Pesticides Cause Cancer? *Consumers' Research* (December): 30–33.

Statistics Canada (1999a). *Causes of Deaths*. Cat. No. 84F0208 (May).

——— (1999b). Deaths, 1997. *The Daily* (May 13).

Tengs, Tammy O., and John D. Graham (1996). The Opportunity Cost of Haphazard Investments in Life-Saving. In R. Hahn (ed.), *Improving Risk Management: From Science to Policy* (Oxford: Oxford University Press).

Torrance, Kelly (1998). Risky News. *Fraser Forum* (October): 12–16.

Vancouver Sun (1998) (June 16): A10.

Wigod, Rebecca (1992). Coming to Grips with the Cold Hard Hand of Cancer. *Vancouver Sun* (June 8): A1, A3.

2   Case Studies in Risk Management

Science and Policy in the Economic Assessment of Transport Regulations

WILLIAM G. WATERS, II

Science and policy

Science is the institutionalized activity of expanding knowledge by investigation, research, and debate. This scientific activity places considerable emphasis on reviewing available knowledge, devising experiments or conducting investigations to shed light on the questions of interest, and publishing or submitting the analysis for peer review. Although we often have "hunches" or hypotheses to investigate, ultimately there is commitment to seeking the truth, that is, accepting whatever one finds and communicating that. Science and research place emphasis on the use of logic and empirical evidence in arriving at a position. The foregoing description could be qualified in many respects but it will provide a point of contrast.

Policy refers to the development of rules, regulations, or other actions by government agencies or representatives, devised in response to perceived needs of the public. The public may encompass broad groups in society or policy may be aimed at helping particular groups if there is broad consensus supporting such a policy. The analysis and decision-making leading to policy often emerge in a highly charged

Notes will be found on pages 70–71.

political atmosphere where perceptions of problems and solutions may be more important than objective descriptions and factual analysis.

There is more to the process of science and policy-making, including questions of principle versus practice. But, these two cryptic descriptions are sufficient to raise a few questions.[1]

Potential conflicts between science and policy

Although one would expect that knowledge, fact-finding, and analysis would be a key part of formulating public policy, the decision-making environment is not always compatible with the requirements for scientific analysis. For one thing, policy-making typically functions on a tight time table: policies must be devised, sometimes on short notice. Governments *will* make decisions, with or without good advice. In contrast, science (meaning conceptual and empirical analysis) cannot always produce definitive answers as learned people may disagree and different empirical analyses may produce different results. Science and knowledge progress by confronting and comparing different approaches. There is no tight time table to invoke closure on scientific debate. It is important that existing knowledge be codified and summarized to help policy makers but, at times, the state of the science (or that of the scientific advisors) may not be able to provide the definitive guidance that is sought.

Projects and policies are viewed through different lenses: academic researchers, politicians, and civil servants have different perspectives and professional backgrounds. This can affect both the objectives pursued and the interpretation of costs and benefits. Even within the civil service, there are different perspectives, which reflect the type of department they represent. Treasury Board staff tend to have a different perspective on proposed projects or policies than the view taken by those in the operating agencies putting the policy proposals forward (Boardman, Vining, and Waters, 1993).

There are other characteristics of the political environment of government policy making that are important to recognize. One is that governments may favour groups or regions or industries that are a political priority. The resultant objectives and actions might not stand up to objective analysis based on broader goals; that is, short-term political priorities can differ from long-term goals and the means to achieve them.

A second important characteristic of the political process is that perceptions and popular opinion matter a great deal. Politicians respond to, and mirror, the public mood. It is common for people to hold beliefs that are inconsistent with the facts. The average person does not engage in scientific inquiry to evaluate the information coming from the media. People form opinions and politicians survive by reading these moods and designing policies that appeal to constituents. The key point is that perceptions are (or, at least, can be) reality in politics. These can drive decisions and they can be in conflict with what careful and scientific investigation would reveal.

A third characteristic of the process of policy making, which can be important at times, is secrecy. A fundamental characteristic of good research and thorough investigation is the regular revelation of progress and conclusions, opening them to criticism. But, in the hypercritical world of democratic politics, often it is necessary to keep options and investigations secret because opponents of government have an interest in anything that can be seized upon to criticize the government of the day.

Related to this is the problem of acknowledging errors. While it is embarrassing to researchers to realize that some of their hypotheses were wrong or evidence misinterpreted, there is a common acceptance that knowledge advances by detecting errors and redirecting effort. In the world of politics, however, error may be seized upon as a sign of weakness or poor judgement by the government. As a result, there is great reluctance to admit error. Often governments must continue to pursue a policy, even when they realize that it is a mistake, because there would be broader strategic costs if they were to admit error.

The implication of the latter two characteristics is that it is all the more important to get policies right the first time.

The growing importance of risk assessment and regulation

Risk assessment and regulation is becoming more important for governments all the time. The reductions in government spending and accompanying decrease in staff in recent years has meant that government has less capacity to carry out the policies it would like. A reduction of direct expenditures or operations by government makes regulatory policies relatively more attractive. Regulations have the seeming attraction of directly targeting something the government wishes to achieve while the costs of implementing the policy are largely borne by those affected by the regulations rather than by the government. This is an attractive feature to a fiscally constrained government; however, it is seen as negative by economists and policy analysts because the government implementing a regulation may be oblivious to—and normally does not bear—the costs imposed on society of adhering to the regulation.

Secondly, the increase in risk assessment and regulation is a paradox of modern wealthy societies. We live in an age when the traditional scourges of human kind—the "four horsemen of the apocalypse"—are largely subdued for residents of wealthy countries. Nevertheless, many of us are quite preoccupied with risks and demanding more from governments on these issues. There are several reasons why this might be the case. The primary one is wealth itself: having escaped the prospect of famine, pestilence, and so on, we enjoy life and are wealthy enough to worry about what would have been minor concerns in previous generations. There is also the argument that modern industry is producing more substances and at least some of them will have harmful effects upon us, given our long life expectancy. Further, our ability to conceive of, and investigate, potentially harmful effects is increasing. We can measure minute particles every more minutely.

For all these reasons, governments are finding risk analysis and regulatory policy of growing importance.

Science and public opinion polling

The Canadian government, and those of the Provinces, place great emphasis on polling to find out what people's feelings or perceptions are about problems and possible policies and, hence, what issues are perceived as important and what policies are politically feasible. While *realpolitik* cannot be ignored, there is a big difference between establishing policy on the basis of widely held beliefs or perceptions and constructing policy on the basis of facts and knowledge. Note that we can be very scientific in gauging and measuring public opinion but this is not the same as basing policy on scientific fact about the problem requiring a policy response.

Some fear that recently there may be a reduced commitment in government to the pursuit of real knowledge and analysis and, instead, officials are concentrating on collecting opinions of the public and of interest groups to guide policy. This includes engaging stakeholders in the formation of policy. Stakeholders might have objective analysis and evidence behind their position but they might also be acting from pure self-interest. Given the everyday pressures that face those on the policy front line, it is not hard to see that public acceptance of policies—whatever scientific validity may underlie their beliefs—could come to be an expedient and seemingly less risky approach to policy formation.

Implications

Civil servants are caught between the politician's desire for quick policies that respond to public perceptions and the academic and research communities' belief that careful, lengthy, and often expensive study is required to assess real policy needs accurately and weigh the cost and benefits of alternative policy actions. Some public issues and policy alternatives can be anticipated so that research and analysis can be carried out in advance and hence influence actual policies when they suddenly rise high on the political agenda. For long-term policy formulation, it should be possible to meld science and research with policy formulation. This does not mean that it is an automatic or a smooth process. Knowledge comes with debate and disagreement along the way. It can be difficult to sort out disagreements among researchers. How does an administrator sort out which econometric equation and results are to be accepted? But time and at least some resources can be allocated to address such issues when the policy deadline is not urgent. But, often there is urgency and it is necessary to make policy decisions with or without consensus from the research community.

Evolution of economic evaluation of public policy

There is much experience with the economic evaluation of government projects and policies. These include the broad policy analysis of macroeconomic studies or aggregate industry/market studies in contrast to microeconomic studies of specific investment projects or policy proposals. A recent example of macro-studies in transportation would be D.A. Aschauer's empirical assessment of infrastructure spending and economic development (Aschauer 1989a, 1989b) and the extensive literature that followed his studies (see Gillen 1996 for a concise review of this literature). There are numerous examples of the empirical assessment of the impact of policies on specific industries or markets.

Microeconomic analysis in transportation has been used extensively. Cost-benefit analysis (CBA) has been used extensively since the 1950s[2] to evaluate infrastructure projects. CBA has also been used to evaluate regulatory policies but examples are fewer in number. Cost effectiveness analysis (CEA) has also been used extensively, especially in the field of transportation safety. The main difference between the two techniques is that CEA frameworks tend to be less comprehensive than CBA frameworks, which are supposed to include all benefits and costs "to whomsoever they may accrue," whereas CEA might focus only on one or two measures of effectiveness. The other important characteristic of CEA is that it does not put dollar values on the measure of effectiveness. For example, a CBA study of an improvement in transportation safety would require that a dollar value be placed on lives saved, injuries avoided, and so on, whereas a CEA study would merely rank different policies in terms of the cost-effectiveness rating such as cost per life saved or cost per accident avoided. This avoids the controversy of valuing intangibles yet still is useful for prioritizing and rationing a scarce budget. However, while CEA is useful for prioritizing within a department, unlike CBA it is not as useful for making comparisons across different measures of outcome.

In terms of the economic evaluation of regulatory policies, there are three main areas of application (which may overlap):

(1) traditional economic regulation (price regulation, controlling entry into, or exit out of, an industry, licensing, consumer protection);

(2) transportation safety (this can include vehicles and operations, safety, infrastructure standards, traffic control;

(3) environmental regulations (these include air-emission standards, both local and global warming, ground contamination, energy, and human dimensions such as noise and health impacts).

Economic evaluation of risk and regulation in transportation

An electronic scan on a number of key words and phrases (cost benefit, risk, environment, transportation, etc.) produced a stack of abstracts many centimetres thick and an electronic search of the literature produces the iceberg's tip of what is actually in the public domain. A short and arbitrary list of the topics revealed is shown in Appendix 1. The list illustrates the diversity of topics that exist.

To draw some lessons from the application of CBA and CEA to the regulation of transport risk, it is instructive to focus on a few specific issues that have been studied a great deal: (1) the research and evidence on the American regulations on fuel economy for automobiles; (2) a policy initiated for energy reasons but subsequently justified for safety reasons (the American 55-mph speed limit); and (3) automotive air bags.

Fuel-economy regulations and their effects

One well-publicized and extensively studied policy has been the American attempt to increase the fuel economy of automobiles through regulations. This has been a long-term policy, not subject to reversals in direction. This is a useful case study with some lessons about regulations and economic evaluations of their effects.

The policy emerged following the fuel "crises" of the 1970s, although even prior to this there were various calls for government intervention to reduce fuel consumption. There was (and is) wide belief that the true social-opportunity costs of petroleum are understated and, hence, fuel is consumed at higher than optimal rates. The arguments include:

(1) the United States is a monopsony or dominant buyer (the converse of a monopoly supplier), which leads to prices below actual marginal cost;

(2) a substantial portion of American defence expenditures is aimed at keeping oil fields in the Middle-East secure and the costs of this protection should be included in the price of gasoline;

(3) oil markets are myopic or influenced by short-term political priorities of supplying nations and, hence, the current market price is below that which is sustainable over the long-run;

(4) much vehicle use is a deductible business expense and, hence, consumers are not paying the full price of fuel;

(5) environmental costs such as local and global air pollution costs are not internalized (Lave and Lave 1999: 262).

If true, gasoline is underpriced with the predictable consequence that larger quantities of gasoline are consumed than would be the case if the price were higher. In the long run, the problem is compounded as complementary decisions and investments are made in response to cheap fuel; for example, motorists would tend to buy less economical cars and use them more intensively, including, possibly, living in locations, and adopting life-styles, more dependent on cheap fuel. One solution that has been suggested

> would be to impose a tax to account for the externalities. Gasoline taxes, however, are unpopular. The CAFE [corporate average fuel economy] standards are thus an attractive alternative for politicians who find a gasoline tax politically inexpedient or who believe that regulation is a more equitable mechanism for reducing future demand. Although the CAFE regulation is more attractive to politicians, economists are quick to note that the cost of achieving the desired goal is likely to be higher with regulation than with a market approach, such as an externality tax. A market approach provides an incentive to change behaviour immediately while giving maximum flexibility to all parties to achieve the desired goals.
>
> A further difficulty is that Congress made a guess that doubling fuel economy was the right regulation. [Today] with oil prices below 1973 levels, after accounting for inflation, the CAFE standards specify fuel economy levels much higher than are demanded by consumers. (Lave and Lave 1999: 262–3)

There are at least two issues here. One is the choice of policy instrument, direct regulation or taxation. The second but related and more subtle issue is the long-term consequences of conflicting policy signals.

The debate between those advocating regulation and those advocating taxation (pricing) is not new. Rather, it is a long-standing conflict between economic advice and policy action. Economic arguments often identify pricing or taxation as a superior tool for responding to a misallocation of resources but it frequently encounters significant objections by policy makers. Some objections have a "scientific" basis; for example, it is claimed that welfare economics arguments for taxation solutions do not take income distribution into account. However, it has also been noted frequently that the effects of income distribution often are exaggerated and quite possibly correctable. There is a deeper dislike of pricing mechanisms by the general public and hence by the politicians who mirror public moods, perhaps because the majority of people do not understand the subtlety of economic arguments. Concerning the CAFE regulations, A.M. Howitt and A. Altshuler (1999: 235) note that people seem to accept the notion that a few corporations can be bullied into achieving desired public-policy goals without the need of burdening the public at large via higher taxation. This may well be a plausible description of the policy environment that lay behind the fuel-economy initiatives but the economics is not sound. The costs of achieving the fuel-economy standards will be borne by the users, whether in gasoline prices or the prices of cars that they purchase. Popular perceptions and the conclusions from economic analysis are in conflict here.

There was also an on-going conflict between the broad imposed policy of increasing fuel economy and the eventual real decline in fuel prices. At first, the fact that fuel prices were not raised probably did not make much difference. The prospect of rationing and scarcity of gasoline supplies would imply a long-run shadow price of fuel above what motorists were paying at the time. But, over time, the feared fuel shortages did not materialize and motorists adjusted to the low fuel prices. Choosing a regulatory policy over taxation is not a "one-off" decision. The inconsistency between regulations and the price incentives to consumers hampered market performance, increasing costs as manufacturers struggled to meet standards inconsistent with personal preferences of consumers responding to relatively low fuel prices. Although more factors than fuel prices are involved, the rising popularity of light trucks and, now, sport utility vehicles are a manifestation of consumers purchasing the larger and less economical vehicles that they desired (trucks had lower fuel-economy standards). That is, over time inconsistencies or behavioural responses by consumers may undermine the costs and effectiveness of initial policies that were incomplete or inconsistent in their construction.

Finally, there is the appearance of side effects that were not recognized initially. In this example, there are trade-offs between policy goals. The goal of increasing fuel economy (whether by regulation or price mechanisms) sets forces into motion that alter the design of vehicles. In this case, increased fuel economy led to smaller and lighter vehicles. But, there is a significant correlation between the size of a vehicle and personal safety in crashes. Crandall and Graham (1989) estimate that the down-sizing of cars to meet fuel-economy standards resulted in a 14 percent to 27 percent reduction in safety.[3]

In summary, the fuel-economy standards for automobiles are a worthy case study of the costs and effectiveness of policy actions even when those policies are consistent over a long period of time. They illustrate the importance of consistency between regulatory policies and pricing and taxation policies. Even if economists' arguments for pricing policies are rejected by policy makers, real complications and costs are likely to emerge if at least some reliance on pricing policies is not employed. This long-standing policy and its consequences are useful for illustrating how human and corporate behaviour can thwart or, at least, complicate intended policies and their costs. Similarly, it provides interesting examples of side effects whereby achieving one goal may conflict with other goals being pursued by other policies, that is, the emergence of "solution-caused problems" (Lave and Lave 1999: 287).

While economists are quick to invoke pricing and taxation as the recommended policy instrument, there are some compelling arguments for at least some role for technology-forcing regulations in the case of fuel economy. Even if automobile manufacturers thought that fuel prices might rise in the future, any individual manufacturer would be taking a high risk to begin to produce vehicles with much greater fuel economy. Government policy stabilized expectations about the future by calling for mandated economy standards. Although one can debate whether or not the standards set were appropriate, they did have the effect of keeping the playing field level so all manufacturers could compete under a consistent set of rules.[4]

The Regulation of Transportation Safety

Government involvement in transportation safety is decades old. There are many examples of economic analysis used to evaluate existing and prospective regulations; but there are also many cases where regulations persist contrary to economic criticism. Reviewing a couple examples of long-standing regulatory policies can shed light on the controversies that can arise around the economic analysis of transport safety.

Background on safety regulation

There are a mix of motives behind government involvement in transportation safety. Many regulations are a response to classic market failures, notably the problems of asymmetric information and externalities. Transport operations often produce situations where consumers may know little about the safety of transport operations but the suppliers know a great deal. Under these circumstances, buyers make decisions lacking full information and this could cause firms to produce goods that are less safe than they should be or claim that operations are much safer than they really are. Market outcomes will not be efficient. The other market failure prominent in safety issues is externalities: users of the transportation system may impose costs on others that they do not take into account in making their decisions. Even if unsafe drivers were to weigh the risks incurred to themselves, they do not take into account the risks imposed on others. Both of these market failures are *potential* rationales for government intervention (*actual* justification if it is found that the benefits out-weigh the costs of intervention).

It is common for safety intervention to include elements of paternalism in the rationales, that is, to protect people from themselves. It can be difficult to separate paternalism from lack of information. If people are observed not taking advantage of safety equipment (e.g., seat belts), is this because they are inadequately informed and would use seat belts if they fully understood the probabilities of injury? Or, are they deemed to be exercising bad judgement and need to be protected from the folly of their own actions?

One of the intriguing but also frustrating characteristics of transport-safety regulation is that policies sometimes lead to behavioural adjustments by users that thwart the intended safety goals. In its extreme form, this is the "offsetting behaviour hypothesis," attributed to Peltzman (1975) but which has been noted and studied by many authors. An example may be a recent popular innovation to improve safety, the Antilock Braking System (ABS), which prevents wheel lock-up during heavy braking and thus enables drivers to have better control. (I ignore controversies over whether or not ABS brakes always lead to improvement; there are some circumstances where this is not true.) If drivers' behaviour were not altered by the presence of the brakes, we would see reductions in crashes, fewer pedestrians hit, and so on. But, what if the drivers modify their behaviour to take advantage of better braking? If drivers accurately understand the technical capabilities and wished to continue driving at the previous level of risk they faced, this would nullify the effects of the brake technology. The even more alarming scenario is that, if motorists overestimate the benefit of ABS brakes, they could end up having even worse safety records. This is a graphic illustration of the possibility of the off-setting behaviour hypothesis. "Society may be happy about the people with antilock brakes who can get to church on rainy days but not about those who use their new-found confidence to terrorize slower drivers" (Small 1999: 153).

There is a further complication with the possibility of behavioural adjustments in response to safety improvements. From the perspective of automobile safety, this means that policies are undermined by drivers' behaviour. On the other hand, from an economic perspective there is still a benefit being realized. If drivers are accurately informed about the risks and how they are affected by a new regulation, the fact that drivers choose to drive faster or closer to one another indicates that they value the time saving or other benefit as more valuable to them than the intended safety benefit (Lave and Weber 1970). That is, a benefit is realized by motorists but they deem it more desirable to "consume" the safety benefit in some form other than safety. This is usually regarded as a failure by automobile-safety advocates but, so long as there are no externalities or other such problems (it is, however, plausible that these factors are at work in many safety concerns), then a CBA might conclude that the policy was worthwhile even if it was failing by its CEA test.

It is useful to review a couple of transport-safety issues that have been widely studied to see some examples of the complications that arise in trying to assess safety policies. These are speed-limit regulations, specifically the 55-mph speed-limit policy that was pursued for several years in the United States, and the more recent controversy over air bags.

Evaluation of the 55-mph speed limit

The 55-mph speed limit in the United States originated in response to the energy crisis of the early 1970s. By slowing down cars, fuel consumption would be reduced. The policy appeared to work although there were other factors at work, notably reductions in traffic as trips were cancelled due to possible fuel shortages and the recession that accompanied the rise in fuel prices.

As fuel shortages eased, the rationale for the policy shifted from energy conservation to safety: the 55-mph speed limit was accompanied by a substantial reduction in crashes and fatalities from 55,500 fatalities in 1973 to 46,400 in 1974 (National Research Council; cited in Lave and Lave 1999: 271). This seemed to confirm the popular view that "speed kills." But, closer analysis revealed that the issue is more complex than was popularly thought (Lave and Lave 1999). In the first few years, the reductions in fatalities could be explained by a number of factors including an already existing downward trend in the accident and fatality rate, and the reduction in travel due to the recession (and fuel shortages early in the period). Another factor was that the speed limit not only reduced the average speed but also reduced the variance of speeds on the road. The data from the early years were not sufficient to test this influence but subsequent studies have confirmed that the variance of speed of vehicles is an important factor, possibly more important than the speed limit. That is, abnormally slow drivers pose a threat just as abnormally fast drivers do.

The increase in speed limits in 1987 provided another opportunity to assess the impact of the speed-limit change. At first glance, it appeared to support the viewpoint that speed kills: fatalities did increase on the interstate highways following relaxation of those speed limits. However, further analysis showed that this was misleading. Fatalities did increase but traffic volumes jumped substantially on these higher-speed highways. That is, people were diverting from slower highways to the faster and normally safer interstate highways. Focusing on total fatalities in a state rather than just on fatalities on the interstate highways and correlating this with states that did and did not increase the speed limit showed that fatalities tended to decrease overall in the states that adopted higher speed limits (Lave and Elias 1997). The explanation was the "ripple effects" whereby people diverted from less safe roads in response to the opportunity to save time; the net result was decrease in the number of fatalities rather than an increase.

Another illustration of substitution affecting safety policies was the proposal that infants travelling on airplanes be required to have their own seat rather than sitting on a parent's lap. This would require that parents purchase an additional seat. As a result, a number of parents travelling on relatively short-haul air routes would divert to automobile travel, a mode less safe than commercial air travel. The net result would be an increase in fatalities rather than a decrease (Windle and Dresner 1991). As a result, the proposed policy was abandoned.

The evidence from the foregoing studies indicates that expected benefits may not be retained, once substitution and system effects are taken into account.

Air bags

The automotive air bag is a remarkable piece of technology. In the event of an impact, sensors detect the sudden deceleration of the vehicle and trigger the inflation of an air bag mounted, for the driver, on the steering wheel and, for the front-seat passenger, on the dashboard. All this takes place, literally, in less than the blink of an eye. To achieve this performance, the air bag must inflate extremely rapidly (with a velocity of about 300 kph). Recently, there has been adverse publicity because a number of people, mostly children and adults of small stature, have been killed by the air bags. The number of deaths reported in North America (61) is small compared to the estimated 1700 lives saved (IIHS 1997). A less well known but similarly adverse fact is that minor and even moderate injuries are worse in air-bag equipped cars than in those not so equipped (Dalmotis 1996). This has given rise to complaints that air-bag performance should be modified and requests by some users that the air bag be disconnected. Air bags are not required equipment in Canada but they are in the United States and, because automobile manufacturing is integrated across the border, new cars sold in Canada are equipped with air bags.

An important issue is the interpretation of the role of air bags: are they viewed as a system supplementary to seat belts or are they to be a primary safety device, a "passive-restraint" system. If seat belts are worn, air bags offer modest additional protection primarily for frontal collisions. If seat belts are not worn, then air bags are significant protection for frontal collisions.

In the United States, although most states have legislation making the wearing of seat belts mandatory, the estimated percent of drivers wearing seat belts is about 68 percent (NHTSA 1996) compared to about 90 percent in Canada. Because a large number of drivers do not wear seat belts, air bags are mandated to protect these drivers. Injuries and even death can occur in low-speed crashes if the occupants are not buckled. Therefore air bags are triggered by impacts at relatively low speeds (typically 12 kph to 20 kph). But, if occupants of the vehicle are wearing seat belts, there is little or no need for air bags in low-speed impact accidents. It has been discovered that the air bag itself is a major source of injury and has even caused a few deaths.

As a result of the publicity about air bags, some steps are underway to modify them. Air bags are being "depowered" to reduce the likelihood of injury when they inflate. However, this means that when the air bag is really needed, in a high speed crash, the air bag may not be fully deployed when the occupant makes contact with the bag. The air bag will be less effective and even dangerous if the occupant hits the air bag as it first deploys. The threshold deployment speed has not been changed—air bags are still set to deploy in relatively low-speed collisions.

The air-bag controversy raises a number of issues. First, is the debate over using technology to make vehicles safer because people refuse to use seat belts. There is extensive information about the efficacy of seat belts but many people still do not wear them. It appears to be paternalism that is motivating the promotion of air bag technology. Users must pay for them in the price of a car even if they are "standard equipment" (i.e., no extra charge). Those who do use seat belts are paying a substantial price for modest additional protection. If air bags were optional equipment, they could weigh pro and con and decide for themselves if the air bags were worth it to them. As it is, this decision has been made for them. Canada does not require air bags largely due to studies that conclude that the benefits are only marginal given that the vast majority of Canadians wear seat belts (Lawson 1993).

The publicity about air bags may distort rather than clarify the problems and benefits of air bags. If people fear air bags and would turn them off if they could, then this would nullify whatever benefits the air bags have. Prior to the recent publicity, the concern was that people might overstate the benefits of air bags: if people thought that air bags would protect them, they might not wear a seat belt. If this offsetting behaviour came to pass, air bags would result in a even more injuries and deaths than if they had not been introduced. This is because seat belts protect occupants in a variety of crash situations, whereas air bags are only really effective for frontal impacts. Fortunately, it does not appear that this offsetting behaviour is widespread.

Another less well known cost of air bags is the cost of repairing vehicles and re-installing the bags once they have deployed. The air-bag sensors must be replaced along with the bags, and typically there is extensive interior damage from the air bags themselves. Repairs can run to several thousand dollars. This means cars more than a few years old are likely to be scrapped rather than repaired and air bags are causing many cars to be scrapped that otherwise would have had several years life left in them. It appears that this cost was not given adequate attention in the original decisions to adopt air bags.

There are technological developments that can improve air bags. Research and development is underway to produce "smart" air bags that could modify the deployment depending on the circumstances. One possibility is to have two rates of inflation, one for slow speed impacts and a more rapid deployment for high-speed impacts. Already some manufacturers have passenger-side bags that deploy only if the seat is occupied and sensors could be used to prevent the bag from deploying if the occupant were out of position and too close to the air bag (these have been the cause of deaths). This raises an interesting issue for rapidly evolving technologies. Arguably, there are some shortcomings in the current modifications that are being made to air bags but it is quite possible that technological solutions will solve the problems more quickly than optimal policies could be designed and implemented based on current air-bag design and performance characteristics.

In sum, the adoption of air bags is an example of a policy to adopt a technological solution because people were not making use of available safety equipment. These people would be protected from themselves by mandating air bags in all vehicles. Mandating air bags means every user must pay for the air bags, whether or not they are wanted or needed. Car owners pay for them in the initial purchase price and in the increase in insurance premiums caused by the need to repair the damage caused by air bags that have deployed. The net merits of air bags are debatable at least; they can be valuable *if* vehicle drivers and occupants do not make use of belts though seat-belts are the first choice. If seat-belts are used, as in Canada, the air bags produce a modest additional benefit. The benefits do not necessarily exceed the costs (Waters, 1997; Lawson, 1993). It may be that many people would elect to buy them but, at present, they do not have this choice.

Lessons

The experience with economic analysis of transport regulations is both encouraging and frustrating. It is encouraging because there is considerable experience with, and examples of, CBA and CEA in evaluating transport regulations. It is frustrating because there are persistent policies where economic analysis has little influence (the fuel economy measures might be an example). Economic analysis has been useful but contradictions such as low fuel prices along with fuel economy regulations are not a formula for cost-effective policies. Nonetheless, a review of some of these studies and criticisms of past policies can identify a number of lessons or guidelines to improve the analysis of public policies.

First, while there is a presumption that we seek the most cost-effective policies, it is important to recognize that there can be widely held misconceptions of problems and their solutions. Because politics mirrors popular sentiment, there are times when there will be a conflict between the facts or science of an issue and what is politically feasible and preferred. Academics have the luxury of ignoring and criticizing such situations but civil servants must make the policy process function and must produce acceptable and good policy in the face of special interests, misperceptions, and perhaps even some "junk science" put forward by advocates of certain policies and positions.

Evaluation of costs, effectiveness, and benefits must focus both on direct and indirect costs and consequences. Many criticisms of past policies arose because indirect costs and behavioural responses, which undermined effectiveness, were overlooked. It is important, however, to consider carefully the direct or first-round implications of some action. In evaluating a proposed policy intervention, it is vital to look closely at the claims of costs and effectiveness. Will the policy have the consequences that are desired? What evidence is being put forward? Is it scientific evidence or opinion that is being presented in support of a policy? Further, how much evidence is there? Are there numerous studies or only one or two? Have they been subject to review and criticism so their scientific validity can be assessed?

Along with questions about effectiveness, it must be asked what the costs of the proposed policy are. Costs manifest themselves in various ways. There are costs borne by the implementing agency, which may be separate from costs borne by enforcement agencies or costs borne by the federal government or provinces. And, costs are imposed on users. These may be money costs or costs in time or inconvenience. It is important to recognize the latter, for two reasons: first, these are real costs—opportunities forgone—whether expressed in money or in minutes; second, even if a government agency wished to ignore costs imposed on users in their evaluation, these costs will affect the behaviour of users and this may be important for evaluating the impact that particular safety policies will have. If a regulation imposes time or similar personal costs on users that can be avoided, then people will try to avoid them and this may undermine the effectiveness of the proposed policy. As noted, there are many examples of people's behaviour modifying the outcome of safety regulations. These are the "downstream" or indirect consequences of some initial policy.

Also, note that, even if it can be demonstrated that a particular policy is cost-effective, this does not mean it is worth doing. CEA is incomplete; a CBA framework tries to measure the value of the benefits derived from a policy and not just whether or not the policy meets some technical criteria. Expressed another way, it is important to assess the worthwhileness of the goals or effectiveness measures that are being pursued.

The more subtle but possibly important effects are the various indirect or "downstream" consequences that follow from a policy, including behavioural responses. Research analysts and policy-makers alike have learned the importance of indirect effects, which often may have been unanticipated and unintended. Often, these indirect effects take time to become apparent. Looking back at the experience in transport regulations, it is the accumulation of indirect and unanticipated consequences that often are the basis for criticisms of policies.

Anticipating behavioural response is an important issue: the nature of regulations is that we are trying to induce people to do something they are not doing at present. It is understandable, even likely, that people will resist interference with their behaviour. The illustration from fuel efficiency is instructive: regulations can modify fuel economy but low fuel prices work counter to this and even encourage automobile-intensive life-styles and choice of car-size can thwart fuel economy. The offsetting-behaviour hypothesis from discussions of transport safety can arise in any field. Policies, however good their intention, will set changes in motion as people respond to the new environment and its signals. In some cases, the behavioural response might thwart the policy intention completely. More typically, it will reduce but not eliminate the desired policy outcomes. In almost every case, this means that policies cannot be as effective as was desired, unless the behavioural responses are anticipated in the design and coordination of policy packages.

In the end, combining good science and good policy is a worthwhile administrative and social goal. There are conflicts along the way, and not all battles can be won but it is a professional responsibility of both researchers and those in the policy-making process to seek a closer link between their respective activities.

Appendix 1
Sample of transportation topics involving economic assessment of risks, costs and benefits

(Gleaned from a review of abstracts generated from a computerized bibliographic search.)

- marine organisms released through ballast water
- ground-water contamination from non-point sources
- truck size and weight limits
- noise and vibration from transport operations and impacts on drivers and nearby residents
- bird strikes at airports
- transport of radioactive materials
- tinted glass on automobiles
- fire danger in underground transit systems
- improving emissions from small engines for use in third-world countries
- air-traffic control standards
- safety of life at sea
- safety implications of environmentally-based regulations on automobiles
- air emissions with alternative fuels
- bridge strength and failure probabilities
- policies to promote car-pooling
- speed-limit enforcement
- "cash for clunkers" to reduce air emissions
- motor-vehicle safety inspections
- air-bag regulations
- bicycle-helmet standards and requirements

- carbon monoxide and other emissions at drive-up facilities (banks, drive-in restaurants, petc.)
- tort liability considerations in developing intelligent vehicle and highway systems (IVHS)
- mandatory use of child seats during air travel
- the implications of economic deregulation for safety enforcement
- profiles of high-risk drivers
- collision risk of oil-tanker traffic
- transportation of people on freight vehicles
- safety of flawed seamless gas cylinders
- traffic signaling, traffic flow, and safety
- motorcycle helmet regulations
- use of cellular telephones and traffic safety
- substance abuse and vehicle operators
- signaling for railroad-grade crossings
- truck-crash rates for diabetic drivers
- mandatory car-trip reduction for large employers
- graduated licensing for automobile drivers
- wind-shear detection for airplanes

Notes

1 For a further discussion of professional backgrounds and how they influence policy analyses, see Weimer and Vining 1992: chap. 1.
2 The origins of cost-benefit analysis (CBA) of public projects began with water-resource projects in the United States, whereas the first applications were in transport in the United Kingdom. The textbooks and articles on CBA in transport often originate outside North America, perhaps reflecting the early application of these techniques. Some countries—notably England, New Zealand, and to some extent, Australia—have extensive experience and reliance on CBA. Many state and provincial highway departments have standardized CBA frameworks and manuals. An institution where CBA is relied upon extensively is the World Bank.

3 The link between vehicle mass and safety is more complicated than this. For example, Greene 1996 (cited at Lave and Lave 1999: 269) notes that CAFE standards tended to reduce the variance in the weights of vehicles on the road. This would tend to make the cars more equal in crashes and thus could entail a safety benefit.

4 Well, not quite a level playing field: focusing on corporate average fuel economy standards gave an advantage to large automobile manufacturers producing a wide range of vehicles, i.e., North American producers. Producers of a narrow range of vehicles were at a disadvantage. A company that produced only large cars (e.g., Mercedes-Benz) could not average this vehicle's fuel economy with those of smaller models. Conversely, manufacturers specializing in small cars (the Japanese manufacturers at the time) did not have the high-end high-markup vehicles to help offset the costs and low margins of the more competitive small-car markets.

References

Aschauer, D.A. (1989a). Is Public Expenditure Productive? *Journal of Monetary Economics* 23: 177–200.

——— (1989b). Public Investment and Productivity Growth in the Group of Seven. *Economic Perspectives* 13, 5: 17–25.

Boardman, A., A. Vining, and W.G. Waters (1993). Costs and Benefits through Bureaucratic Lenses: Example of a Highway Project. *Journal of Policy Analysis and Management* 12, 3: 532–55.

Crandall, R.W. (1984). Automobile Safety Regulation and Offsetting Behaviour: Some New Empirical Estimates. *American Economic Review* (May: Papers and Proceedings): 328–31.

Crandall, R.W., and J.D. Graham (1989). The Effect of Fuel Economy Standards on Automobile Safety. *Journal of Law and Economics* 32 (April): 97–118.

Crandall, R.W., and L. Lave, eds. (1981). *The Scientific Basis of Health and Safety Regulation*. Washington, DC: Brookings Institution.

Gillen, D.W. (1996). Transportation Infrastructure and Economic Development: A Review of Recent Literature. *Logistics and Transportation Review* 32, 1: 39–62.

Dalmotas, D.J. (1996). Performance of the Combination Manual Three-Point Seat Belt and Supplementary Restraint System Based on US Field Accident Data. Discussion Paper (January). Transport Canda, Road Safety and Motor Vehicle Regulation Directorate, Ottawa.

Greene, D.L. (1996). *Transportation and Energy*. Lansdowne, VA: ENO Transportation Foundation.

Howitt, A.M., and A. Altshuler (1999). The Politics of Controlling Auto Air Pollution. In J.A. Gomez-Ibanez, W.B. Tye and C. Winston (eds.), *Essays in Transportation Economics and Policy: A Handbook in Honor of John R. Meyer* (Washington, DC: Brookings Institution): 223–55.

Insurance Institute for Highway Safety [IIHS] (1997). *Airbag Statistics*. Digital document: www.hwysafety.org/PASSVEH/Abstates.htm.

Lave, C., and L. Lave (1999). Fuel Economy and Auto Safety Regulation: Is the Cure Worse than the Disease? In J.A. Gomez-Ibanez, W.B. Tye, and C. Winston, eds., *Essays in Transportation Economics and Policy: A Handbook in Honor of John R. Meyer* (Washington DC: Brookings Institution): 257–89.

Lave, C., and P. Elias (1997). Resource Allocation in Public Policy: The Effects of the 65-mph Speed Limit. *Economic Inquiry* 35 (July): 614–20.

Lave, L., and W.E. Weber (1970). A Benefit Cost Analysis of Auto Safety Features. *Applied Economics* 2: 265–75.

Lawson, John (1993). Cost-Benefit and Cost-Effectiveness Assessments of Potential Regulation Requiring Air Bags in Passenger Cars in Canada. *Chronic Diseases in Canada* 14, 4 (supp.): S93–S100.

Leone, R.A. (1999). Technology-Forcing Public Policies and the Automobile. In J.A. Gomez-Ibanez, W.B. Tye, and C. Winston, eds., *Essays in Transportation Economics and Policy: A Handbook in Honor of John R. Meyer* (Washington DC: Brookings Institution): 291–323.

National Highway Traffic Safety Administration [NHTSA] (1996). Effectiveness of Occupant Protection Systems and Their Use. Third Report to Congress (December). Washington, DC: United States Dep't of Transport. Digital document: www.nhtsa.dot.gov./cars/rules/rulings/208con2e.html.

Peltzman, S. (1975). The Effects of Automobile Safety Regulation. *Journal of Political Economy* 83: 677–725.

Small, K. (1999). Project Evaluation. In J.A. Gomez-Ibanez, W.B. Tye, and C. Winston, eds., *Essays in Transportation Economics and Policy: A Handbook in Honor of John R. Meyer* (Washington DC: Brookings Institution): 137–77.

Waters, W.G., II (1997). Overblown! Examining the Costs and Benefits of Automotive Air Bags in Canada. In *Proceedings*, Canadian Transportation Research Forum (Saskatoon, SK: University of Saskatchewan Printing Services): 625–43.

Weimer, D.L., and A.R. Vining (1992). *Policy Analyses: Concepts and Practice* (2nd ed). Englewood Cliffs, NJ: Simon and Schuster.

Windle, R.J., and M.E. Dresner (1991). Mandatory Child Safety Seats in Air Transport: Do They Save Lives? *Journal of the Transportation Research Forum* 31, 2: 309–16.

Second-hand Smoke and Cancer
The Research Evidence

John C. Luik

Of all the questions that might be asked about the problem of environmental tobacco smoke (ETS)—second-hand smoke or passive smoke, as it is called—perhaps the most interesting are these two: since science does not establish that ETS is a risk for lung cancer in non-smokers,

(1) why does a large majority of the public believe that it is such a risk and

(2) why do governments, not only in North America, but around the world, regulate public smoking as if it put non-smokers at risk of lung cancer?

The answer to these questions is to be found in the actions of the United States Environmental Protection Agency (EPA) and the anti-smoking movement, both of whom have manufactured a risk and orchestrated a health scare through failing to provide truthful answers to the central questions that should guide public policy about the risks of ETS or indeed about any other risk, namely:

(1) does second-hand smoke put non-smokers at risk of lung cancer and

(2) if it does, is the risk substantial enough to worry about?

I want to argue that second-hand smoke provides a splendid example of junk science producing junk public policy.

In order to examine how the EPA and the anti-smoking movement have manufactured the ETS lung-cancer risk, I want to look at two case studies, first, the court case in which the EPA's classification of ETS as a human carcinogen was overturned and, second, the 1998 study by the International Agency for Research on Cancer (IARC) that failed to find a statistically significant link between lung cancer and second-hand smoke. In the first instance, the public-health community and the anti-smoking movement manufactured a health risk and, in the second instance, they attempted to discredit their own scientific study when it failed to support their manufactured risk.

Both of these cases, the EPA court case and the reaction of the anti-smoking and health community to the IARC's ETS study are interesting because they reveal the same key characteristics of junk science—the misrepresentation of scientific findings, the misrepresentation of scientific procedure, and the desire, at all costs, to suppress dissent in the service of junk policy. Let us begin with the EPA court case.

The EPA in court: the Osteen decision

The decision: an analysis

On the face of it, the decision by Judge W.L. Osteen appears to be simply another piece of the seemingly unending stream of tobacco litigation: Flue-Cured Tobacco Cooperative Stabilization Corporation et al., Plaintiffs, v. United States Environmental Protection Agency, Defendant. The language is difficult, the arguments complex and technical, and the issue itself appears completely disconnected from the lives and concerns of ordinary citizens. But, behind Judge Osteen's carefully measured words, behind even the specific controversy that the judgment addresses are issues of enormous significance to every citizen of a democratic society who relies on his government to tell him the truth. For the Osteen decision at its core is about truth: it is about how the government uses science to determine whether something constitutes a risk to our health; it is about how the scientific procedures for finding truth and the administrative processes for disseminating truth can be corrupted; and it is about the consequences for public policy of institutionalizing such corrupt science. This analysis begins with a discussion of the concept of corrupt science, then turns to the regulatory processes addressed by the decision, and finally examines the substantive scientific issues of the decision.

Corrupt science

Inasmuch as we wish to argue that the Osteen decision supports the characterization of the EPA's ETS procedure and science as corrupt science, it is important to be clear at the outset about what constitutes corrupt science. By corrupt science we mean bogus science, science that knows that its data misrepresent reality and its procedures are deviant but that nonetheless attempts to pass itself off as genuine science. It is science that has an institutionalized motivation and justification for allowing ends extrinsic to science to determine the findings of science, for allowing science to be subject to an agenda not its own, for allowing science to tell lies with clear conscience. It is essentially science that wishes to claim the public-policy advantages of genuine science without conforming to the scientific procedure or doing the work of real science.

There are at least four characteristics of corrupt science. First, corrupt science is science that moves not from hypothesis and data to conclusion but instead from a mandated and acceptable conclusion to selected data back to the mandated and acceptable conclusion. It is science that starts with a conclusion, indeed, starts with a mandated policy and sees its job as that of finding and presenting only that evidence that is considered supportive of that conclusion. That is to say, it is science that fundamentally distorts the scientific procedure through using selected data to reach the "right" conclusion, a conclusion that by the very nature of the data necessarily misrepresents reality.

Second, corrupt science misrepresents the nature of what it seeks to explain. Rather than acknowledging alternative evidence or problems with its evidence that would cast doubt on its conclusions, and rather than admitting the complexity of the issue under review and the limits of the evidence, corrupt science presents what is at best a carefully chosen partial truth as the whole truth necessary for public policy. In effect, public policy is manipulated into reaching certain conclusions on the basis of data that has been fabricated, falsified, misrepresented, or massaged so as to speak in a fashion that is fundamentally at odds with the way things really are. Corrupt science in this sense adopts, according to Teich & Frankel, "the scientific counterparts of what lawyers call 'sharp practices' ... incomplete citation of previously published work; bias in peer review of ... manuscripts; or skewed selection of data to hide or disguise observations that do not fit the author's conclusions" (1992: 4).

Third, corrupt science not only misrepresents reality but also misrepresents its own procedures in arriving at its conclusions. Instead of acknowledging the selectivity of its procedures and the official desire for demonstrating predetermined conclusions, it invests both its procedures and its conclusions with a mantle of indubitability. It hides, as it were, behind what both scientists and the public believe scientific procedure to be and, in doing so, it builds an aura of respectability around a decidedly disrespectable procedure. The results appear to be reliable because the procedure appears to be objective, open, and candid—in short, scientific. The selective, the arbitrary, the irrational, and the contrived appear to be certifiably absent since the procedure is "scientific." Substance and procedure are thus mutually supporting and, taken together, the scientific findings that result from the scientific procedure present a formidable barrier to public policy dissent.

Fourth, whereas legitimate science creates a climate in which debate and dissent is welcome, in which disagreement is dealt with on the basis of the quality of its evidence and argument and in which *ad hominem* argument is considered inappropriate, corrupt science seeks to create formidable institutional barriers to dissent through excluding dissenters from the process of review, characterizing dissent as working against the public interest, and contriving to silence dissent not by challenging its scientific merits but by questioning its character and motivation.

These four characteristics of corrupt science manifest themselves in a variety of ways which include: claiming that a statistical association is a causal relationship; a highly selective use of data; fabrication of data; falsification of data; misrepresentation of data; selective citation and referencing; claiming that a risk exists regardless of exposure level; claiming that a large number of statistically non-significant studies constitute a significant evidentiary trend; claiming that a series of inconclusive or weak studies justify a strong conclusion; relaxing generally accepted statistical conventions without compelling reasons; being unwilling to consider non-conforming data seriously; implying that the status of an authority justifies its evidence independently of the strength of that evidence; suggesting that weak evidence warrants decisive regulatory action; claiming that a finding based on one population is necessarily true of a different population; suggesting that certain risks are exempt from the normal regulatory and public-policy process; and conjoining the roles of the public-policy advocate and scientist.

The Issues

The issues in dispute in the litigation before Judge Osteen centred on the EPA's 1992 report, *Respiratory Health Effects of Passive Smoking: Lung Cancer and Other Disorders,* in which the EPA, using the authority provided to it under the Radon Gas and Indoor Air Quality Research Act of 1986, examined the health effects of ETS and classified it as a Group A carcinogen (USEPA 1992). Classification as a group A carcinogen meant that the scientific evidence supported the conclusion that ETS causes lung cancer in human beings. The plaintiffs argued that both the procedure used by the EPA to examine the health effects of ETS and its finding that ETS causes cancer in human beings were flawed. Specifically, the plaintiffs alleged that: the EPA exceeded its statutory authority under the Radon Research Act; the EPA failed to follow the Radon Research Act's procedural requirements; the EPA violated established administrative law procedures by reaching a conclusion about the health effects of ETS before conducting its scientific examination of the evidence; and the EPA's classification of ETS as a Group A carcinogen was not the product of reasoned science and decision-making.

Issues about the procedure

Questions about the procedure involved at least three separate issues: the extent of the EPA's authority under the Radon Research Act; the nature of the Radon Research Act's procedural requirements and the EPA's conformity to these requirements; and the question of whether the EPA reached a decision about the health effects of ETS before beginning the scientific procedure, and whether such a decision violated administrative law procedures.

The EPA's authority under the Radon Research Act

The language of the Radon Research Act appears, at least within the statutory context, to be relatively straightforward. Yet, as Judge Osteen observed, the parties reading the same plain language of the Act, came "to opposite conclusions" as to its meaning (Osteen 1998: 8). The Act authorizes the EPA to establish a research program on radon and indoor air quality that has three components: research and development concerning the identification, characterization, and monitoring of the sources and levels of indoor air pollution; research relating to the effects of indoor air pollution and radon on human health, and dissemination of information to assure the public availability of this research (Osteen 1998: 4). The Act does not authorize the EPA to establish any regulatory program based on the research conducted under the Act. In order to assist it in discharging its responsibilities under the Act, the EPA is required to create two advisory groups, one of which is to be made up of representatives of federal agencies that are concerned with indoor air quality, and the other of which is to be made up of "individuals representing the States, the scientific community, industry, and public interest organizations" (Osteen 1998: 5). As the court notes, the purpose of the Act was to have the EPA provide United States Congress and the public with clear, objective information about indoor air quality and the effects of indoor air quality on human health (Osteen 1998: 10). The Act was not intended to provide regulatory authority to the EPA: the EPA's role was neither that of advocate of certain positions nor of public-policy maker. Rather, the EPA was to create a research program that would result in clear, neutral information about indoor air quality.

The plaintiffs did not dispute the right of the EPA to establish a re-search program on the possible effects of ETS on indoor air quality. They did, however, contest its authority to engage in a carcinogen risk assessment and classification on the grounds that these are regulatory actions that go beyond the authority of the Radon Research Act. The court, however failed to accept this line of argument.

> The court disagrees with Plaintiffs' argument that risk assessment constitutes a regulatory activity and is thus prohibited under the Radon Research Act. Both the NRC's [National Research Council] Redbook and EPA's Risk Assessment Guidelines identify regulato-ry activity as being comprised of two elements: risk assessment and risk management. Prohibition of certain conduct does not in-clude prohibition of lesser included activities. (Osteen 1998: 15)

Moreover, the also court noted that the Radon Research Act also contains specific directives to the EPA that warrant its carcinogenic classifications.

> First, Congress required EPA to characterize sources of indoor air pollution ... Since they emit gasses and particulates, burning cig-arettes are a source of indoor air pollution. By determining wheth-er these emissions cause cancer in people exposed to burning cigarettes, EPA is characterizing a source of indoor air pollution. Second, Congress required the EPA to determine indoor pollutant effects on health ... In determining whether health is affected by a pollutant, the researcher must identify whether a causal relation-ship exists between the pollutant and deteriorating health. Put simply, the researcher must determine how, if at all, a pollutant af-fects health. Once a researcher has identified how a pollutant harms human health, the risk is most often identified. This is es-pecially true regarding carcinogens. The Radon Research Act's general language authorizing EPA to characterize sources of pol-lutants, research effects on health, and disseminate the findings encompasses classifying pollutants based on their effects. (Osteen 1998: 12–13)

Thus, the court found that the Radon Act, by providing authority for characterizations of indoor pollutants and their possible health consequences, provides authority for the EPA to engage in risk as-sessment. As the Court noted, "the Act requires more of the EPA than merely describing effects. Congress intended EPA to disseminate findings, or conclusions, based upon the information researched and gathered. Utilizing descriptions of health effects to make findings is risk assessment" (Osteen 1998: 12). While the EPA is not provided with authority to engage in risk management, it is allowed to conduct risk assessments.

The Radon Research Act's procedural requirements and the EPA

The Radon Research Act requires that the EPA create two advisory groups to assist it in its research and other statutory activities. One of these groups is to be "comprised of individuals representing the States, the scientific community, industry, and public interest organizations" (Osteen 1998: 5). The plaintiffs alleged that the EPA failed to comply with this requirement of the law. The EPA replied that it met its procedural obligations by consulting with its own Science Advisory Board.

Before considering the court's analysis of this issue, it is important to be clear precisely what is at stake here. In one sense, this is a narrow legal argument about the conditions that satisfy a procedural requirement of the law. But, in another sense there is something far more important at stake. The procedural requirements for risk research and assessment are not incidental or peripheral to the research or the risk classifications that result from such a research procedure. Indeed, they are integral inasmuch as adherence to accepted scientific procedures and standards serves to preserve the integrity of the research findings.

In framing the legislation, the United States Congress understood that if science is to preserve its transparent and objective role in the public-policy process it must follow a procedure that was itself transparent and objective. In effect, because of the danger of the scientific procedure being subverted by a non-scientific agenda, the scientific procedure needs to occur in an arena in which all voices are heard and no position is excluded *a priori*. The Congress' mechanism for ensuring the legitimacy of the scientific procedure was to have that procedure occur within, and be accountable to, a representative body that included all, not just some, of those likely to be effected by the research and any consequent regulation. As Judge Osteen, quoting the Court of Appeals for the District of Columbia, noted:

> The most important aspect is the requirement of consultation with knowledgeable representatives of federal and state government, industry and labor. This goes far beyond the usual requirements of public notice and opportunity for comment set forth in the Administrative Procedure Act, and represents the Congressional answer to the fears expressed by industry and labor of the prospect of unchecked federal administrative discretion in the

field. These rather unique requirements of the Act are an important part of the ultimate legislative compromise, and must be giv-
en their due weight. (Osteen 1998: 32)

The representative advisory group serves, then, as an important check on
the corruption of science in that, by bringing everyone to the table and
then structuring its research program and determining its risk assessment on the record, the advisory group dramatically reduces the opportunities for manipulation of procedure, policy determination *a priori*, data
misrepresentation and evidentiary selectivity. The failure to comply with
the Radon Act's procedural requirements is not simply a legal quibble;
failure to comply goes to the heart of the question of whether the EPA's
research and risk assessment on ETS is an instance of corrupt science.

The EPA did not deny that it failed to create the required advisory
group and Judge Osteen noted that the "EPA's procedural failure constitutes a violation of the law" (Osteen 1998: 37). The crucial question
is, why would the agency act in a way so clearly in violation of the law?
We would suggest that the EPA failed to create a representative advisory group because such a group, first, would have objected to and made
transparent the improper research and risk-assessment procedure to
which the EPA was committed; and second, would have prevented the
ETS carcinogen classification. There are three pieces of evidence that
support this conclusion.

First, the EPA obviously understood how the advisory group would
operate and what was at stake in forming an advisory group. At a minimum, as Judge Osteen noted, an advisory group would have ensured
that the research and risk-assessment procedures were on the record,
preventing the gaps in the record that raise what the judge calls the "ugly possibility" of inappropriate methodology and selective evidence. By
failing to create an advisory group, the EPA allowed itself to work in the
dark—to work, both literally and figuratively, off the record.

But, by failing to create an advisory group, the EPA also ensured
the exclusion from its research and risk-assessment procedures of critics of its ETS position, which in this case included many others in addition to the tobacco industry. In effect, there would be no contradictory voices, no disturbing dissent to the predetermined scientific
procedure. The Tobacco Institute's attorney, John Rupp, complained to
assistant administrator William Rosenberg about the procedural unfairness of ignoring the industry's role in the research and risk assessment procedure, noting that "at no time has there been an opportunity
for a scientific discussion of fundamental issues regarding ETS"
(Kluger 1996: 693). But, of course, the corruption of the procedure was
deliberate: the EPA had no interest in having a "scientific discussion of

fundamental issues" with anyone who might provide compelling and credible evidence against its pre-determined position.

Second, the EPA, realizing that its manipulation of the research and risk-assessment procedure looked like an attempt to justify a pre-determined position, attempted to mislead the court about the steps it did take to ensure industry representation. The EPA told the court that it "formed an advisory group within the [Science Advisory Board] which included representatives of all the statutorily identified constituencies" (Osteen 1998: 21). This group, the Indoor Air Quality/Total Human Exposure Committee (IAQC), according to the EPA, contained three members (out of nine) who represented the tobacco industry. But the court concluded that this was not in fact true.

> EPA claims that one of the listed members, Dr. Woods, represent-ed industry. However, this is not possible since Dr. Woods left in-dustry for employment with a university almost a year before the first draft of the ETS Risk Assessment was made available for re-view by IAQC ... EPA further asserts that two other individuals represented industry. The ETS Risk Assessment IAQC listing does not contain the names of these individuals. The individuals are not listed in the IAQC ETS reviews' transcripts, nor does EPA assert or direct the court's attention to evidence that these individuals provided any participation in the ETS Risk Assessment.(Osteen 1998: 27–28)

The EPA's contention that Dr. Woods represented the tobacco in-dustry, even though he had taken up an academic appointment, is in-teresting in that it appears to represent a belief that one can never really leave the industry, that even whilst no longer in the industry's employ one's views will be the industry's views. The same peculiar notion un-derlies the EPA's further claim to the court that, because certain mem-bers of the IAQC were "associated with organizations that had received some industry funding pursuant to contract," they could be considered industry representatives (Osteen 1998: 28). As the Court observed, this "does not convert these individuals into industry representatives" (Osteen 1998: 28). Moreover, even if the IAQC had functioned in the way the EPA claimed, it would have been, according to the court, a

> poor proxy for industry representation. EPA sought parties near the "middle" of the spectrum when establishing SAB [Science Ad-visory Board] panels and allegedly avoided representation from ei-ther end of the spectrum. As a general rule, the tobacco industry occupies that end of the spectrum contesting the carcinogenicity

of ETS and EPA's motives. A committee aspiring to represent the middle of the ETS debate necessarily suppresses the tobacco industry's perspective. Further, industry's ability to submit comments to a "neutral" committee, which itself had access to EPA, is not equivalent to industry access to EPA. (Osteen 1998: 32)

But, of course, the EPA did not wish for the industry to have access for its corruption of the procedure was precisely designed to "necessarily suppress" the industry's perspective and participation in the research and assessment activities. Despite the EPA's claims, the record shows the IAQC did not and, indeed, could not function as the required advisory group since its representation did not include industry and its parties were chosen on the basis on their occupying positions near the middle of the spectrum.

The third and strongest piece of evidence supporting the claim that the EPA failed to create the required advisory group because such a group would have exposed and opposed its fraudulent research and assessment program is the fact that the agency came to the conclusion that ETS was a human carcinogen prior to beginning its research and risk-assessment procedure. Indeed, this is the clearest piece of evidence for the claim that the EPA's entire work with respect to ETS is an instance of corrupt science inasmuch as it reveals both that the EPA moved from policy and risk assessment (ETS causes cancer in humans) to research rather than vice versa, and that the Agency attempted to conceal this. As Judge Osteen noted:

> Rather than reach a conclusion after collecting information, researching, and making findings, EPA categorized ETS as a "known cause of cancer" in 1989. EPA, *Indoor Air Facts No. 5 Environmental Tobacco Smoke*, ANR-445 (June 1989) (JA 9, 409–11). EPA's Administrator admitted that EPA "managed to confuse and anger all parties to the smoking ETS debate ..." EPA Memorandum from William K. Reilly, Administrator, to Secretary Louis W. Sullivan, 2 (July 1991) (JA 6, 754). The Administrator also conceded, "[B]eginning the development of an Agency risk assessment after the commencement or work on the draft policy guide gave the appearance of ... policy leading science ...". (Osteen 1998: 88)

Having already reached a conclusion about ETS in the absence of the required research program, the EPA could simply not risk using the legally required advisory group. At the very least, such a group with members representing the tobacco industry would leave a public record of vigorous scientific debate about the risks of ETS to human populations, a debate that might well make both the public and the scientific community skeptical about the EPA's conclusions. At the most, a duly constituted advisory group might actually be so unconvinced by the agency's conclusions that it would overturn them. As the court observed, there is a clear "logic" to the EPA's pattern of conduct that was driven by the recognition that there was simply too much at stake to risk the possible interference in a pre-determined policy process of an advisory group.

> In this case, EPA publicly committed to a conclusion before research had begun; excluded industry by violating the Act's procedural requirements; adjusted established procedure and scientific norms to validate the Agency's public conclusion, and aggressively utilized the Act's authority to disseminate findings to establish a de facto regulatory scheme intended to restrict Plaintiffs' products and influence public opinion. (Osteen 1998: 89–90)

It is simply not credible, then, that the EPA failed to note the significance of its action in failing to create the required advisory group.

The substantive issues

It is possible, of course, that the corruptions of the procedure that the court found, while serious, were nonetheless simply incidental and not material to the EPA's risk assessment. In effect, even though the EPA behaved badly in preventing the research process, the end product of that process—the risk assessment—was nonetheless legitimate. In order to resolve this issue the court needed to determine whether "consultation with the representative group would have likely produced a different result" (Osteen 1998: 38). And, in order to determine this, the court was required to examine the substance of the EPA's risk assessment. In effect, if the plaintiffs' claims about the quality of the EPA's risk assessment are true, namely that the assessment is arbitrary, capricious, and unreasoned, then it follows that the plaintiffs' legally required participation in the research and assessment procedure would have made a substantive difference. As Judge Osteen noted, the first issue

> is whether EPA's consulting a representative committee, on which industry's concerns were represented during the research process, likely would have caused EPA to change the conduct or conclusions of its ETS assessment. The key to this determination is whether industry representatives could have presented a meritable criticism and advice. (Osteen 1998: 43)

What, then, of the industry's criticism of the EPA's ETS science? Was it meritable? The credibility of the EPA's risk assessment centres on three types of claims: first, about the biological plausibility of equating Mainstream Smoke (i.e. that inhaled by smokers) with ETS; second, about the epidemiological evidence regarding the health effects of ETS; and third, about the EPA's epidemiological methodology.

EPA's Biological Plausibility Thesis

The EPA's biological plausibility thesis is crucial to its risk assessment since it establishes an indispensable chain of argument. This runs as follows: first, the biological plausibility of equating Mainstream Smoke (MS) with ETS justifies the EPA's *a priori* hypothesis that ETS is a Group A carcinogen; second, this hypothesis justifies the EPA's use of one-tailed significance tests (see Appendix, page 105); and third, the use of one-tailed significance tests leads to the use of a confidence level or 90 percent as opposed to a confidence level of 95 percent. As the court noted, "these issues are more than periphery. If EPA's *a priori* hypothesis fails, EPA has no justification for manipulating the Agency's standard scientific methodology" (Osteen 1998: 65). Thus, if the biological plausibility argument is without merit, the entire risk assessment is seriously imperilled.

The plaintiffs raised three objections against the bioplausibility thesis, saying: "(1) [EPA] ignored Assessment findings about the differences between MS and ETS; (2) EPA ignored evidence rejecting any chemical similarity; and (3) EPA did not define the criteria used to reach conclusions about the similarity/dissimilarity/indeterminacy of MS and ETS" (Osteen 1998: 45). The plaintiffs' claims here were supported to a large extent both by the assessment and by prior EPA risk classifications. For instance, in chapter 4 of its report the EPA noted that "the rapid dilution of both SS [side-stream smoke, i.e. smoke coming from a smouldering cigaette] and exhaled MS into the environment and changing phase distributions of ETS components over time raise some questions about the carcinogenic potential of ETS under actual environmental exposure conditions" (Osteen 1998: 45, quoting USEPA 1992 at 4-29) Again, the assessment record notes that the primary author of chapters 5 and 6, Kenneth Brown, argues that "there are differences between active and passive smoking that may affect carcinogenic risk that are not fully understood." (Osteen 1998: 46–47, quoting Draft Report *Responses to Public Comments etc.*) Clearly the assessment's own authors appear to doubt the bioplausibility thesis. These doubts are also shared by others and the plaintiffs introduced evidence citing scientific literature that also rejected the bioplausibility hypothesis.

Finally, there is an absence of any defined criteria as to how the chemical similarity of MS and ETS was established. This gives rise to the suspicion that the EPA changed its position on the alleged similarity of MS and ETS depending on what sort of argument it was attempting to make. As Judge Osteen noted, "It is striking that MS and ETS were similar only where such a conclusion promoted finding ETS a carcinogen" (Osteen 1998: 61). Indeed, this suspicion is given considerable credence by the fact that in previous risk assessments the "EPA did not classify agents in Group A because they contain the same constituents as other Group A carcinogens" (Osteen 1998: 49).

In response to these arguments, the EPA claimed that the bioplausibility thesis is supported in three ways. First, since active smoking is a cause of lung cancer in humans, it is reasonable to assume that ETS is a cause of lung cancer in humans because ETS is chemically similar to MS. Second, there is evidence that non-smokers who are exposed to ETS absorb and metabolize significant amounts of it. Third, laboratory tests have shown that ETS causes cancer in animals and damages DNA. The EPA also rejected the assertion that it failed to provide criteria for determining the similarity of MS and ETS, arguing that it set out four criteria (Osteen 1998: 51–52, 54).

Judge Osteen found each of these arguments to be unconvincing due to the fact that "there is limited evidence in the record supporting EPA's final basis for its bioplausibility hypothesis" (Osteen 1998: 57). In other words, whatever the *post hoc* explanations devised for purposes of litigation, the scientific record of the assessment process does not support the EPA's claims of bioplausibility. Indeed, as the court notes, it is not simply that there is limited evidentiary basis in the record to support the EPA's thesis—there is also substantial evidence in the assessment record that contradicts the EPA's plausibility thesis.

For instance, the scientists on the IAQC's final review panel themselves expressed significant reservations about the similarity of MS and ETS: "The data in Chapter 3 'do not ... adequately support the conclusion that the two are chemically similar ... [T]he data that are in there, speaking as a chemist, they simply don't make the case ... [T]he data ... simply do not demonstrate that they are similar'" (Osteen 1998: 62).

What was most disturbing to the court was what might be called the convenience factor, the fact that the bioplausibility hypothesis was maintained in the assessment only when it served the purposes of the EPA in finding ETS a carcinogen and was abandoned in other places. The EPA attempted to justify these inconsistencies in the record on the basis of both quantitative and qualitative components of risk assessment but both these were completely rejected by the court: "Neither the Assessment [n]or the administrative record explains why physicochemical inquiries require a bifurcated analysis instead of a combined analysis as per the Guidelines, or why MS and ETS are similar for purposes of hazard identification, but not for purposes of quantitative risk assessments" (Osteen 1998: 60). Moreover, the claims about ETS causing cancer in laboratory animals did not support the EPA's hypothesis either, since the "studies detected no evidence of lung cancer ... and the Assessment does not explain, nor does EPA direct the court to any evidence within the record explaining, how SS [side-stream smoke] condensate demonstrates similarities between MS and ETS" (Osteen 1998: 57–58).

It is not simply the convenience factor, however, that disturbed the court. There was also the issue of circularity. Sensing that the case against ETS could not be sustained on the basis of the bioplausibility thesis, the EPA sought to reinforce the thesis with epidemiological studies, claiming that the epidemiological evidence supported the bioplausibility thesis. This reasoning was patently circular in that the EPA's "logic" turns on the independent integrity of the bioplausibility argument. As the EPA used the bioplausibility argument to relax the standards of statistical significance for the epidemiological studies, it could hardly then use the contrived significance of those studies to justify bioplausibility. In short, the biopausability thesis was being asked to do too much. It could not both justify a manipulation of the epidemiological data and derive its support from that same data.

> The court is disturbed that EPA and Kenneth Brown buttress the bioplausibility theory with the epidemiology studies. EPA's theory must be independently plausible. EPA relied upon similarities between MS and ETS to conclude that it is biologically plausible that ETS causes cancer. EPA terms this theory its *"a priori* hypothesis" in justifying Chapter 5's methodology. Chapter 5's methodology allowed EPA to demonstrate a statistically significant association between ETS exposure and lung cancer ... Chapter 5's analysis rests on the validity of the biological plausibility theory. It is circular for EPA to now argue that epidemiology studies support the Agency's *a priori* theory. Without the theory, the studies would likely have done no such thing. (Osteen 1998: 58)

What emerges from the both the assessment record and the litigative record on bioplausibility is a second pattern of corrupt science. Consider the court's conclusions:

> The court is faced with the ugly possibility that EPA adopted a methodology for each chapter, without explanation, based on the outcome sought in that chapter. This possibility is most potent

where EPA rejected MS-ETS similarities to avoid a "cigarette-equivalents" analysis in determining carcinogenicity of ETS exposure. Use of cigarette-equivalents analysis may have lead [sic] to a conclusion that ETS is not a Group A carcinogen ...

EPA's assertion that "EPA did explain the numerous criteria it used in assessing similarity" ... is without merit. EPA merely parrots the findings made in Chapter 3 of the ETS Risk Assessment. The record presents no evidence of EPA establishing similarity criteria before the Assessment ...

The record does not support EPA's arguments that EPA took MS-ETS differences into account and, despite them, concluded ETS is a known human carcinogen because non-smokers are exposed to and absorb carcinogens. EPA conceded that dilution, aging and exposure characteristics fundamentally distinguish ETS from mainstream smoke, and "raise ... questions about the carcinogenic potential of ETS." ... The record does not explain how, after raising these questions, EPA could classify ETS a known human carcinogen based on similarities between SS and MS ...

If confronted by a representative committee that voiced industry concerns, EPA would likely have had to resolve these issues in the record. It is not clear whether EPA could have or can do so. These issues are more than periphery. If EPA's *a priori* hypothesis fails, EPA has no justification for manipulating the Agency's standard scientific methodology. (Osteen 1998: 60–65)

What is most striking about the court's language is the repeated use of phrases like "the record presents no evidence," the "record does not explain how," and the "EPA's assertion is without merit," all of which point to the unreasoned, unscientific character of the EPA's bioplausibility hypothesis. Now it might be argued that the court's language and analysis point to nothing more disturbing than incompetent science, that there is nothing here that rises to the level of corrupt science. While the process of the assessment might be corrupt, the substance of the assessment's science is merely incompetent, not corrupt.

Though in some senses appealing, this interpretation of the EPA's science is untenable for three reasons. First, the convenience factor is a clear mark of corrupt science. Rather than taking a consistent position about the alleged MS-ETS similarities, the EPA crafted positions depending on the required outcomes of particular chapter in its report. Rather than basing its MS-ETS equivalency on some chemical basis, the EPA founded it instead on a pre-conceived policy outcome: namely, that ETS causes cancer in humans. Despite the contrived explanations offered to the court, the only way in which the contradictory claims about MS-ETS similarities make any sense is within the pre-determined position of finding ETS a carcinogen. And this is without question the defining characteristic of corrupt science—mandated conclusion driving scientific explanation. In effect, Judge Osteen had discovered that the bioplausibility hypothesis was a pseudo-scientific front protecting a scientifically unjustified position, hence his reference to the "ugly possibility."

Second, the circularity of the bioplausibility and epidemiological arguments and EPA's tenacious defence of their interconnection is unlikely to be the product of mere incompetence. The logical unacceptability of such reasoning is obvious to anyone operating at the EPA's level of policy and scientific sophistication. The EPA is clearly aware of the fact that it can only sustain its carcinogenicity finding through the bioplausiblity thesis; it is clearly aware of the fact that its bioplausibility thesis provides the rationale for manipulating the statistical outcomes of the epidemiological evidence; and it is clearly aware of the fact that it claims the bioplausiblity thesis is in turn supported by the manipulated epidemiological evidence. If the argumentative circle were less tight the circularity might be less apparent. But to characterize such openly illogical and manipulative practices as the product of inadvertence or incompetence is to ascribe to the EPA a level of inconceivable methodological schizophrenia.

Third, the consistent willingness of the EPA during the trial to misrepresent its positions, its evidence, and its reasoning on bioplausibility to the court, together with its apparent unconcern with tortured and clearly untenable explanations, distinguishes its actions from the simply incompetent. Even the persistent language of the court ("the record does not explain how," "the EPA's assertion is without merit") indicates a polite disdain for the agency's contorted defense of its insupportable assertions. To take but one example: despite the agency's claims that criteria for MS-ETS had been established prior to the assessment, there is no evidence of such a criteria having existed. Indeed, as the court noted, no such criteria were presented at the IAQC final review panel, where the panel's neutral scientists raised fundamental and unanswered questions about the chemical similarity of MS and ETS. Thus, even allowing for the significant gaps in the assessment record, the record that does exist is at odds with the EPA's central hypothesis.

A similar instance of significant non-confirming evidence being completely ignored was the review of the EPA's own Risk Criteria Office, which recommended against the approach taken in the assessment (Osteen 1998: 64). As the court finally concluded, it is apparent that the arguments submitted during litigation do not represent the argumentative process or position developed during the assessment. Rather they are fundamentally misrepresentations designed to make the unreasonable look reasonable, *"post hoc* rationalizations devised during litigation"* (Osteen 1998: 73).

What the evidence shows, therefore, is that the EPA report was the result of corrupt science. Not only were the EPA's procedures corrupt, its arguments about, and evidence—perhaps, more appropriately, lack of evidence—for, bioplausibility, display a pattern of corruption.

EPA's epidemiological evidence

The second issue on which the validity of the EPA's ETS assessment turns is the extent of the epidemiological evidence that the EPA examined. By the time that the EPA risk assessment appeared, there were 58 studies that examined the risks of lung cancer in ETS-exposed populations. Of these, 33 looked at the risk of lung cancer to non-smoking females married to male smokers and, of these 33, the EPA based its assessment on 31 studies that were available at the time that it conducted its second IAQC review. One of the 31 studies was not ready in its complete form so that the agency used interim results only. In order to draw conclusions from all of the studies, the EPA submitted them to meta-analysis.

Given that the EPA based its analysis on only 31 of the available 58 studies, it is worth noting which studies were excluded and why. The studies excluded fell into three groups: 12 studies examined the cancer risks of females exposed to ETS in the workplace; 13 looked at cancer risks of females exposed to ETS during childhood; and two looked at cancer risks of females married to smokers. The EPA is remarkably silent as to why these 27 studies were excluded, the assessment noting only that more were included than excluded.

Now the EPA's IAQC noted that one of the conditions necessary for meta-analysis is a "precise definition of criteria used to include (or exclude) studies" (Osteen 1998: 67). But, it is clear from the assessment record that the EPA undertook the meta-analysis in the absence of any articulated criteria as to which studies to include. As the IQAC observed, "[s]pecific criteria for including studies was not provided. The importance of this was reinforced at the Committee meeting when a reanalysis was presented on a different set of studies than those in the report. This resulted in a change in the overall risk estimate. Decisions as to study inclusion should be made *prior* to analysis, based on clearly stated criteria" (Osteen 1998: 67, quoting USEPA 1991: 32–33).

The importance of having criteria is thus twofold. On the one hand, it is necessary for the validity of the meta-analysis because it forces a clear examination of the differences and similarities in the data that are being combined. On the other hand, it provides an important procedural element of transparency by certifying that the database is not biased towards some pre-determined outcome. This last requirement is particularly important in this case, as the EPA had already committed itself to a conclusion about ETS before it began its risk assessment. If the agency cared at all about scientific and policy integrity, it would have taken exceptional care in this phase of its assessment to conform to the procedural requirements outlined as necessary by its own IAQC.

But, it did not. As the plaintiffs noted, this failure to create criteria and the consequent unexplained exclusion of important epidemiological data provides strong evidence of arbitrary, unreasoned decision-making: "Plaintiffs contest that EPA excluded studies and data on workplace and childhood exposure to ETS, as well as the 'two largest and most recent' US spousal smoking studies, because inclusion would have undermined EPA's claim of a causal association between ETS exposure and lung cancer" (Osteen 1998: 68). In an attempt to deny the claim of arbitrariness designed to insure a pre-determined outcome to the assessment, the EPA offered the court five *post hoc* reasons for excluding these 27 studies and including the remaining 31.

First, the data in the childhood and workplace studies were said to be "less extensive and therefore less reliable" (Osteen 1998: 68). The court noted that the EPA's evidence for this claim was unconvincing both on the question of extent and reliability (Osteen 1998: 68–69). Second, the EPA argued that the workplace studies were excluded because of potential "confounders," i.e. methodological errors or problems that undermine a meta-analysis). Again, the court found no support in the record for this claim. Third, the EPA explained that workplace studies were excluded because most did not classify subjects by the amount of their exposure. Here as well, the court noted that this reasoning was not part of the assessment record. Fourth, the EPA claimed that the childhood studies were excluded because they were founded on distant and perhaps unreliable memories and represented a more limited exposure than spousal exposure (Osteen 1998: 70), But, as the court noted, there is nothing in the record to support the claim that "childhood exposure data should be ignored" (Osteen 1998: 70). Again, the record does not reveal that the EPA used reliability of memory of total lifetime exposure as a selection criterion. Indeed, if memory reliability were to be used as a criterion, many of the studies would have to be excluded, as all rely to some extent on recollection.

Fifth, regarding the spousal studies completed after the comment period had passed and the EPA already had a considerable database, the agency justified its use of preliminary data from only one of the three studies (the Fontham study) on the grounds it was the largest American ETS study and used methodology superior to any other study (Osteen 1998: 71). These claims however, were again not supported by the record. As the EPA failed to create criteria by which to select studies, it could hardly claim that the Fontham study's methodology was superior. For, without criteria in which the weight given to methodology is clearly articulated, such a claim appears to be nothing more than another explanation designed purely for the purposes of litigation. Indeed, as Judge Osteen noted, given that there was no record of the methodology employed in the other two studies, it would be impossible even to compare methodologies (Osteen 1998: 71).

This returns us to the critical influence of the EPA's violations of procedure on its substantive conclusions. With the open, representative procedure required by law and a full deliberative record, the EPA would have found it virtually impossible to be arbitrary and, indeed, even to appear arbitrary. Disputes about criteria and study selection against that criteria would be answerable at least in principle. As Judge Osteen noted:

> EPA's study selection is disturbing. First, there is evidence in the record supporting the accusation that the EPA "cherry picked" its data. Without criteria for pooling studies into a meta-analysis, the court cannot determine whether the exclusion of studies likely to disprove EPA's *a priori* hypothesis was coincidence or intentional . . .
>
> In making a study choice, consultation with an advisory committee voicing these concerns would have resulted, at a minimum, in a record that explained EPA's selective use of available information. From such a record, a reviewing court could then determine whether EPA "cherry picked" its data, and whether EPA exceeded its statutory authority. (Osteen 1998: 72–73)

Of course, even allowing the EPA the benefit of the doubt about its motives does not clear it of other failures. By excluding nearly half of the available studies, the EPA failed to follow its own risk-assessment guidelines and contravened the Radon Research Act. The Act states that the EPA should gather data and information on all aspects of indoor air quality, while the agency chose selectively to ignore significant amounts of data: "At the outset, the court concluded risk assessments incidental to collecting information and making findings. EPA steps outside the court's analysis when information collection becomes incidental to conducting a risk assessment" (Osteen 1998: 72–73).

In the absence of both a procedure ensuring objectivity and fairness, and criteria for methodological soundness, it is difficult not to conclude that the EPA's insistence on including the Fontham study was based less on reasoned decision-making than on its desire to support its *a priori* conclusion about ETS. Without the Fontham study, the epidemiological evidence would not have produced the desired conclusion. Further, including all three of the large American studies along with the workplace and childhood exposure studies would have made EPA's carcinogen classification of ETS impossible. Hence, the court's observation that, for the EPA, information collection became incidental to conducting a risk assessment. (Osteen 1998: 72–73).

Is this assessment of the EPA's methods and motivation too harsh? Consider the following scenario. You announce a scientific conclusion prior to examining the scientific evidence supporting that conclusion. Upon examining the scientific evidence, you find that the bulk of the evidence (in this case, epidemiological studies) does not support your conclusion. You now have two options: one, to withdraw or modify your conclusion; two, to adjust the evidence to support your conclusion. You decide to maintain your conclusion. This means that the embarrassing counter-evidence must be dealt with. To do this you create, off the record, two classes of evidence, evidence that is helpful to your conclusion and evidence that is unhelpful to your conclusion. Evidence that is unhelpful to your conclusion is not used; evidence that is helpful becomes the foundation of your case. When asked later to explain why certain pieces of evidence were examined and became the basis of your conclusion, you put forward a series of explanations, although there is no evidence that any of these actually drove your original selection.

We would argue that what emerges from the court record is just this scenario—a predetermined conclusion driving a selective procedure of evidence-gathering, in which the key to selection is not scientific integrity but support for the EPA's pre-determined conclusion. It is this scientifically corrupt procedure in which, as Judge Osteen noted, evidence collection and examination become incidental to truth-finding.

The EPA's Epidemiological Methodology

The third and final issue upon which the validity of the EPA's ETS risk assessment hinges is the agency's epidemiological methodology. The plaintiffs raised seven specific methodological issues, charging that the EPA deviated from accepted scientific procedure and its own risk assessment guidelines in a manner designed to ensure a pre-ordained outcome (Osteen 1998: 73–74). Despite the significant problems already identified with the assessment, however, Judge Osteen thought it unnecessary to delve further into what he calls the EPA's epidemiological web. But, there were two methodological issues so serious and in which the EPA's conduct was so unjustified that the court considered they merited further examination.

The first of these issues was the question of confidence intervals. The plaintiffs alleged that the EPA, without explanation, switched from using standard 95-percent confidence intervals to 90-percent confidence intervals in order to enhance the likelihood that its meta-analysis would appear statistically significant. This shift assisted the EPA in obtaining statistically significant results that could be used to support a Group A classification (Osteen 1998: 74).

With a 95-percent confidence interval, there is a probablility of only 5 percent that the result of a test is a product of chance. Generally, researchers are unwilling to accept higher probabilities of error. In its 1990 draft of the risk assessment, the EPA used a 95-percent interval but in subsequent drafts they switched to a 90-percent confidence interval. This change was criticized by Geoffrey Kabat, who served on the IAQC and also contributed to the risk assessment: "The use of 90 percent confidence intervals, instead of the conventionally used 95 percent confidence intervals, is to be discouraged. It looks like [a]n attempt to achieve statistical significance for a result which otherwise would not achieve significance" (Osteen 1998: 75, quoting Kabat 1992 at 6 [July 28, 1992] [JA 12, 185]).

Why, then, in the face of such internal criticism, would the EPA change its confidence intervals? In its risk assessment, the EPA argued that this usage was justified by the *a priori* hypothesis that a positive association existed between exposure to ETS and lung cancer (Osteen 1998: 75). But, as noted earlier, this explanation fails because it is circular. In a second attempt, the EPA explained to the court that use of the 95-percent confidence interval with the one-tailed test would have produced an apparent discrepancy: statistically significant study results using the standard p-value of .05 might nevertheless have a 95-percent confidence interval that included a relative risk of one (Osteen 1998: 75–76) In short, these studies would have failed to confirm that ETS was a significant health risk. As Judge Osteen observed:

> The record and EPA's explanations to the Court make it clear that using standard methodology, EPA could not produce statistically significant results with its selected studies. Analysis conducted with a .05 significance level and a 95% confidence level included relative risks of 1. Accordingly, these results did not confirm EPA's controversial *a priori* hypothesis. In order confirm its hypothesis, EPA maintained its standard significance level but lowered the confidence interval to 90%. This allowed EPA to confirm its hypothesis by finding a relative risk of 1.19, albeit a very weak association. (Osteen 1998: 77)

What drove the EPA to change its confidence intervals and its ep-idemiological methodology is thus the same thing that drove it to select certain epidemiological studies in preference to other studies: the de-termination, regardless of the costs to scientific integrity and its statu-tory responsibilities, to justify its pre-determined position that ETS was a human carcinogen. Indeed, the record shows that even after care-fully selecting its studies, the EPA still could not make its ETS case without abandoning normal scientific procedures. Again, the court not-ed that the record does not provide any reason for the EPA's abandon-ment of the 95-percent confidence interval (Osteen 1998: 78), despite the agency's clear responsibility to explain changes in methodology used during the conduct of a risk assessment. But, the EPA can no more explain why it changed confidence intervals than it can explain any-thing else about its procedure and findings. To do so would be to admit to scientific corruption.

Further reason to believe that the EPA's science was corrupt is to be found in the court's comments about the second problem with the EPA's epidemiological methodology. As a result of its statistical analy-sis using a 90-percent confidence interval, the EPA concluded that the relative risk (RR) of ETS was 1.19, and it was this finding that provided a large measure of its justification for the Group A classification (Os-teen 1998: 76). Yet, as the plaintiffs noted, the EPA failed to provide any reason why such a weak RR justified a Group A classification. Ev-ery other Group A carcinogen had been required to exhibit a much higher relative risk (Osteen 1998: 76) and a recent candidate for Group A status with an RR range of between 2.6 and 3.0 had not been classi-fied as a Group A carcinogen. Further, Dr. Kabat of the IAQC had noted: "An association is generally considered weak if the odds ratio is under 3.0 and particularly when it is under 2.0, as is the case in the relation-ship of ETS and lung cancer" (Osteen 1998: 76–77).

Clearly then, there is no precedent for Group A classification on the basis of such a weak RR. But, why should the consistency, adherence to normal procedure, and evidence-based decision-making be thought im-portant at this final stage? Consider what had preceded this final step in the assessment procedure: certain epidemiological studies had been deemed relevant and others irrelevant on the basis of no clear criteria; the relevant epidemiological studies had been analyzed at a 90-percent confidence level rather than the usual 95-percent confidence level; and this, in turn, had produced a RR of 1.19, which in no other circumstance would be judged sufficient to justify Group A classification.

Two things about this process of scientific corruption were partic-ularly troubling to the court. First, and most obviously, with such a weak RR, the problems with study selection and methodology meant that the EPA could not show a statistically significant association between ETS and lung cancer in non-smokers (Osteen 1998: 78). In other words, the risk assessment was invalid.

Second, while the Radon Act authorizes the EPA to collect information, conduct research, and disseminate findings, the EPA's epidemiological basis for its risk assessment actually represented a suppression, if not a misrepresentation, of information. The EPA did not disclose certain facts either in the record or in the assessment: its inability to demonstrate a statistically significant relationship under normal methodology; its rationale for adopting a one-tailed test; and the shaky foundations for its RR rating for ETS. Instead of disclosing information, the agency withheld significant portions of its findings and reasoning in striving to confirm its *a priori* hypothesis (Osteen 1998: 79).

Two of the most characteristic features of corrupt science are its misrepresentation of reality and its misrepresentation of its procedure. Rather than acknowledging alternative evidence or problems with its evidence that would cast doubt on its conclusions, and rather than admitting the complexity of the issue under review and the limits of the evidence, corrupt science presents what is at best a carefully chosen partial truth as the whole truth necessary for public policy. In effect, public policy is manipulated into reaching certain conclusions on the basis of data that have been fabricated, falsified, misrepresented, or massaged to appear in a guise fundamentally at odds with reality. Corrupt science misrepresents not only reality but also its own procedures in arriving at its conclusions. Instead of acknowledging the selectivity of its procedure and the official insistence to demonstrate a predetermined conclusion, corrupt science invests both its procedure and its conclusions with a mantle of indubitability.

This is precisely what the court found in this case. The EPA failed to disclose its procedures and its failure to make its case under normal scientific procedures. It also failed to disclose its reasoning for changing its normal procedures, both methodological and with respect to the RR level required for Group A status. Most importantly, it failed to reveal how dependent its findings were on these departures from the norm. As a result, what the EPA presented as fact would be accepted by the casual observer as being scientifically supported when in actuality the truth was fundamentally different.

Conclusion

Judge Osteen began his analysis of the EPA's risk assessment by asking whether a different procedure would have produced different results; in effect, he asked whether the EPA's science was open to question. In his conclusion, he pulled together his findings both about the procedure and the substance of the EPA's risk assessment, to determine whether the risk assessment demonstrated reasoned decision making. He entered judgment in favour of the plaintiffs and vacated the EPA's ETS risk assessment. The Judge's major findings were:

(1) In 1988, EPA initiated drafting policy-based recommendations about controlling ETS exposure because EPA believed ETS is a Group A carcinogen. (Osteen 1998: 87)

(2) Rather than reach a conclusion after collecting information, researching, and making findings, EPA categorized ETS as a "known cause of cancer" in 1989. (Osteen 1998: 88)

(3) EPA determined it was biologically plausible that ETS causes lung cancer. In doing so, EPA recognized problems with its theory, namely dissimilarities between MS and ETS. In other areas of the Assessment, EPA relied on these dissimilarities in justifying its methodology. (Osteen 1998: 80)

(4) EPA did not explain much of [sic] the criteria and assertions upon which EPA's theory relies. (Osteen 1998: 80)

(5) EPA claimed selected epidemiologic studies would affirm its plausibility theory. The studies EPA selected did not include a significant number of studies and data which demonstrated no association between ETS and cancer. (Osteen 1998: 80)

(6) EPA did not explain its criteria for study selection, thus leaving itself open to allegations of "cherry picking." (Osteen 1998: 80–81)

(7) Using its normal methodology and its selected studies, EPA did not demonstrate a statistically significant association between ETS and lung cancer. (Osteen 1998: 81)

(8) This should have caused EPA to reevaluate the inference options used in establishing its plausibility theory. (Osteen 1998: 81)

(9) EPA then claimed the bioplausibility theory, renominated the *a priori* hypothesis, justified a more lenient methodology. (Osteen 1998: 88)

(10) EPA claimed, but did not explain how, its theory justified changing the Agency's methodology. (Osteen 1998: 81)

(11) With a new methodology, EPA demonstrated from the selected studies a very low risk for lung cancer based on ETS exposure. Based on its original theory and the weak evidence of association, EPA concluded the evidence showed a causal relationship between cancer and ETS. (Osteen 1998: 88–89)

(12) In conducting the ETS risk assessment, EPA disregarded information and made findings on selective information; did not disseminate significant epidemiologic information; deviated from its Risk Assessment Guidelines; failed to disclose important findings and reasoning; and left significant questions without answers. EPA's conduct left substantial holes in the administrative record. While doing so, EPA produced limited evidence, then claimed the weight of the agency's research evidence demonstrated ETS causes cancer. (Osteen 1998: 90)

(13) So long as information collection on all relevant aspects of indoor air quality, research, and dissemination are the lodestars, the general language of the Radon Research Act authorizes risk assessments. (Osteen 1998: 89)

(14) Gathering all relevant information, researching, and disseminating findings were subordinate to EPA's demonstrating ETS as a Group A carcinogen. (Osteen 1998: 90)

(15) In the Radon Research Act, Congress granted the EPA limited research authority along with an obligation to seek advice from a representative committee during such research. Congress intended industry representatives to be at the table and their voices heard during the research procedure. EPA's authority under the act is contingent upon the agency hearing and responding to the represented constituents' concerns. The record evidence is overwhelming that IAQC was not the representative body required under the Act. Had EPA reconciled industry objections voiced from a representative body during the research procedure, the ETS risk assessment would be very possibly not have been conducted in the same manner nor reached the same conclusions. (Osteen 1998: 91)

Corrupt science re-visited

Does the pattern of conduct described here consistently constitute corrupted science? We would argue that it does. Indeed, we would suggest that the EPA's ETS risk assessment is a case study in the corruption of science. Recall that corrupt science involves four characteristics: (1) movement from policy to science rather than science to policy; (2) misrepresentation of reality through misrepresentation of evidence; (3) misrepresentation of procedures; and (4) attempts to suppress dissent through attacks on the character of the dissentor and the motivation for dissent rather than on its logic and the evidence. The court's findings are decisive in each of these areas.

(1) Movement from policy to science

The record clearly shows that the EPA began with a conclusion about ETS (quotations 1, 2, 14 above) rather than with a question. As the court noted, the EPA's collection and assessment of evidence was merely incidental window-dressing to the procedure of conducting a risk assessment. (Osteen 1998: 72–73) Everything that the EPA did was designed to bring about the desired conclusion.

(2) Misrepresentation of reality

First, the EPA proposed a bioplausibility hypothesis that was unsupportable, then sought to bolster the thesis with epidemiological evidence while simultaneously claiming that the same evidence supported bioplausibility (quotations 2, 3, 8, 9 above). Further, the EPA attempted to mislead the court about the evidence for the bioplausibility thesis and its inconsistent use of the theory.

Second, rather than present the entire evidentiary record, the EPA arbitrarily excluded certain epidemiological studies that demonstrated no association between ETS and cancer (quotations 5, 6, 7, above). The EPA provided no credible reasons for its exclusion of certain studies and inclusion of other studies.

Third, having found that even its selected studies failed to demonstrate an association between ETS and lung cancer, the EPA re-analyzed its studies using a 90-percent confidence interval rather than a 95-percent interval. The agency provided no explanation for its change in methodology. This allowed the agency to demonstrate a statistically significant risk of lung cancer in non-smokers exposed to ETS (quotations 7, 9, 10, 11, above).

Fourth, the EPA used the resulting RR of 1.19 as the major basis for its Group A classification of ETS although every other Group A carcinogen had required a higher RR and its own IAQC member, Dr. Kabat, indicated that a RR of 1.19 indicated a weak association. The EPA failed to provide the court with convincing reasons for this inconsistency (quotations 10, 11, 12, above).

Fifth, the EPA failed to disclose its inability to demonstrate statistical significance under normal scientific procedures and the fact that its weak RRs were obtained only after changing methodology. Indeed, the agency withheld significant portions of its findings and reasoning (Osteen 1998: 79; quotations 12, 13, above).

(3) Misrepresention of processes

First, the EPA failed to conform to the procedural requirements of the Radon Act, requirements that were designed to create an objective and transparent procedure of risk assessment in which all sides had the opportunity, on the record, to examine the evidence (quotation 15, above). Further, the EPA attempted to maintain that it had discharged its procedural responsibilities for openness and objectivity through the IAQC, although the IAQC contained no industry representation and that its concerns on several points were ignored by the agency.

Second, the EPA's risk assessment failed to disclose the nature of its scientific procedure, namely, that it moved from conclusion to evidence rather than from evidence to conclusion, and that everything was subordinate to demonstrating that ETS was a Group A carcinogen. (Osteen 1998: 90; quoatations 1, 2, 14, above)

Third, the EPA's risk-assessment procedure failed to provide a record of the rationale for its decisions to ignore the criticisms and reservations of its own Risk Criteria Office and IAQC members, its decisions about its data selection, its decisions about epidemiological methodology, and its decision to assign Group A status to ETS in the presence of a weak association. In the absence of such a record, it is impossible to conclude whether the EPA acted rationally (quotations 12, 15, above).

Fourth, the EPA failed to reveal the circular argumentative procedure involved with the bioplausibility thesis, the arbitrary procedure of its data selection, and the methodological departures from standard scientific practice (quotations 7, 10, 11, 12, above).

(4) Suppressing dissent

First, the EPA viewed the tobacco industry's scientific positions as untenable not on the basis of evidence or logic but simply because they were advanced by the industry. As industry attorney Rupp's letter indicated, at no time was there an opportunity for a scientific discussion of the fundamental issues regarding ETS (Kluger 1996: 10). The EPA's attitude to the legitimacy of the industry's science is neatly captured in the reply of an assistant EPA administrator, William Rosenberg, to Rupp: "Frankly, the tobacco industry's argument would be more creditable if it were not so similar to the tobacco industry's position on direct smoking" (Kluger 1996: 693).

Second, the EPA's certainty about ETS, in advance of the evidence, created such a belief in the unfalsifiability of its *a priori* hypothesis that it apparently encouraged a climate in which even members of its own advisory panel like Dr. Geoffrey Kabat, who disagreed with its procedures and conclusions, were challenged not on the basis of their scientific arguments but on their alleged and in fact non-existent connection to the tobacco industry. As Jacob Sullum writes, "In this context anyone who questioned the case against ETS risked being portrayed as a tool of the cigarettes—even if, like Kabat, he had never received a dime from them" (Sullum 1998: 172). Inasmuch as the *a priori* hypothesis was a revealed dogma, dissent could have no legitimate foundation. Character, not coherence and consistency, was the criteria against which disagreements were measured.

Corrupt science?

Thus, the case for corrupt science is compelling. Each of the characteristics of corrupt science is present in multiple instances, wound together within a consistent pattern. It would be difficult, indeed, to provide an alternative account that provides so coherent an explanation for so many of the uncontested facts of the case.

The Controversy around the IARC study

The Osteen decision was not the only 1998 setback to the ETS junk-science/junk-policy machine. A second blow to the claim that second-hand smoke was a risk for lung cancer for non-smokers came from the unlikely source of the World Health Organization's International Agency for Research on Cancer (IARC).

The study by the IARC on the relationship between ETS and lung cancer in non-smokers is the largest study ever conducted outside of the United States. The study, spanning ten years and involving 12 cities in seven European countries, involved 650 cases and 1542 controls, and was designed to provide a definitive answer to the question of the risks of lung cancer for non-smokers from second-hand smoke. The study is, thus, extremely important in answering our questions as to whether second-hand smoke is a risk to the health of non-smokers.

In its 1998/1997 biennial report published in March 1998, the IARC published a summary of its ETS study IARC 1998). The study found no statistically significant increase in the risk of lung cancer for non-smokers exposed to ETS in four settings: workplace, home, home and workplace together, and childhood. Of particular interest from a regulatory standpoint was IARC's finding that ETS exposure in indoor public settings such as restaurants did not result in a statistically significant risk of lung cancer for non-smokers.

In itself, there is nothing extraordinary about these results; indeed, they are similar to the majority of other ETS studies. What is, however, extraordinary is the response from the international public-health community and anti-smoking movement that followed a story about the IARC study in the United Kingdom's *Sunday Telegraph* on March 8, 1998.

In an article headlined Passive Smoking Doesn't Cause Cancer—Official, the *Telegraph* reported:

The world's leading health organization has withheld from publication a study which shows that not only might there be no link between smoking and lung cancer but that it could even have a protective effect.

The findings are certain to be an embarrassment to the WHO, which has spent years and vast sums on anti-smoking and anti-tobacco campaigns. The study is one of the largest ever to look at the link between passive smoking—or environmental tobacco smoke (ETS)—and lung cancer, and had been eagerly awaited by medical experts and campaigning groups.

Yet the scientists have found that there was no statistical evidence that passive smoking caused lung cancer.

Responding the *Telegraph*'s story, which was reported in Canada in the *Ottawa Citizen*, the British group, Action on Smoking and Health (ASH), complained to the Press Complaints Commission that the *Sunday Telegraph*'s claims were "false and misleading," a complaint that was subsequently rejected by the Commission. The United Kingdom's Chief Medical Officer, Sir Kenneth Calman, claimed that IARC's results had been "misreported" and the WHO characterized the *Telegraph* article as "false and misleading," asserting that "passive smoking does cause lung cancer, do not let them fool you."

Reaction from the Canadian anti-smoking movement was equally strong. David Sweanor, the Senior Legal Counsel for the Non-Smokers' Rights Association (NSRA), wrote in a memorandum to the Toronto NSRA office:

A Citizen reporter called me at home, twice about this "story" yesterday. He said they had this as an exclusive from the *Telegraph* . . .

I explained that they were being "had." That Neil Collishaw at WHO was not aware of any such study, that it had too small a sample size to be statistically significant, that there were major authoritative reports that looked at all of the data, that this had "tobacco industry PR machine" written all over it . . .

This is tabloid journalism. It misinforms the public . . .

IARC may or may not have done such research. If they did, the methodology is such that it was bad science and would not have passed peer review. Of 650 lung cancer patients, likely about 600 were there due to direct smoking.

I spoke with Neil this morning. He does not know anything about this "WHO commissioned" research. (Sweanor 1998)

Several things about Mr. Sweanor's comments are worth noting. First is the apparent ignorance, not only of the anti-smoking movement, which claims comprehensive knowledge about tobacco science, but also of a senior Canadian official at WHO, Neil Collishaw of a major, 10-year scientific study about ETS. It is also curious that Mr. Sweanor appears to know quite a bit about what is apparently wrong with a non-existent piece of research.

Second is the apparent ignorance about how epidemiology works and what statistical significance means. For one thing, the "small-size" argument is incorrect as any risk assessment can be made statistically significant by increasing the sample size. IARC set the sample size itself so it can hardly *post facto* complain about the size not producing statistical significance. Again, the 650 cases were, by the very nature of the study's design, carefully chosen to be non-smokers, not smokers as Sweanor claims. Indeed, if Sweanor believes that 92 percent of all cases in ETS studies are misclassified—that is, that they are really smokers rather than non-smokers—as his claim that 600 of the 650 cases were smokers suggests, then the case against ETS completely collapses since all studies would be invalidated by misclassification bias. In effect, they would be studies about smokers and not about non-smokers. Contrary to Sweanor's claim, the IARC's study is not bad science; it is rather customary epidemiology.

Third is the outright inaccuracy of Sweanor's claims. The *Citizen* was not being "had": the study was done by IARC and not by the tobacco industry; it was not publicized by the tobacco industry but by WHO; the newspaper did not misinform the public but accurately reported IARC's own findings; and, finally, the IARC's study did pass peer review, being published in the *Journal of the National Cancer Institute* (Boffetta 1998).

What Mr. Sweanor's claim of "bad science" and what claims of "false and misleading" reporting by ASH and WHO really mean is that the IARC's study is terribly inconvenient science because it exposes, in the most dramatic fashion, the manufactured nature of the case for the risk of lung cancer from ETS. Not only does the IARC's study destroy the claim that there is a "scientific consensus" that ETS causes lung cancer in non-smokers but it also puts an end to the anti-smoking movement's false claim that the only studies showing ETS not to be a risk are those funded by the tobacco industry.

With so much at stake, it is imperative for the anti-smoking league that the IARC's study be discredited at all costs through the techniques of junk science, even though the study is the product of one of the health community's premier research organizations. What we see at work are the usual techniques: misrepresentation of date, misrepresentation of process, and questioning of character rather than research quality. Thus, IARC itself in reporting its research claims that its relative risk for non-smokers exposed to ETS is 1.16, without explaining that since the confidence interval is 0.93 to 1.44, the results should be interpreted as meaning either an increase or a decrease in risk and, more importantly, that the results are not statistically significant, that is, it is impossible to distinguish them from chance. In effect, by failing to comment on the confidence interval and the issues of statistical significance, IARC conveys the fundamentally misleading impression that its study found an increased risk of 16 percent of lung cancer in non-smoking subjects exposed to ETS. Hence WHO can claim that passive smoking "does cause lung cancer, do not let them fool you." But, clearly the only people being fooled are those who do not understand epidemiology and who take IARC's claims at face value. The only scientific conclusion to be drawn from the IARC's study is that it shows no association between ETS exposure and lung cancer in non-smokers. Claims by the IARC and WHO otherwise are simply junk science: scientific findings baldly misrepresented for policy purposes.

Moreover, Sweanor's claim that IARC's study procedure is "bad science" because it is flawed by poor study design and sample size appears to be another instance of inaccuracy. The IARC's study is the second largest ETS study ever done; it ran over ten years and both the sample size and the study procedure were carefully designed by IARC. It is only because the results are inconvenient that the procedure is retroactively described as flawed.

Finally, not only Sweanor's comments about the *Citizen* being "had" and that this story "had 'tobacco industry PR machine' written all over it" but also the world-wide effort by the health community and the anti-smoking movement either to link the IARC's study or its publicity to the tobacco industry are themselves junk-science techniques. Rather than looking at the quality of the evidence, one focuses instead on the connections and character of the scientist in an attempt to discredit and suppress dissent. What makes this strategy so bizarre in this instance is that the anti-smoking movement was forced to discredit the source of its own scientific claims.

Conclusion

To return to where we started, both of these case studies show—in quite different respects—not only why sizeable majorities of most democratic societies believe that second-hand smoke causes cancer in non-smokers but how these beliefs have originated. In the first instance, the techniques of junk science—misrepresentation of scientific reality, misrepresentation of scientific procedure and suppression of dissent— were used to establish an untruth. In the second instance, these same techniques of junk science were used to protect that untruth. Both instances raise fundamental and deeply troubling issues for a public health community and anti-smoking movement apparently undisturbed by their willingness to engage in producing junk science for the sake of winning their war against tobacco.

Appendix   One-tailed and two-tailed tests

A null hypothesis is a precisely stated assertion associated with a statistical test; results of that test are intended to determine whether the null hypothesis should be accepted (regarded as true) or rejected (regarded as untrue).

Because we are more comfortable accepting demonstrations that statements are false than otherwise, statisticians usually arrange their experiments so that the null hypothesis is contrary to the underlying thesis. Thus, rejection of the null hypothesis corresponds to confirmation of the thesis.

Suppose that like the EPA we want to demonstrate that exposure to ETS increases the risk of lung cancer. Since we cannot examine everyone exposed to ETS, we design a statistical experiment to determine whether our thesis seems to be true. Our null hypothesis is: Exposure to ETS does not increase the risk of lung cancer. Next, we select random samples of individuals exposed to ETS and random samples of individuals not exposed to ETS. if equality holds between the two samples—that is, if the rates of lung cancer are not different—we have failed to demonstrate our thesis. If, on the other hand, individuals exposed to ETS have significantly higher rates of lung cancer, we can reject the null hypothesis.

In posing a null hypothesis for statistical testing one always states an alternative hypothesis that is to be accepted if the null hypothesis is rejected. The alternative hypothesis must encompass the entire range of alternative to the null hypothesis. In this case, the correct alternative hypothesis is that the risk of lung cancer in populations exposed to ETS and populations not exposed ETS are *different*; that is, populations exposed to ETS might have *increased* risks of lung cancer or they might have *reduced* risks of lung cancer.

This is an example of a two-tailed analysis since exposure to ETS can either increase or decrease the risk of lung cancer. In using a one-tailed test, the EPA failed to state the correct alternative hypothesis to its null hypothesis. The EPA, in effect, *assumed* that ETS exposure could only increase the risk (one tail) of lung cancer. Since a substantial number of studies have shown a *decreased* risk with ETS exposure ... two-tailed tests are required. (Luik 1993/1994: 54)

References

Boffetta, P., et al. (1998). Multicenter Case-Control Study of Exposure to Environmental Tobacco Smoke and Lung Cancer in Europe. *Journal of the National Cancer Institute* 90, 19: 1440–50.

Gori, Gio B., and John C. Luik (1999). *Passive Smoke: The EPA's BEtrayal of Science and Policy*. Vancouver, BC: The Fraser Institute.

DeRosa, C. (1990). Memorandum to William H. Farland, Director, Office of Health and Environmental Assessment (April 27).

Kabat, G. (1992). *Comments on EPA's Draft Report: "Respiratory Health Effects of Passive Smoking: Lung Cancer and Other Disorders."* S[cience] A[dvisory] B[oard] 9.15 at 6 July.

Kluger, R. (1996). *Ashes to Ashes: America's Hundred-Year Cigarette War, the Public Health, and the Unabashed Triumph of Philip Morris*. New York: A. Knopf.

Luik, John C. (1993/1994). Pandora's Box: The Dangers of Politically Corrupted Science for Democratic Public Policy. *Bostonia* (Winter): 54.

Osteen, W.L. (1998). *Order and Judgment in: Flue-cured Tobacco Cooperative Stabilization Corporation et al. V. United States Environmental Protection Agency and Carol Browner, Administrator, Environmental Protection Agency*. U.S. District Court, Middle District of North Carolina, Winston-Salem Division (July, 17). Reprinted after page 102 in Gori and Luik 1999.

Sullum, J. (1998). *For Your Own Good*. New York: Free Press.

Sweanor, David (1998). Memo to Non-Smokers' Rights Association (NSRA). Digital document published, with permission, by Randel Marlin at newsgroup ncf.sigs.propaganda+media.

Teich, A.H., and M.S. Frankel (1992). *Good Science and Responsible Scientists. Meeting the Challenge of Fraud and Misconduct in Science*. Washington, DC: American Association for the Advancement of Science.

United States Environmental Protection Agency [USEPA] (1991). An S[cience] A[dvisory] B[oard] Report: Review of Draft Environmental Tobacco Smoke Health Effects Document.

——— (1992). *Respiratory Health Effects of Passive Smoking. Lung Cancer and Other Disorders* (December 1992). Washington, DC: Office of Research and Development.

International Agency for Research on Cancer (IARC) (1998). *Biennial Report, 1996–1997* (March). Lyon: World Health Organisation.

Much Ado about (Almost) Nothing
Greenpeace and the Allegedly Toxic Teethers and Toys

W.T. STANBURY
with Elaine Atsalakis, Dian Choi, Vivian Lau,
Tammy Lee, Sindy Li, Olivia Tsang

1   Introduction

The issue of allegedly toxic teethers and toys made headlines in Canada, the United States, Europe, and a few other countries in 1997 and 1998. The extensive coverage in the news media was the result of Greenpeace's "Play Safe" campaign.[1] The campaign was apparently triggered by a study conducted by Greenpeace that found high levels of toxic chemicals in children's toys. Specifically, the concern revolved around the phthalate softeners found in polyvinylchloride (PVC), a common plastic used to make teethers and toys for children. Greenpeace was also concerned with the hazardous levels of lead and cadmium found in PVC.[2]

The chapter is organized as follows. Section 2 briefly describes the product in question, polyvinylchloride (PVC), and notes its extensive

Notes will be found on pages 129–31.

use in the toy industry for over a decade. Section 3 provides some background to Greenpeace's campaign against allegedly toxic teethers and toys, focusing on Greenpeace's research, said to be the primary motivation for the "Play Safe" campaign.

Section 4 describes Greenpeace's "Play Safe" campaign in Canada in 1997 and 1998. It was part of a multi-nation effort in North America and Europe coordinated by Greenpeace International. Section 5 describes the responses of Health Canada, which has primary regulatory responsibility for hazardous products relating to children.

Our analysis of Greenpeace's "toxic toys" campaign in Canada is found in section 6. Finally, in section 7 we set out our conclusions.

2   The product in question: PVC

Polyvinylchloride (PVC) is the second most common type of plastic and is used in a wide variety of products: packaging, credit cards, car interiors, flooring and blinds.

PVC alone is a brittle plastic. When used to produce items such as toys, which require a softer plastic, softeners or plasticizers are added to achieve the needed flexibility. Although a variety of chemicals are used as softeners, phthalates are the most common. The most commonly used phthalates are diethylhexyl-phthalate (DEHP), di-isodecyl phthalate (DIDP), and di-isononyl phthalate (DINP). DINP, the current most commonly used phthalate, has been found to cause damage to the liver and kidneys of laboratory animals, although it does not follow that the same result would appear in humans. When used by humans in laboratories, bottles of DINP are required to carry warning labels (website, Phthalates). The main concern with PVC is that phthalates are not chemically bound to it; instead, they sit side by side with the polymer. PVC also contains lead and cadmium. Together, phthalates, lead, and cadmium can leach out of the PVC and be ingested by children using teethers or sucking on small toys.

Greenpeace's position is this: "The entire life-cycle of PVC plastic is a polluting process. Its production involves highly toxic additives and generates hazardous chlorinated emissions and wastes. When burned in accidental fires or incinerators, PVC products are a significant source of dioxins" (Greenpeace, press release, September 17, 1997).

PVC is extensively used in the toy industry by all the major toy makers such as Mattel, Inc. (makers of Barbie, Fisher-Price, and Disney products), Hasbro, Inc. (which includes Playskool and Tonka), and Galoob Toys, Inc. (makers of Power Rangers) (Christensen 1998: 38). Studies have shown that about 93 percent of soft vinyl toys sold in Canada contain between 4 percent to 44 percent of product weight of DINP (Everson 1998a: A1).

Many things we use in everyday life contain toxic chemicals.[3] The real issue is whether their use results in exposure to those chemicals and then whether the amount of exposure could cause illness or death. Then, we need to know how many people are harmed in various ways. While Greenpeace in a host of countries made repeated claims of harm, no evidence was presented of actual harm. Yet DINP had been used in PVC toys for well over a decade.

3   Background to Greenpeace's campaign

(a)   Toxic Teethers: Part of a larger Greenpeace campaign against PVC

Greenpeace Canada (and Greenpeace in other nations) was attempting to stop the usage of PVC plastics long before the "Play Safe" campaign began in September 1997. PVC plastics are believed by Greenpeace to be harmful to the environment because of the release of dioxins in both the production and disposal process. Greenpeace claims that the "entire life-cycle of PVC plastic is a polluting process" (Greenpeace, press release, September 17, 1997; Rice 1995)

It is important to understand that the "Play Safe" campaign is really only another skirmish in Greenpeace's war on dioxins, which began in the mid-1980s. In fact, Greenpeace has been able to stigmatize dioxin as the most toxic chemical on the earth, largely because of the ineffectiveness of governments' risk communication efforts (see Powell and Leiss 1997: chap. 3). Greenpeace's sustained and often misleading attack on dioxin has followed a complex course from a critique of the release of chlorine by pulp mills (ca. 1987) to criticisms of the release of phthalates by PVCs (1993 to 1998). Its series of publications beginning in 1987 "take up the following set of relationships, for example: (1) pulp and paper—chlorine, (2) pulp and paper—dioxin, (3) dioxin—chlorine, (4) chlorine—incineration, (5) dioxin—incineration, (6) PVC—incineration, (7) PVC—dioxin, (8) PVC—chlorine, (9) chlorine—hormone disruptors, (10) PVC—hormone disruptors" (Powell and Leiss 1997: 62).

A precursor to the "Play Safe" campaign occurred 18 months earlier (March 25, 1996) when Greenpeace Canada appeared before a joint meeting of the health board and city's services committee at Toronto city hall and requested that the City ban the use of water and sewage pipes made of PVC (see Corcoran 1996; Powell and Leiss 1997: chap. 3). Greenpeace claimed that "toxic piping" produces "dangerous toxins" that imperil humans and wildlife by, among other things, reducing sperm counts and increasing cancer rates. The Vinyl Council of Canada, a division of the Society of the Plastics Industry of Canada, told the City that the assessment of experts and governmental agencies is that PVC

piping does not endanger human or animal health and does not produce dangerous quantities of dioxin (Corcoran 1996).

Greenpeace claimed that PVC piping contains cancer-causing
"plasticizers." However, Environment Canada's review of PVC concluded that it is not a health hazard and is not bioaccumulative or toxic.
Other studies have concluded that incineration of vinyl does produce
unsafe amounts of dioxin. While Greenpeace did not persuade Toronto
to stop using PVC piping, it was able to persuade the City to adopt a
policy of not incinerating any of its PVC waste.

(b)   Greenpeace's original research

Greenpeace's "Play Safe" campaign in 1997 and 1998 was said to be
based on research conducted on PVC toys for Greenpeace at Exeter
University in the United Kingdom.[4] For the test, 71 toys were purchased from 17 countries worldwide, of which 63 were made of, or contained, PVC. The tests revealed that 10 percent to 40 percent of most
of the PVC toys was toxic material, namely phthalate (website, Some
Quick Facts). The phthalate most commonly found in the toys was
di-isononylphthalate (DINP). The study for Greenpeace, performed on
laboratory animals, found that di-isononylphthalate caused liver and
kidney damage and hindered reproductive development. Since phthalates are released by excessive sucking or chewing, this study caused
Greenpeace to be concerned over the possible damage to children.

The possibility that PVC toys are toxic is not new to the toy industry. Di-ethylhexylphthalate (DEHP) was used before it was replaced in
1985 with DINP after Greenpeace had found that liver damage occurred in rats that ingested this chemical.

(c)   Other Greenpeace research

Additional research commissioned by Greenpeace Germany, and carried out by two separate German laboratories, supported the findings
of the study done at Exeter University. Their tests concluded that "PVC
toys leach hazardous additives" (Lisa Finaldi, Greenpeace International, quoted in a Greenpeace press release, December 12, 1997). Twelve
out of 23 toys made of PVC that were tested were found to be "leaching
chemical additives at levels five to six times the recommended limits
set by German official authorities" (Greenpeace website, Chemical
Leaching).

Three points should be noted here. First, the size of the sample used
for testing by Greenpeace Germany was very small. Second, there were
several studies of the leaching of phthalates (cited in Health Canada
1998a) that did not get the results claimed by Greenpeace Germany or
Greenpeace International. Third, weak science—or even "junk science"

(see Huber 1991)—can be effective in causing fear in a risk controversy and in helping to set the agenda for both industry and government.

4 The campaign in Canada, 1997–1998

The "Play Safe" campaign in Canada[5] began on September 17, 1997 with a press release based on its research on soft PVC toys and teethers for children. Press conferences were held in New York and London. The press release was reported in newspaper stories and on television news. It appears that the opening of the campaign was timed to coincide with the peak toy-buying period before Christmas.

On September 23, 1997, Greenpeace Canada sent letters to leading Canadian retailers of toys (Toys 'R' Us, Wal-Mart and Zellers) demanding they withdraw all soft PVC infant toys from sale (press release, September 23, 1997). On October 9, 1997, Greenpeace submitted a copy of its study of PVC toys and teethers to Health Canada. Almost immediately Health Canada began a reassessment of the safety of soft PVC toys and phthalates (see section 5).

Receiving no response from the toy retailers, Greenpeace activists took direct action and hung a banner at a Toronto Toys 'R' Us store on November 27, 1997, urging the company to "Stop Selling Toxic Toys." They also removed PVC toys from the Toys 'R' Us shelves. The action highlighted the fact that all Toys 'R' Us stores in Denmark, Holland, and Belgium had withdrawn soft PVC plastic toys for children under age three from sale. The Greenpeace activists loaded shopping carts with PVC toys and hung signs reading "Play Safe: Buy PVC-Free" on the shelves. They also confronted the Toys 'R' Us manager, calling on the retailer to follow the example of European chains.[6]

On June 1, 1998, Greenpeace activists interrupted the annual meeting of the International Council of Toy Industries in Toronto to demand the withdrawal of PVC toys from store shelves.

About a year after the campaign began, Greenpeace formed alliances with five of Canada's leading organizations concerned with the health of children and with the environment: Canadian Institute of Child Health, Learning Disabilities Association of Canada, Canadian Association of Physicians for the Environment, Canadian Childcare Federation, and Canadian Association of Family Resource Programs (McIlroy 1998a). Together, the group called on Health Minister Allan Rock on November 16, 1998 to force stores to remove PVC children's products. Health Canada reacted the same day with an "advisory" (see section 5).

On October 21, 1998, Dr. Paul Johnston, a British toxicologist retained by Greenpeace, gave a public lecture on the issue of toxic chemicals at the Vancouver Public Library sponsored by the BC Environmental Network. He was one of the authors of the report on toys and teethers made out of PVC commissioned by Greenpeace in 1997. Johnston said adoption of the precautionary principle made sense because no one seems to know the effect on humans who handle, chew, bite, and suck on toys containing phthalates (Fayerman 1998).

On November 13, 1998, the *National Post* (A10) quoted the federal health minister Allan Rock who wrote, in a letter to Greenpeace: "It would be premature, at this time, for Health Canada to formulate a position" on phthalates in children's toys. In the same article, the *National Post* quoted American expert Richard Mass (retained by Greenpeace) saying that chemicals are transferred to children's mouths when they suck or chew on teethers or rubber toys. This conclusion was reached after 131 PVC toys were tested for levels of lead and cadmium. The results showed that 18 percent of the toys not only contained high levels of lead but phthalates as well. These levels were said to be high enough to cause substantial brain damage to children and hormone developmental problems.

The same article reported the results of Health Canada's tests (reported on November 16, 1998, see section 5), which found that 17 out of 24 products contained 200 parts per million of lead compared to the Canadian standard of 15 parts per million. Yet Health Canada did not conclude that the products were risky to children because the products they tested were mainly intended for older children (Everson 1998a).

On November 14, 1998, Health Canada (1998a) published its updated risk assessment on di-isononylphthalate in vinyl children's products. The study had taken 11 months. (It is discussed in section 5.) Also on November 14, the *Globe and Mail* (A13) reported the challenge by biochemist Joe DiGangi of Greenpeace USA of the method used by the US Consumer Product Safety Commission to set the maximum allowable level for humans (take the largest dosage level that does not appear to cause problems in rats and divide by 100). He said "this one-hundredth is a made up number; it's a standard they've invented." DiGangi argued that substances that cause cancer in laboratory animals should not be allowed in items that children could chew.

On November 16, Greenpeace Canada demanded in a press release (1) that products that contain PVC should be removed from sale and from use by small children, (2) that the government ensure that the manufacturers are labeling the content of the product in order to inform the parents, and (3) that government set a limit on the amount of lead, cadmium, and phthalates used in products (press release, November 16, 1998). Greenpeace Canada also challenged the federal Minister of Health, Allan Rock, to take action against PVC toys.

On the same day, Health Canada issued an advisory bulletin on children's toys made of PVC (see section 5). The Vinyl Council of

Canada (1998b) also issued a press release on November 16, 1998 stating that the "preponderance of scientific evidence supports the safe use of DINP." Not surprisingly, on November 16, 1998, the lead story on CBC-TV's national news (*The National*) was toxic toys. The same issue was a front-page story in the *Toronto Star*, though only page three in the *Globe and Mail*.

The next day, the *Globe and Mail* (A1, A3) quoted Greenpeace toxics expert, Matthew Bramley as saying that "Health Canada has done nothing about the various serious dangers from astonishingly high levels of lead and cadmium." It also quotes him to the effect that toys containing PVC are hazardous to children (McIlroy 1998b).

On November 18, 1998, columnist Marcus Gee sought to put the toxic toy issue into perspective by describing the much greater risks faced by children in poor countries: for example, two million die each year for lack of immunization against simple diseases like measles. Gee wrote:

> If it wasn't clear before, the vinyl toy scare has made it so: Canada has become a nation of hypochondriacs. Enclosed in a bubble of wealth and privilege, we have become neurotic about our health and the health of our cosseted, overprotected children. While millions of children around the world waste away from measles or pneumonia or diarrhea, we fret that our little darlings will succumb to a deadly rubber ducky or a toxic Barbie House (Gee 1998: A31).

During the same week, in a speech in Toronto to a meeting of the Canadian Institute of Law and Medicine, Dr. Cornelia Baines, professor of public health sciences at the University of Toronto, said that "unfettered junk science" is distorting health care, interfering with industry, and causing life-saving products to be removed from the market (cited in Corcoran 1998).

On November 21, 1998, *Financial Post* columnist Terence Corcoran (D8) indicated that, based on the view of a Health Canada official, children would have to suck on the same soother for at least three hours a day for several years before any significant risk would be involved. Even then, the likelihood of sufficient exposure to DINP to cause illness (not death) would be one in a million. As well, tests on mammals such as hamsters and monkeys, which are closely related to humans, did not show any negative effects from exposure to phthalates.

The issue of toxic teethers and toys became nearly invisible in the news media after Health Canada issued its advisory bulletin in mid-November 1998. Greenpeace Canada, however, soon came up with another product said to be leaching phthalates.

On February 22, 1999, Greenpeace Canada issued a press release saying that lab tests it had commissioned showed "extraordinarily high levels of DEHP (diethylhexyl) phthalate" in PVC bags used to deliver medicines intravenously and for transfusions (see also Le Gault 1999). It claimed: "over 160 North American health organizations including the American Public Health Association and the American Nurses Association, are calling today on hospitals to switch from PVC products to safer approved alternatives" (McIlroy 1999). Again, Greenpeace used Dr. Matthew Bramley as a spokesman.

5   Health Canada's responses

Determined efforts by an interest group to create a risk controversy put pressure on the government agency responsible for regulating or otherwise dealing with such risks. In Canada, the agency on the "hot seat" was the Health Protection Branch of Health Canada (Aubuchon 1999). The federal government does not have a good record in dealing with risk controversies, particularly with respect to the important activity of risk communication (Powel and Leiss 1997; Lundgren 1994; Covello, von Winterfeldt and Slovic 1987; Gutteling and Wiegman 1996).

(a)   The risk assessment

Less than a month after Greenpeace Canada launched the "Play Safe" campaign on September 17, 1997, Health Canada initiated its own tests on PVC toys in Canada to verify the levels of phthalates leached into the mouths of children.[7] "Whenever there is a lead in products we're always concerned," said Francois Dignard of the Health Department.[8] Health Canada said that it wanted to propose a "Strategy for Reducing Lead in Children's and other Consumer Products," which would be completely voluntary, rely principally on industry, and not come into full effect until 2001. Health Canada has called for phasing-out the use of lead where it poses unacceptable health hazards and where alternatives to lead are available but they refuse to regulate. After this announcement, Health Canada became all but invisible for eleven months when its research was completed.

On November 14, 1998, Health Canada published an eight-page risk assessment on DINP in vinyl children's products (1998a). Specifically, this investigation was conducted to determine the health risk of DINP from soft PVC children's products as a result of mouthing by a child. The risk assessment included an analysis of the total DINP content in PVC children's products, human exposure to DINP, a hazard assessment of DINP, the cancer risk of DINP, an evaluation of the risks, and a probabilistic analysis of risk. The study found that there is no significant correlation between the total DINP content in a given PVC children's product and its release rate. In other words, it does not matter that Greenpeace found 40 percent of the content of some toys to be phthalates; this does not determine how much exposure children actually receive because that depends on the amount that leaches out of the toy or teether and is ingested.

Health Canada also concluded that a reasonable extrapolation from the cancer risk found in the animal model to humans cannot be made given currently available information (1998a). The investigation did find, however, that the quantity of DINP released from soft PVC products designed specifically to be mouthed by young children may pose a risk to the health and safety of children between the ages of three months and one year (Health Canada 1998a). As a result, Health Canada issued an advisory bulletin two days later.

(b) The advisory bulletin

On November 16, 1998, Health Canada issued an advisory bulletin (1998b) saying that children under eight kilograms could be at risk if they sucked on a rattle or teether containing DINP for more than three hours a day. It stated that testing on animals showed that intense exposure to DINP could lead to kidney and liver damage. Also, parents were advised to remove soft vinyl items that were not designed for sucking and chewing from playpens and cribs from the reach of small children because children could easily have oral contact with them. However, at the time when the advisory was released,[9] the risk from sucking and chewing was not reported.

Health Canada sent out faxes to 75,000 Canadian retail outlets to "urge" them to "withdraw the teethers and rattles from their stores (Kennedy 1998).[10] It also sent out an advisory warning to parents and caregivers. Health Canada also requested physicians to post the notice, "Health Canada Notice to Parents and Caregivers with Very Young Children," in their offices and in daycare facilities. The warning informed parents and caregivers to dispose of "products designed for sucking or teething," as Health Canada had concluded that "intense DINP exposure can cause potential damage to the kidneys and liver" (Health Canada 1998b).

PVC products containing the phthalate DINP cannot be distinguished from others since contents are not marked on the products. For this reason, Health Canada recommended that all soft vinyl toys be removed from younger children's cribs. Health Canada gave manufacturers six months to find a replacement for the phthalate DINP in the manufacturing of soft PVC toys (Health Canada 1998b). It also put on its website the names of soft PVC toys and teethers that do not contain phthalates.[11]

Health Canada said that it issued the advisory only as a precautionary measure because it found no scientific proof of DINP posing a health risk to small children (Everson 1998a: A1). The department wanted to inform the parents and caregivers that some risk (not quantified) was associated with vinyl toys.

(c) Information bulletin

Also on November 16, 1998, Health Canada released an information bulletin[12] on lead and cadmium (1998c). It noted that the international standard (European Standard EN-71) for the allowable amount of releasable lead in children's toys is 90 ppm (parts per million) and for cadmium, 75 ppm. The bulletin pointed out that the presence of lead or cadmium in the toy does not necessarily mean that children who mouth or suck such toys are at risk since the amounts leaching out may be below the standard.

Health Canada stated that its testing of numerous soft vinyl (PVC) products, including children's toys and garments, found that:

> While some of these tested products were found to contain lead, the vast majority of the tested products were found not to have extractable lead that exceeded the international standard of 90 ppm. (Heath Canada 1998a: 2)

Health Canada indicated that in May 1997 it had initiated its "Strategy for Reducing Lead" as a preventative measure to reduce the exposure of children to lead in toys and other consumer products.

6   Analysis of Greenpeace's campaign

(a) How big a risk?

The claims of Greenpeace suggest that a serious risk is being posed to children by the leaching of phthalates from toys made of PVC in which DINP has been used as a softening agent. But rationality requires both citizens and governments to ask how big is the risk. In particular, (a) what harm(s) can occur (e.g., slight illness versus certain death), (b) what is the likelihood (or probability) of such harm(s), (c) how many people are exposed to such harm(s), and (d) how many people are likely to be harmed?[13]

The quantity of phthalate to which children are exposed from toys and teethers is minute. A Health Canada official said (in November 1998) that if a person had a PVC toy in his mouth continuously for 18 years, that individual would have about one chance in one million of developing an illness as a result (Corcoran 1998). Children usually stop putting toys in their mouths after their first three years. Further, plastic toys are not constantly in their mouths. Thus, the chance of a child developing an illness as a result of toys and teethers is near zero. Even Greenpeace, on its website, admitted as much: "The Dutch Government released the results of the study on a standardized and validated test ... the study concludes that there is presently no reliable laboratory test available for measuring phthalate release" (website, Government Action ...).

When assessing the dangers of PVC toys, one should also observe past generations who had PVC toys. The fact is that PVC toys have been softened with DINP for some 13 years and there has not been any reported cases of illnesses due to contact with PVC toys in children.

As important as the estimate of very tiny risk involved in this case is the timing and origins of the estimate. The estimate was not made public until November 1998, over a year after Greenpeace launched its "Play Safe" campaign. Further, the estimate was offered by a Health Canada official in response to questions at a press conference. In other words, Health Canada made no effort early in Greenpeace's campaign to try to help parents understand the possible harm (illness, not death) and the low probability of that harm (one chance in a million). This is hardly a model of risk communication. Nor did Health Canada offer any figures on other risks to children that might have helped parents put the alleged risk from "toxic toys" into perspective.

(b) Comparing risks

The comparison of different types of risks is difficult because the perception of risks is necessarily subjective and there are large differences in the way people characterize risks (number of dimensions and the utility for combinations of dimensions).[14] But without some effort to make comparisons we lose all sense of perspective. It simply cannot be true that each of the millions of different risks in the world is unique for each person. If such were the case, rational public policy (risk management) is impossible.

What can we say about the attributes of the alleged risks relating to phthalates in PVC toys and teethers? These appear to be the key characteristics:

(1) This is a risk to the health of children under age three—this is a category of risk very likely to seem a threat or an outrage (see Sandman 1986).

(2) The risk comes from a man-made chemical, which are always seen by the public as much more threatening than the many more poisonous chemicals in nature (see Ames and Gold 1996).

(3) The risk is invisible—the toxic chemical leaches out of the plastic and is ingested when children "mouth" the toys or teethers. Invisible threats are perceived as more serious.

(4) The risk is largely voluntary: parents and other adults give soft PVC toys to children. Other toys deemed to be safer can be substituted. Involuntary risks are almost always perceived as vastly more serious than objectively comparable risks that are voluntarily assumed (see Fischer et al., 1991).

The "good news" is that millions of children have been "mouthing" soft PVC toys or teethers containing phthalates for at least a decade. Neither Greenpeace nor any national health authority have published any data showing illnesses reasonably related to phthalates leaching from toys or teethers. Not one death has been attributed to such leaching. Nor has any research—even that by Greenpeace—suggested that the leaching of phthalates has a long latency period, i.e., that the harm shows up years after the exposure.

So what do we have? Is this is another example of Greenpeace–induced fear overwhelming both logic and the absence of hard evidence of any harm, let alone serious harm? Several nations in Europe have legislated against either a phantom or a truly minute risk. In December 1999, the EU Health and Consumer Protection Commissioner imposed an emergency ban on soft plastic toys made with phthalates, ignoring the unanimous advice of the European Commission's scientific committee that had earlier found no evidence of danger to children (Milloy 2000: C7).

It has been argued that one of the criteria for good risk management is for government to ignore very tiny risks (i.e., those of less than one chance in a million of harm). Why? Because, by expending regulatory time and citizens' money on unimportant risks, much more important ones will not be addressed. No wonder that Professor John Graham (1996) has described the American government's approach to selecting risks for regulatory action as "a syndrome of paranoia and neglect." Canada's approach is very similar (Stanbury 2000).

While all the controversy over phthalates was occurring in 1998, Health Canada was conducting a study of the injuries to children from dog bites and attacks. In April 1998, the Health Protection Branch searched the database of the Canadian Hospitals Injury Reporting and Prevention Program (CHIRPP) for 1996 to identify the number of persons injured from dog bites or attacks (Health Protection Branch 1998). They accounted for 1.0 percent of all injuries in the CHIRPP database. The number of injuries by age group is shown in table 1. The data indicate that some 350 young children (under age 4) are injured each year by dogs (a risk voluntarily accepted by parents). By compari-

Table 1   Number of injuries from dog bite per age group (1996)

≤ 1 year	80	10–14 years	292
2–4 years	273	15–19 years	65
5–9 years	353	≥ 20 years	174

Source   Health Protection Branch, Health Canada

son, there are no reports of illness or injury due to phthalates from PVC toys or teethers. Yet Health Canada has never issued an advisory on the risks of dog bites and attacks to young children.

The data also indicated that 30.1 percent of the injuries (all ages) were inflicted by the victim's dog or family dog and 35.1 percent came from the dog of a friend, neighbour, or relative. Some 73.1 percent of injuries consisted of a bite (mainly to the head, face, neck) while 18.0 percent consisted of a laceration (again primarily to the face).

Of the 1,237 persons injured by a dog, 56 (or 5.8 percent) had to be admitted to hospital. Note that one-half of these were children under age four (the same group said to be at risk from toxic toys and teethers). The good news is that no fatalities resulted from dog bites.

To see how small the risk relating to certain teethers and plastic toys was, consider the following: on average the odds of a child dying from all causes under the age of one is 1 in 140 for boys and 1 in 180 for girls (Thomas and Hrudey 1997: 3). The annual odds of a child dying between the ages of 5 to 9 years are 1 in 5,500 for boys and 1 in 7,300 for girls (again, these figures are for all risks). For additional perspective, consider two more risks: in the United States, the risk that a baby will be born with Down's syndrome is 1 in 600; the risk that a newborn will have a serious birth defect is one in six (Laudan 1997: 153–56).

Analysts find it hard to explain the underlying rationale for the process by which society (through government) decides to focus regulatory efforts on certain risks while ignoring risks that have a higher probability of harm, where the harms are more serious, and where more people are harmed (injuries, illness, death). They are becoming increasingly critical (particularly in the United States) of the process that generates such idiosyncratic results.

(c)   Criticisms of Health Canada's responses to Greenpeace Canada's campaign

One criticism of the Health Canada risk assessment is that it covered only DINP. It did not address Greenpeace's concerns about lead and cadmium in toys. Activists claim that this is too significant a problem to be overlooked; these chemicals are identical to those found in vinyl mini-blinds that caused dozens of cases of lead poisoning in children in the United States (Ross 1996) and eventually brought a call for a public health warning in 1996 (Everson 1998a: A10). Health Canada's response to this criticism is that it had found that "there was no danger posed by lead in toys, in part because unlike DINP, the lead is not easily extracted from a product, even if children chew on it" (McIlroy 1998a: A1, A3).

In terms of the method of research used, Health Canada's findings have more validity compared to those of Greenpeace. Health Canada conducted its investigation using conventional research methods, with extensive testing and without any suspect assumptions. However, Health Canada did overlook an important aspect of this issue. Its study failed to consider how long young children actually suck or chew on toys. This flaw is revealed in the Human Exposure section of the study, where "the average levels of DINP released into saliva were obtained from 20 adult volunteers" in order to determine human exposure. The fact that adults were used in the study was addressed by Health Canada, saying that the "difference between adults and children in the manner of chewing or sucking on a toy were not considered to introduce a significant error in the estimate of exposure" (Health Canada 1998a: 2). Perhaps, but this does not address the likely greater duration of time children under age three have a teether or soother in their mouth.

Some critics claimed that Health Canada overreacted to Greenpeace's claims. Some even go as far as to say that Health Canada ran a junk science campaign[15] that is "distorting health care, and interfering with industry" (Corcoran 1998: D8). These critics highlight the fact that there is no report of any child becoming sick from exposure to PVC toys. Despite a Greenpeace news release claiming that babies who sucked on a soother for three or more hours daily might receive too much DINP, Corcoran (1998) states that Health Canada failed to mention the critical point that a baby would have to suck on the same soother for years to achieve anything that could even remotely be considered risky.

So why did Health Canada react the way it did, notably issuing the advisory bulletin. Francois Dignard, of Health Canada's consumer products division, stated: "It's an unnecessary risk, so [they're] taking a precautionary measure. [They're] not about to sit back and do nothing" (Kennedy 1998: A9c). For those who have young children, or are fond of them, this is likely to be a strong enough defence (even though it ignores the costs of over-reaction).

Note also that several European countries had already taken stronger action in the face of similar campaigns by Greenpeace. For example, in July 1998, Austria imposed a ban on the use of phthalates in

PVC toys and teethers; Denmark did the same in June 1998. The EU proposed such legislation in June 1998.

Two weeks after Health Canada put out its advisory bulletin, the United States Consumer Product Safety Commission (1998a, 1998b) released its study of the DINP phthalate used in the production of children's products. The study concluded that few if any children are at risk from the chemical because the amount that they ingest does not reach a level that would be harmful.

To put the advisory bulletin on PVC toys containing DINP into perspective, it is useful to note that in 1997 and 1998 Health Canada issued a total of eight warnings or advisories with respect to children and 25 with respect to adults (data compiled from Health Canada's website). Almost all were warnings rather than advisories. In other words, advisories are rare compared to the stronger action of warnings (which also include product withdrawals).

Business columnist Terence Corcoran (1998: D8) expressed concern that the government, by listing the brands of teethers and rattles that it deems to be safe, implies that all products not on the list are unsafe. This may create a very undesirable situation where the government will find itself approving all toys and maybe even all products (Corcoran 1998: D8).

Health Canada's advisory was another case where risk management was based on the need to deal with false perceptions created by an activist group (which is not accountable for its actions). This action begs the question: why didn't Health Canada go on the offensive with its own media campaign aimed at countering the misinformation and faulty inferences promulgated by Greenpeace? The federal government has never been loath to use taxpayers' dollars to trumpet its "successes," or to "market" a wide variety of policies. Why the reluctance to communicate good science, to explain how tiny was the risk and to help people to think more clearly about this and other risks promoted by activist groups?

(d) The problem of "junk science"

The "Play Safe" campaigns by Greenpeace in Canada, the United States, and Europe were said to be based on scientific research conducted for Greenpeace International (and later for Greenpeace Germany). Certainly, Greenpeace made heavy use of its research in its press releases and its press conferences often featured scientists (usually those closely associated with Greenpeace) making statements said to be based on scientific research. But a closer analysis indicates that Greenpeace's science is probably better described as "junk science" (see Le Gault 1999).

The best evidence for this conclusion is the inconsistency between the conclusions drawn by Greenpeace from its research and those drawn by scientists working for various official bodies notably Health Canada, the United States Consumer Product Safety Commission, the European Union's Scientific Committee on Toxicity, Ecotoxicity and the Environment,[16] and the study for the Dutch Technical Consensus Committee appointed by The Netherlands Minister of the Environment.

> Junk science is the mirror maze of real science, with much of the same form but none of the same substance ... It is a hodgepodge of biased data, spurious inference, and logical legerdemain, patched together by researchers whose enthusiasm for discovery and diagnosis far outstrips their skill. It is a catalog of every conceivable kind of error: data dredging, wishful thinking, truculent dogmatism, and, now and again, outright fraud. (Huber 1991: 2– 3)

"Junk science's one very real power is to stir up fear" (Huber 1991: 212). Much junk science focuses on the fear of harm—often rather farfetched—rather than harm itself. In the age of risk consciousness, the number of things to become fearful of is almost without limit: chemical toxins, electromagnetic fields, microwaves, trace contaminants, possible carcinogens, birth defects, solar radiation, and suppression of the immune system from various causes.

People want—often desperately want—explanations for phenomena that affect them or may affect them adversely. Uncertainty creates much anxiety. Even a non-scientific explanation of cause and effect is preferred to a scientific "we just don't know what causes that problem."

(e) Postscript: Science and rationality triumph?

On June 22, 1999, the 17-member panel convened in November 1998 by the American Council on Science and Health issued its report in two plastic softeners, DINP and DEHP. In summary, the chair of the panel stated: "Consumers can be confident that vinyl toys and medical devices [e.g., intravenous plastic bags] are safe" (Upham 1999: A1). The report stated that the scientific evidence that showed that DINP can cause cancer in rats—a point strongly emphasized by Greenpeace—"has little relevance for humans." Vinyl toys that contain the softener DINP "are not harmful to children under normal use" (Upham 1999: A1).

7   Conclusions

We focus on three main issues here: (a) the tactics Greenpeace uses in its campaigns relating to risk controversies, (b) a summary of some of the federal government's problems in dealing with risk controversies pushed by groups like Greenpeace, and (c) an assessment of whether Greenpeace's "Play Safe" campaign was a success from Greenpeace's perspective.

(a) Greenpeace's tactics

This study illustrates the way Greenpeace has been able to initiate and dominate risk controversies in a number of areas since the mid-1980s. Here we try to summarize how Greenpeace has conducted these campaigns and note any differences in the "Play Safe" campaign.

In general, Greenpeace positions itself, first, as an alarm raiser on the cutting edge of new problems, second, as an "outsider" group that is never contaminated with pragmatic compromise, and, third, as most willing to use confrontation and direct action. At the same time, Greenpeace is in competition for "share of mind" and share of donations with a considerable number of environmental groups and with activist groups generally (see Jordan and Maloney 1997).

(1) Greenpeace makes use of a wide range of tactics with the apparent objective of obtaining extensive coverage in the news media. Publicity is the life blood of Greenpeace (see figure 1). Greenpeace is famous for its "stunts" aimed at gaining visibility, primarily pictures, in the news media. In the "Play Safe" campaign, the following "stunts" were used: (a) "invasion" of toy stores; use of banners and signs; removal of toys (sometimes by a staff-member dressed as Santa Claus), (b) large banner

---

Figure 1: The Iron Triangle of Staff-Type Environmental Groups

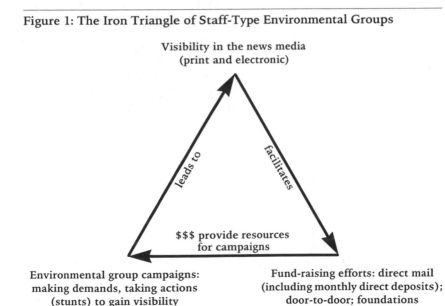

Visibility in the news media
(print and electronic)

$$ leads\ to \qquad facilitates $$

$$$ provide resources
for campaigns

Environmental group campaigns: making demands, taking actions (stunts) to gain visibility

Fund-raising efforts: direct mail (including monthly direct deposits); door-to-door; foundations

draped over the Ministry of Health's building in Rome, (c) having a group of activists disrupt the annual meeting of the toy manufacturers' association, and (d) creating a display to counter those of toy-makers at toy fairs. The other influence techniques used in the "Play Safe" campaign included:

- a large number of press releases; some press conferences;

- studies (said to be independent, scientific investigations);

- letters, visits to retailers, manufacturers;

- forming alliances or coalitions;

- having staff or consultant toxicologists give speeches and interviews; and

- advocacy advertisements.

(2) Greenpeace International often coordinates the efforts of a number of national Greenpeace organizations. The anti-PVC toys campaign involved Greenpeace organizations in many countries besides Canada: United States, Belgium, Austria, The Netherlands, Germany, Italy, United Kingdom, and the Philippines as well as the European community. The multinational approach gives the appearance of international or even worldwide concern. It also increases the odds that one government will "crack" under pressure and take action along the lines proposed by Greenpeace. Greenpeace then treats this as a "precedent" or example for other countries. This tactic was used in the "Play Safe" campaign.

(3) Greenpeace gives the appearance of relying on science or scientific research. Science provides a rational underpinning for Greenpeace's calls for immediate action often based on stunts aimed at gaining visibility in the news media. However, Greenpeace's "science" is biased (to support its pre-determined conclusion) and based on selective quotations, selective references. It also ignores contrary evidence. All of this is done in a sophisticated way.[17]

(4) Greenpeace makes a major effort to make its science-based claims understandable by the general public and the news media. Governments are generally poor at this important element of risk communication.[18] Greenpeace's studies are heavy on implications and conclusions for policy. However, the studies do not stray very far from the outer boundary of prevailing scientific consensus, according to Powell and Leiss, (1997: 63). Thus, Greenpeace provides a "partisan, yet plausible construction of science with sharply drawn conclusions [all of which is] cleverly communicated."

One key to Greenpeace's impact is that there is nothing comparable produced and communicated by any other actor (including government and industry). Where neither government nor industry assumes responsibility for effective risk communication with the public, Greenpeace's successes are close to victories by default. In the "Play Safe" campaign, industry challenged Greenpeace's claims but the Canadian government did not.

(5) Greenpeace relentlessly exploits the asymmetries between its position in society and the position of governments and industry. These asymmetries relate to at least the following:

- the tactics that may be employed to win the support of the public;

- the nature of the appeals (often to emotion—trying to induce fear) made to influence the public;

- the attitude of the public toward interest groups like Greenpeace, i.e., much more tolerant of aggressive, direct-action tactics, strong language, and looseness with respect to the truth; and

- the much greater accountability of government organizations for their behaviour—being Greenpeace means never having to say you are sorry, no matter the extent of the group's misbehaviour.

More radical groups like Greenpeace are not necessarily expected by the public to be rational and to provide factual support or logical arguments. In the "Play Safe" campaign, however, Greenpeace emphasized the scientific research it had done and on which it said it based its demands for government action. Greenpeace can use hit and run or guerilla tactics not available to others such as business firms or associations. Greenpeace can try almost any appeal to see what resonates with the public. If it fails to get the desired response, Greenpeace will try something else next week or next month. In the "Play Safe" campaign, there is no doubt that an effort was made to make parents fearful for the safety of their children.

Greenpeace can create pressure on established organizations to prove something is "safe" even though this is conceptually impossible. It can emphasize the existence of risk without quantifying it or putting it into perspective. In the "Play Safe" campaign, Greenpeace emphasizes the most remote possibilities as if they are clear and present dangers. Greenpeace's power is based largely on its ability to create fear in the minds of ordinary citizens. In general, it plays on ignorance and distrust of government. Greenpeace targets issues likely to be most vulnerable, e.g., children, medical supplies that give life.

(6) Critics confuse the substance of Greenpeace's claims or demands and the factors that greatly influence campaigns, namely extensive media coverage that is vital to fundraising. Money is the life blood of this staff-type interest group whose leaders and employees are entirely self-selected. No members participate in governance, only the senior staff. This is a marketing organization operating in a competitive market—for "causes" (see Jordan and Maloney 1997).

For Greenpeace, lack of visibility in the news media equals lack of effect and lack of effect means donors cannot see their money at work. Figure 1 describes the "iron triangle," which links visibility in the news media to efficacy in raising funds. Such money pays for the various campaigns. Central to all campaigns is the need to gain visibility in the news media. Coverage is easier where the media operate on the principle that the news is a branch of entertainment. Sensationalism and graphic images sell—"if it bleeds, it leads."

The news media's reportage of risk controversies is important for several reasons. first, the public is heavily dependent upon the mass media for information and opinions on these controversies; it is the primary filter between the various participants and citizens. Second, the reportage also provides some clues as to how the public understands these controversies. Third, governments' efforts at risk communication must rely heavily on this channel that, by its nature, must be selective and so introduces biases into the messages conveyed to the public.

(b)   The government's problems

Greenpeace's skill in initiating and advancing risk controversies is able to create enormous pressures on governments and other established organizations. They must respond in some fashion, no matter how ridiculous the claim by an interest group, particularly if that group can claim some scientific support for its position. Moreover, they must operate in a rational fashion as responsible, professional organizations. The need to respond immediately puts the established organization on the defensive. It is easier to plant doubt or create fear than it is to offer rational explanations, particularly when they involve tiny probabilities, imperfect knowledge, and the need to make trade-offs. Creating uncertainty or the awareness of uncertainty is a primary means of creating fear.

When fear dominates an issue, rationality is cold comfort to the concerned, anxious, and distraught individuals since it operates in a different part of the brain. Fear leads to the bypass of reason, engendering the atavistic fight-or-flight response, a holdover from our primitive past (see Hall 1999).

The Canadian federal government has a poor record in terms of effective communications in recent risk controversies (Powell and Leiss

1997). It did not acquit itself well in the "Play Safe" campaign: it communicated too little, too slowly, and its communications were not well designed to help a fearful public understand and cope with the issue. It must be appreciated that it is hard for government to deal with interest groups[19] and others engaging in "down and dirty" tactics (Leiss 1995).

Major players in risk controversies, in communicating with other parties, have exploited the inherent uncertainties in the estimates of risks, and the lack of even reasonably complete databases to advance their interests as they see them. Sometimes they conceal what they do know or suspect (Leiss 1995: 688).

The federal government should devote some resources to an effort to predict which issues are likely to become important in the future—particularly those likely to be "crisis" issues.[20] Issues do not arise spontaneously. They always have a "pusher" (or a coalition of pushers). Greenpeace has been a notable pusher of a number of risk issues (e.g. dioxins, chlorine, and various types of PVC). Moreover, it has been argued that "the hottest risk issue of the coming decade [will be] endocrine disruptors"—and Greenpeace published a report on this issue ("Our Stolen Future . . .") in 1996 (Powell and Leiss 1997: 61). Part of the federal government's forecasting efforts should be a "Greenpeace Watch" because of (a) its malign record on dioxins and PVC including toxic teethers, medical products (bags, tubes for injections); (b) Greenpeace's scale of operations and the international scope of many of its campaigns, and (c) ability to move governments to regulatory action even when it is unjustified.

(c) Effectiveness of Greenpeace's efforts

The success or effectiveness of any interest group's efforts to influence public policy are usually difficult to determine, often because of time lags and the presence of other variables that influence changes in public policy. More generally—and particularly when assessing a Greenpeace campaign—it is important to ask what criteria the group might use to measure its performance. For Greenpeace, the following criteria could be relevant:

- fund-raising (which requires extensive media coverage);

- provoking over-reaction by businesses (many Greenpeacers are really watermelons—green on the outside but red on the inside);

- changes in public policy;

- increased credibility and legitimacy; and

- capturing or setting the agenda in a policy issue.

A campaign could move government to modify its policies in the direction desired by Greenpeace or it could alter the activities of major corporations. Yet, the same campaign could fail to persuade people to give money to Greenpeace and, without funds, Greenpeace would soon not be able to carry on. The reverse could be true: a campaign may be useful in raising money even if no substantive results are achieved.

An important objective for Greenpeace is to set or change the agenda in some area of public policy;[21] i.e. get everyone responding to their issue or question. Since this, too, is a competitive process, Greenpeace's reputation in the competitive market for "causes" is enhanced and its "share of mind" is increased. Even when Greenpeace does not succeed in changing public policy in the short-run, it often succeeds in defining the terms of the debate in the future. This occurs at least in part because of the failure of government (and industry) in risk communication.

It is clear that the "Play Safe" campaign in 1997 and 1998 produced substantive results in terms of (a) the behaviour of certain toymakers and retailers, particularly in Europe, and (b) certain governments. For example, Austria, Denmark, and Sweden imposed a ban on the use of DINP in toys and teethers for children under age three. Spain banned five types of teethers.

Note that all the countries that took the strongest actions with respect to "toxic toys" were in Europe. By comparison, Canada did a re-assessment and issued an advisory bulletin. The United States did not go beyond a study of the toxicity of phthalates in PVC toys and concluded that no official action was warranted. It is possible that Health Canada may not have issued the advisory and published a list of toys not containing DINP if the Health Protection Branch was not in "disarray" when it had to deal with Greenpeace's "Play Safe" campaign (see McIlroy 1998b).

The "Play Safe" campaign raised public awareness in Canada of Greenpeace's position on PVC. However, Greenpeace studies have been the subject of strong criticism since researchers found significant flaws in the methods used. It is not clear that these flaws caused Greenpeace to lose credibility with the general public and the news media, both of which are more important than government. The media provide the publicity and the public provides the money to finance the organization.

For Greenpeace, the "Play Safe" campaign appears to have been a success in the following ways. First, because of its mass media penetration, many parents have discarded or stopped purchasing PVC toys for their children. Despite the evidence against Greenpeace's findings, parents are understandably unwilling to take the risk of endangering their children. Second, Greenpeace has also convinced many toy retailers worldwide to "voluntarily" (under serious pressure) stop selling PVC toys. Third, Greenpeace's poorly conducted studies appear to have triggered many more credible studies that may soon settle this controversial toxic-toys issue. We do not know if "Play Safe" was successful in terms of raising money for Greenpeace because Greenpeace's financial statements do not provide sufficient detail.

With the November 16, 1998 advisory bulletin and implicit recall, Greenpeace Canada can reasonably claim to have cowed Health Canada, which took the actions knowing that "the probability of anything happening is very small" (Gee 1998: A31). Health Canada could not ignore the issue. But, it did very little to challenge Greenpeace's grossly exaggerated claims.

After reviewing all the evidence and putting the risks into perspective, it is hard to avoid the conclusion that governments in a number of nations, by banning phthalates in toys and teethers, over-reacted to a minute risk of a modest harm. This was another example of weak risk management in the face of a skilled and determined interest group. Fear of harm to children created sufficient fear of political repercussions in a number of countries to result in over-regulation. Thus, rationality in policy-making took another beating.

Acknowledgments

The associate authors, Elaine Atsalakis, Dian Choi, Vivian Lau, Tammy Lee, Sindy Li, Olivia Tsang, are B.Com. students in the Faculty of Commerce and Business Administration, University of British Columbia. Each student prepared a short paper on this issue for a class taught by W.T. Stanbury in 1998. I am indebted to Cynthia Hendricks for careful and prompt word processing.

Notes

1 Greenpeace consists of Greenpeace International, which holds the copyright in the name and has its offices in Amsterdam, and the separate Greenpeace operations in over 30 nations. These entities are referred to as Greenpeace Canada, Greenpeace USA, Greenpeace Germany, Greenpeace UK and so on. All of the Greenpeace entities are "staff" groups, i.e., they are controlled entirely by the employees. While donors are often called "members," they have no say in the governance of any Greenpeace entity, except indirectly by no longer making donations. It is these donations that finance the Greenpeace entities. Note, however, that Greenpeace International is financed by a "tax" of variable percentage on the gross revenues of each Greenpeace operation in industrialized nations. Part of Greenpeace

International's revenues (about $30 million in 1997) are used to help finance Greenpeace operations in developing countries or those where environmentalism is less well developed (about $7 million). From 1993 to 1998, Greenpeace Canada did not pay any "tax" to Greenpeace International; rather, it was receiving contributions from Greenpeace International ($4.7 million from 1993 to 1997) to augment the revenues raised within Canada as these had fallen sharply in the early 1990s (Gao 1998).

2 Greenpeace Canada's website says that it wants "to ensure the ability of the Earth to nurture life in all its diversity." In 1997 and 1998 Greenpeace Canada had three main campaigns: Climate and Energy, Biodiversity, Fish, and Forests, and Toxics and Health. The "Play Safe" initiative was part of the Toxics and Health campaign.

3 Bruce Ames, a leading toxicologist, points out that the risks posed by natural carcinogens are far greater than those related to man-made substances. See Ames and Gold 1996.

4 Greenpeace, press release, September 17, 1997. The study was received by Greenpeace International in April 1997 but not made public until September. See McAndrew 1997 and Greenpeace Research Laboratories 1997.

5 Greenpeace Canada states (on its website, www.greenpeace.org) that it has 130,000 members. It described its method of fundraising as follows: Greenpeace "signs on new members through direct mail, door and phone canvass, workplace giving and monthly giving. We also raise money through bequests and gifts of life insurance." Greenpeace noted that it accepts no government or corporate funding.

6 "Toys 'R' Us has strong guidelines to protect the health of European children, but weak ones for Canadian children," said Greenpeace campaigner Beverly Thorpe, who monitors international action on the PVC issue. (Greenpeace, press release Company Withdraws Products in Europe—but Not Canada, November 27, 1998.

7 On risk assessments, generally, see Health Canada 1993; Kunreuther and Slovic 1996; Presidential/ Congressional Commission on Risk Assessment and Risk Management 1997).

8 "Vinyl Toys to Be Tested for Lead, Cadmium," Globe and Mail, (October 10, 1997): A8.

9 According to its website, Health Canada issued only three advisory bulletins in 1997 and 1998.

10 The Canadian Toy Association (1998) on the same day recommended that member companies begin to use alternative plasticizers temporarily in soft teethers and rattles designed for children under eight kilograms. It also recommended that the Minister of Health establish an international panel of scientific experts to develop worldwide standards for plasticizers used in soft teethers and rattles.

11 By January 9, 1999, some 174 toys and teethers from over a score of manufacturers were listed on Health Canada's website as containing no DINP (phthalates).

12 This is another form of communication with the public. Information bulletins do not result in actions by Health Canada beyond monitoring.

13 These are standard questions in any reasonable risk assessment. See Presidential/Congressional Commission on Risk Assessment and Risk Management 1997.

14 Generally, see Fischhoff et al. 1981, Slovic 1987, Slovic 1993, Slovic, Kraus and Covello 1990.

15 See the discussion of junk science in (d) below.

16 The issue with this study, which raised concerns about the leaching of phthalates, lies in the standard to which the results were compared.

17 Le Gault (1999) states that the key features of junk science are fear, specious logic, and misleading information.

18 While appearing to use science, Greenpeace benefits from the very limited knowledge of science or even scientific thinking in the vast majority of citizens. This also applies to reporters.

19 The advantages of interest groups over even respected individual scientists in communicating with the public will inevitably give the interest groups an opportunity to dominate the presentation of science. The groups also claim both the public and science.

20 Generally, see Stanbury 2000.

21 See Powell and Leiss 1997: chap. 3.

References

Ames, Bruce N., and L.S. Gold (1996). The Causes and Prevention of Cancer: Gaining Perspectives in the Management of Risks. In Robert W. Hahn (ed.), *Risks, Costs, and Lives Saved* (New York: Oxford University Press; Washington: AEI Press): 4–45.

Aubuchon, Sylvie (1999). The Health Protection Branch and Risk Management in Canada: An Overview. Unpublished paper for BAPA 501, Faculty of Commerce, University of British Columbia.

Australian Toy Association (1998a). ICTI's Position on the Use of Vinyl in Toys. www.austoy.com.au/industry.htm (May).

———— (1998b). TIE News Release: Commission Threatens Europe's Toy Market: Misinformation and Scaremongering behind Greenpeace Campaign. www.austoy.com.au/industry.htm (June 2).

Bonvie, Bill (1998). Toxics in Toyland. *Vegetarian Times* 250 (June): 14.

British Plastics Federation (1997). BPF Statement on PVC Toys and Phthalates. www.bpf.co.uk/bpf.htm (September 17).

British Toy and Hobbey Association [BTHA] (1997). Toy Industry Welcomes EU Action on PVC. Press release (October 10). Digital document: www.btha.co.uk/pr/pvc2910.html

Canadian Toy Association (1998). Canada's Toy Industry Takes Action on Soft Teethers and Rattles. News Release (November 16).

Christensen, Jackie H. (1998). Toxic Toy Story. *Mothering* (Sept./Oct.).

Corcoran, Terence (1996). Now, a Killer Vinyl Scare. *Globe and Mail* (March 26): B12.

—— (1998). Merry Christmas from Junk Science. *Financial Post* (Nov. 21: D8.

—— (1999). Killer toys and Other Games that Activists Play. *Financial Post* (June 22: C7.

Covello, V.T., D. von Winterfeldt, and Paul Slovic (1987). Communicating Scientific Information about Health and Environmental Risks: Problems and Opportunities from a Social and Behavioural Perspective. In V.T. Covello et al. (eds.), *Uncertainty in Risk Assessment, Risk Management and Decision Making* (New York: Plenum Publishing): 39–61.

Everson, Brad (1998a). Soft Plastic Toys Pose Risk to Children, Greenpeace Says. *National Post* (November 13): A10.

—— (1998b). Soft Vinyl Toys Dangerous, Health Canada Warns. *National Post* (November 17): A1.

—— (1998c). Health Canada Joins a Growing Chorus with Warning about Plastic Toys. *National Post* (November 17): A6.

Fayerman, Pamela (1998). Ban Sought on Soft Plastic Toys. *Vancouver Sun* (October 21): B4.

Fischer, Gregory, et al. (1991). What Risks Are People Concerned About? *Risk Analysis* 11 (April): 303–14.

Fischhoff, B., et al. (1981). Lay Foibles and Expert Fables in Judgments about Risks. In T.J. O'Riordan and R.K. Turner (eds.), *Progress in Resource Management and Environmental Planning* (New York: John Wiley).

Gao, Yuan Yun (Gloria) (1998). Computer Analysis of Greenpeace Income Statements. Unpublished paper for Comm. 394, Faculty of Commerce, University of British Columbia.

Gee, Marcus (1998). Spare Me the Panic over Vinyl Toys. *Globe and Mail* (November 18): A31.

Gots, Ronald E. (1993). *Toxic Risks: Science, Regulation, and Perception.* Boca Raton, FL: Lewis Publishers.

Graham, John D. (1996). Making Sense of Risk: An Agenda for Congress. In Robert W. Hahn (ed.), *Risks, Costs and Lives Saved* (New York: Oxford University Press): 183–207.

Greenpeace Demands Toy Recall (1997). *Toronto Star* (October 10): A16.

Greenpeace Questions Safety of Toys (1997). *Halifax Chronicle Herald* (October 10): C18.

Greenpeace Research Laboratories (1997). Determination of the Composition and Quantity of Phthalate Ester Additives in PVC Children's Toys. Technical Note 06/97 (September).

Gutteling, J.M., and O. Wiegman (1996). *Exploring Risk Communication.* Boston: Kluwer.

Hall, Stephen S. (1999). Fear Itself. *New York Times Magazine* (February 28): 42–47, 69–72; 88–90.

Health Canada (1993). Health Risk Determination. Ottawa: Health Canada.

—— (1998a). Updated Risk Assessment on Di-isononyl Phthalate in Vinyl Children's Products (November 14). Ottawa: Consumer Products Division Product Safety Bureau, Health Protection Branch.

—— (1998b). Health Canada Advises Parents and Caregivers of Very Young Children to Dispose of Soft Vinyl (PVC) Teethers and Soft Vinyl (PVC) Rattles. www.hc-sc.gc.ca/advisory/index.htm (November 16).

—— (1998c). Information Bulletin: Lead and cadmium. www.hc-sc.gc.ca/english/archives/releases/lead.htm (November).

Health Protection Branch (1998). Injuries Associated with Dog Bites and Dog Attacks. www.hc-sc.gc.ca/hpb/ledc/brch/injury/dogbit_e.html.

Huber, Peter W. (1991). *Galileo's Revenge: Junk Science in the Court Room*. New York: Basic Books.

International Council of Toy Industries [ICTI] (1997). Statement in Response to Greenpeace September 17, 1997 Press Conferences and Claims Concerning Toys Made with Polyvinyl Chloride (PVC). Digital document: www.newswire.ca/releases.

Jordan, Grant, and William Maloney (1997). The Protest Business? Mobilizing Campaign Groups. Manchester/New York: Manchester University Press.

Kennedy, Mark (1998). Vinyl Teethers, Rattles Pulled from Store Shelves. *Calgary Herald* (November 17): A11.

Kraus, N., et al. (1992). Intuitive Toxicology: Expert and Lay Judgments of Chemical Risks. *Risk Analysis* 12, 2: 83–93.

Kunreuther, H., and P. Slovic, eds. (1996). New Directions in Risk Management. *The Annals of the American Academy of Political and Social Science (Special Issue)* 545 (May).

Laudan, Larry (1997). *Dangers Ahead: The Risk You Really Face on Life's Highway*. New York: John Wiley.

Le Gault, Michael (1999). Greenpeace's Medical Scare. *Financial Post* (April 10): D7.

Leiss, William (1995). "Down and Dirty": The Use and Abuse of Public Trust in Risk Communication. *Risk Analysis* 15, 6: 685–92.

Lundgren, Regina (1994). *Risk Communications: A Handbook for Communicating Environmental, Safety and Health Risks*. Columbus, OH: Battelle Press.

Martin, Keven (1998). Parents Warned, Some Teething Toys Harmful. *Calgary Sun* (November 17): 3.

McAndrew, Brian (1997). Soft Plastic Toys Risky Greenpeace Study Says. *Toronto Star* (September 17): A2.

McIlroy, Anne (1998a). Baby Rattles May Be Toxic, Health Canada Warns Parents. *Globe and Mail* (November 17): A1, A3.

—— (1998b). Safety's Tarnished Stamp of Approval. *Globe and Mail* (November 18): A1.

—— (1999). Intravenous Bags, Tubes Toxic, Greenpeace Research Finds. *Globe and Mail* (February 23): A2.

Milloy, Steven (2000). Unreasonable Precautions. *Financial Post* (February 7): C7.

Mittelstaedt, Martin (1999). Ottawa Knew Risk Very Slight in Toy Case. *Globe and Mail* (April 26): A6.

Oriellet, Eric (1995) Organizational Analysis and Environmental Sociology: The Case of Greenpeace Canada. In M.D. Mehta and CE. Ouellet (eds.), *Environmental Sociology* (North York, ON: Captus Press): 321–38.

Powell, Douglas, and William Leiss (1997). *Mad Cows and Mother's Milk: The Perils of Poor Risk Communication*. Montreal/Kingston: McGill-Queen's Press.

Presidential/Congressional Commission on Risk Assessment and Risk Management (1997). *Final Report: Framework for Environmental Health Risk Management* (Vol. 1). Washington, DC: P/CCRARM. Retrieved as digital document from www.riskworld.com/Nreports.

PVC Study Rejected (1997). *Chemical Week* 159, 37 (October 1): 41.

Rice, Bonnie (1995). Polyvinyl Chloride (PVC) Plastic: Primary Contributor to the Global Dioxin Crisis. Distributed by Greenpeace.

Ross, Igioma (1996). Blinds Could Pose Lead Hazard. *Globe and Mail* (June 26): A6.

Roth, E., M.G. Morgan, B. Fischhoff, L. Lane, and A. Bostrom (1990). What Do We Know about Making Risk Comparisons? *Risk Analysis* 10: 375–87.

Sandman, Peter (1986). Explaining Environmental Risk (November). Washington, DC: US Environmental Protection Agency, Office of Toxic Substances.

Slovic, P. (1987). Perception of Risk. *Science* 236 (April 17): 280–86.

—— (1993). Perceived Risk, Trust and Democracy. *Risk Analysis* 13, 6 (December).

Slovic, P., J. Flynn, C.K. Mertz, and L. Mullican (1993). *Health Risk Perception in Canada*. Ottawa: Health Canada.

Slovic P., N. Kraus, and V.T. Covello (1990). What Should We Know about Making Risk Comparisons? *Risk Analysis* 10, 3: 389–92.

Stanbury, W.T. (1993). *Business-Government Relations in Canada* (2nd ed.). Toronto: Nelson Canada.

—— (2000) Reforming Risk Regulation in Canada: The Next Policy Frontier? (This volume)

Stanbury, W.T., and I.B. Vertinsky (1995). Assessing the Impact of New Information Technologies on Interest Group Behaviour and Policy Making. In T.J. Courchene (ed.), *Technology, Information and Public Policy* (Bell Canada Papers on Economics and Public Policy) (Kingston: John Deutsch Institute for the Study of Economic Policy): 293–379.

Thomas, Simon P., and Steve E. Hrudey (1997). *Risk of Death in Canada: What We Know and How We Know It*. Edmonton: University of Alberta Press.

Toloken, Steven (1998). 11 States Bring PVC Toys under Tighter Scrutiny. *Plastics News* 10, 5 (March 30).

Upham, S. Phineas (1999). Vinyl Toys Pose No Danger to Children Scientists Find. *National Post* (June 22): A1, A2.

U.S. Consumer Product Safety Commission (1998a). News from CPSC. www.cpsc.gov/cpscpub/prerl/prhtml99/99031.html (December 2).

—— (1998b). The Risk of Chronic Toxicity Associated with Exposure to Di-isonyl Phthalate (DINP) in Children's Products: Executive Summary (December). Bethesda, MD: CPSC.

Vinyl Council of Canada (1998a). Member Bulletin: Phthalates in Children's Products (November 16). Mississauga, ON: VCC.

—— (1998b). VCC Initiatives on Soft Vinyl Products for Very Young Children. News Release (November 16). Mississauga, ON: VCC.

Vinyl Toys Contain Chemical that Causes Liver Damage in Rats (1998). *New York Times* (November 14): A13.

Genetically Engineered Angst
From Frankenstein to Frankenfoods

Douglas Powell

On May 20, 1999, John Losey and colleagues from Cornell University published a brief letter in the scientific journal, *Nature* (Losey et al. 1999). The report concerned a laboratory study in which the leaves of milkweed plants in a greenhouse were artificially dusted with pollen from corn plants at levels approximating what the researchers thought happened in nature. Some of the pollen was from conventional corn—whatever "conventional" might mean—and some was from corn genetically engineered to contain the protein toxin from the common soil bacterium, *Bacillus thuringiensis*.

Three-day-old Monarch caterpillars were placed on the leaves and allowed to feed for four days. The researchers reported that 44 percent of the Monarch larvae fed leaves dusted with pollen containing *Bacillus thuringiensis* died. No caterpillar died that ate leaves dusted with regular corn pollen or the control leaves. Larvae feeding on the leaves dusted with pollen containing *Bacillus thuringiensis* also ate much less and were less than half the size of larvae that fed on leaves with no pollen. (No attempt was made, however, to compare the pollen coverage of the leaves in the lab to that which might commonly exist in or near a cornfield.)

The authors correctly recognized that the study was limited in applicability and that field tests would be required to determine the significance of these results found in an artificial environment. Upon publication, Dr. Losey was quoted as saying, "We can't forget that Bt-corn and other transgenic crops have a huge potential for reducing pesticide use and increasing yields. This study is just the first step, we need to do more research and then objectively weigh the risks versus the benefits of this new technology" (Cornell University 1999).

Despite his cautionary statement, Losey found his results transformed into tales of mutant killer corn and sacred butterflies. The *New York Times* led on the front-page with a story entitled, Bambi of the Insect World Threatened (Bambi, of course, having a particular cultural resonance for many in North America who grew up on a "Disneyfied" view of nature). To this date, demonstrators from Greenpeace continue to dress-up as Monarch butterflies and feign death simultaneously at a pre-arranged time, usually for the convenience of television cameras. Great street theatre, poor public policy, ignoring that numerous subsequent studies and analyses have concluded that the risk to Monarch butterflies is minuscule, especially when compared to known risks such as destruction of wintering grounds in Mexico.

This combination of scientific *naïveté*, media hyperbole, and allegations of corporate conspiracy has come to characterize public discussions of genetically engineered foods or, as they are sometimes called, genetically modified organisms (GMOs). Such labels can be confusing because all foods are genetically modified, whether through traditional breeding, chemically induced changes, or genetic engineering.

The Pusztai affair

International public discussion of genetically engineered foods increased dramatically through the latter part of 1998. There was, for example, the Pusztai affair.

On August 10, 1998, Dr. Pusztai of the Rowett Research Institute in Aberdeen, Scotland, reported that, after he had fed five rats for 110 days on potatoes genetically engineered to contain one of two lectins known to be toxic to insects, some of the rats showed stunted growth and impaired immune systems. Dr. Pusztai reported his findings not in a peer-reviewed scientific journal but on the *World in Action* television program. After an internal review of the data by Rowett Research Institute, it emerged that not only had Dr. Pusztai ignored the conventional route of scientific peer review but also that the experimental design lacked appropriate controls. Potatoes themselves are full of poisonous chemicals in quantities that vary depending how they are grown, a phenomenon known as somaclonal variation, and must therefore be uniformly grown for any feeding trail to be informative. As well, rats do not like to subsist on raw potatoes and their diet must be supplemented. By August 12, 1998, Dr. Pusztai had been suspended and was subsequently forced to retire.

The Pusztai affair spawned significant media coverage and numerous allegations. On February 12, 1999, a group of twenty international scientists released a letter supporting the work of Dr. Pusztai and specifically charged that the process of genetic engineering itself and, in particular, the use of the 35S cauliflower-mosaic-virus promoter was to blame. The 35S promoter is widely used in the genetic engineering of plants to turn specific genes on and off. Because of this widespread use, regulators in Western countries already demand evidence that any 35S insertion is stable and well understood. Further, other feeding experiments involving the 35S promoter have not found the problems described by Pusztai and supporters (see www.plant.uogueph.ca/safefood/gmo/gmo-index.htm). Most importantly, though, the potatoes grown by Dr. Pusztai would not have passed regulatory scrutiny in Canada, or the United States, or the United Kingdom and would never have been approved. Subsequently, the Royal Society concluded that "Dr. Arpad Pusztai's widely publicized research into the effects of feeding rats Genetically Modified (GM) potatoes appears to be flawed, and it would be unjustifiable to draw from it general conclusions about whether genetically modified foods are harmful to human beings or not" (Royal Society 1999).

Pubic response to GMOs in Canada

Public discussion of genetically engineered foods in Canada increased dramatically in the fall of 1999 (figure 1). Canadian coverage was significantly bolstered when Greenpeace and the Council of Canadians, two activist groups, held a public demonstration in front of a Loblaw supermarket in an affluent area of downtown Toronto. Typical of the statements made by the demonstrators was that of Jennifer Story, health protection campaigner for the Council of Canadians, who asserted that, "Genetically engineered foods have not been proven safe for human health and the environment. As the largest grocery chain in Canada, Loblaw has the obligation to take the lead, and take genetically engineered food off the shelf" (Greenpeace and Council of Canadians (1999).

Such media accounts, regardless of accuracy and tone, influence the formation of public perceptions. There have been many surveys of public opinion about biotechnology in general and, more specifically, about agricultural biotechnology. In his comprehensive history of biotechnology, Bud (1993) begins by asking, "What other single word is itself the subject of worldwide polling?" (for a review, see www.plant.uoguelph.ca/safefood/gmo/gmo-index.htm).

Figure 1   Distribution of top five plant-agriculture stories by topic from *Associated Press*, the *Globe and Mail*, *Kitchener-Waterloo Record*, *New York Times* (May 1, 1996 to December 31, 1999; *n* = 1,623)

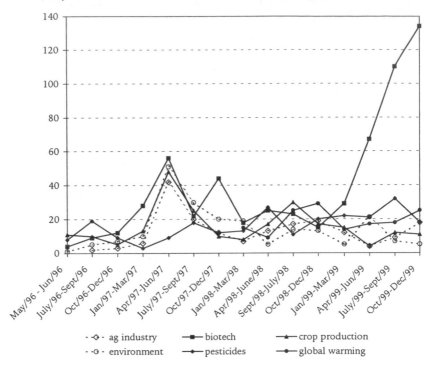

Although relatively few Canadians have heard or read about biotechnology (Powell 1994; May 2000) opinions regarding specific biotechnology applications have consistently appeared much stronger. Kelley (1995) concluded that Australian voters had firm opinions about biotechnology and noted that in a democracy, voters routinely make decisions about policies about which they have no detailed academic understanding. Consumers will continue to make decisions about biotechnology, whether they are "better educated" or not.

The public notions of agricultural biotechnology, consistently articulated as concerns about uncertainty, playing God, and the involvement of powerful interests, leads to the perception, frequently used in media accounts, of science out of control. Such concerns are valid. Genetic engineering is a powerful technology—and that is the source of potential benefit and unrestrained angst. It is also why the technology is regulated. As Norman Ball of the University of Waterloo (Ball 1992) has noted, all revolutionary technologies create three public responses in succession: unrealistic expectations (all new technologies are over-sold), confusion, and, eventually, finding a way to cope. Biotechnology has been greatly oversold but, as with other new technologies, a public discussion over time shifts from one of risks versus benefits to a more realistic approach of extracting whatever benefits a technology can bring while actively and prudently minimizing risks.

From *Frankenstein* to Frankenfoods

Of course, such a pattern of social response to new technologies is hardly novel. First published in 1817, Mary Shelley's *Frankenstein* contained many warnings about science out of control. At a time when fundamental advances in organic chemistry were leading some scientific charlatans to say they had discovered the secret of life, Shelley, a member of England's radical intellectual elite, had Professor Walden, Frankenstein's teacher, say:

> The ancient teachers of this science promised impossibilities and performed nothing. The modern masters promise very little; they know metals cannot be transmuted and that the elixir of life is a chimera. But, these philosophers, whose hands seem only made to dabble in dirt, and their eyes to pore over the microscope or crucible, have indeed performed miracles. They penetrate into the recesses of nature and show she works in her hiding places. They ascend into the heavens; they have discovered how the blood circulates and the nature of the air we breathe. They have acquired new almost unlimited powers; they can command the thunders of the heaven, mimic the earthquake, and even mock the invisible world with its own shadows.

Through the new-found wonders of chemistry, Professor Frankenstein creates a monster that pursues him and, finally, he pays the price for hubris with his life. And, over the years, that is a repeatable pattern—cycles of scientific hubris and humility.

Today, as farmers throughout North America embrace the tools of agricultural biotechnology—in Canada, for example, about one-third of the corn, 20 percent of the soybeans, and 60 percent of the Canola grown in 2000 will be genetically engineered—environmental and activist groups dub the products "Frankenfoods," consistent with the narrative about Frankenstein that resonants deep within humans. Yet despite the rhetoric of "untested" and "Frankenfood bad"—rhetoric designed to alert rather than inform—one can readily substantiate the more accurate claim that genetically engineered foods, in many instances, are better for the environment, contain lower levels of natural toxins and are, indeed, rigorously tested. The first two claims—that genetically engineered foods are better for the environment and contain lower levels of natural toxins—will be discussed later. Of testing though, it can be said shortly that genetically engineered foods are much more rigorously tested than are the so-called conventional foods. (United States National Academy of Sciences 2000).

What is a genetically modified food?

Genes are functional units of deoxyribonucleic acid (DNA) that can encode for proteins or serve a regulatory function affecting the expression of particular genes at a particular time. Genes are arranged along structures known as chromosomes. The characteristics of all living organisms, including humans, are determined by information contained within the DNA inherited from their parents, in concert with environmental interactions. DNA directs how cells develop and controls the way characteristics, such as eye color, are passed on from one generation to the next.

The molecular structure of DNA can be imagined as a zipper. Each tooth of the zipper is represented by one of four letters (A, C, G, or T). These four letters represent the four small molecules, adenine, cytosine, guanine, and thymine, that form the teeth of the DNA zipper. Opposite teeth form either an AT or GC pair. DNA dissolved in water can be "unzipped" by heating and "zipped" by cooling. However, DNA will not zip correctly unless AT or GC pairs are formed (Betsch and Webber 1994).

Since the beginning of the twentieth century, scientists have been cataloging and trying to understand how the 100,000 or so genes in human cells interact with the biochemical environment to create individual human beings, each with their own specific traits such as hair and eye colour, fingerprint patterns, and so on. Similarly agricultural scientists have been working to understand the genetic basis of various traits in plants and animals. Biotechnological methods of genetic engineering are relatively new techniques that plant breeders use to make direct modifications of DNA, a living thing's genetic materials. Scientists make copies of genes for desired traits and introduce the gene copy into an organism such as a food crop. The new gene is usually a single gene whose function is well understood, such as a gene that carries tolerance for herbicides or resistance to insects. These new techniques avoid one of the major problems encountered by plant breeders who use cross hybridization: no unwanted or undesirable genes are introduced along with the desired gene. In addition, scientists can make copies of genes from any organism—plant, animal, or microbe—that may yield a desired trait and introduce that gene into a food crop.

Regulation of biotechnology

The structure and nature of DNA was elucidated in the decades between 1940 and 1960 and geneticists Cohen and Boyer created the first genetically engineered organism in 1975. In 1974, a self-imposed moratorium by the scientific community, led by Paul Berg, on experiments in genetic engineering and the subsequent Asilomar conference in California (February 1975), largely concerning the risks from genetic engineering in terms of laboratory safety and accidental escape, led to wide-spread public debate. The moratorium was lifted the following year, when the United States National Institutes of Health (NIH) issued guidelines for experimentation with genetically engineered organisms (Davis 1991; Krimsky 1991). The European Commission issued similar guidelines (Cantley 1999). The Genetic Manipulation Advisory Group was formed in the United Kingdom while the NIH formed the Recombinant DNA Advisory Committee in the United States. Each group developed regulations for federally funded research. After years of safety research, in 1986 the Organisation for Economic Cooperation and Development (OECD) determined that "there is no scientific basis for specific legislation to regulate the use of recombinant organisms" (OECD 1993). The World Health Organization and OECD, in conjunction with thousands of governmental and academic experts working over the past 20 years, have developed regulations and guidelines for plant biotechnology (Groote, Feldbaum, and Arke 1999).

Mutagenesis

Genetic variability is required to enhance traits deemed desirable by humans. Geneticists can travel the world searching for plants, animals, or microorganisms that posses a trait of interest such as increased productivity or disease resistance. Desirable variability can be selected over generations of breeding. Genetic engineering, using the tools of molecular biology, allows further sources of genetic variability to be introduced into a particular organism.

There are, however, other techniques to create genetic variability between the black-and-white of traditional breeding and genetic engineering. Since the 1940s, mutagenesis breeding has been used to induce genetic variability, especially in the cereals, by exposing seeds to doses of mutagens—compounds that induce mutations in DNA—such as ionizing radiation or mustard gas. The practice is still used today as are other techniques. Should such products also be regulated? Or, is it the process of genetic engineering itself that is inherently risky. Proponents and critics have sparred on this point since the advent of genetic engineering but the scientific community and North American regulators have consistently maintained that it is the end-product, not the process, that should be regulated. Varieties of potatoes and celery, for example, have been produced through traditional breeding that were later discovered to contain unacceptably high levels of natural compounds. The view that the end-product should undergo a safety assessment regardless of how it was produced has been enshrined in the Canadian Novel Food Act (1999) and was more recently reaffirmed by an expert panel of the United States National Academy of Sciences (2000).

Opinion and products

When asked if food products of biotechnology are available in supermarkets, Americans answer "yes," "no," and "I don't know" (figure 2), again evidence of the confusion wrought by technological change. But, when asked what products were available, Americans (IFIC 1999) listed vegetables, tomatoes, and produce as the top three items (figure 3). Yet, it is the bulk commodities—corn, soy, and Canola—that make up the bulk acreage of genetically engineered crops in both Canada and the United States. Genetically engineered whole tomatoes are unavailable in both countries. Yet, people think they are, for two reasons. First is the association with the FlavrSavr tomato, briefly released for commercial sale in 1994 after prolonged public and media discussion. Second, and more important, is that consumers are repeatedly asked: "Do you want fish genes in your tomatoes?" This evocative example is repeat-

Figure 2   Responses to the survey question: "As far as you know, are there any foods produced through biotechnology in the supermarket now?" (n = 1,000)

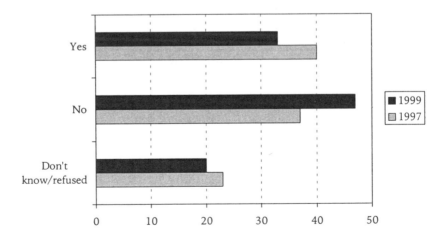

Source   IFIC 1999.

edly used by Greenpeace and others in campaign literature and media accounts. Yet the actual experiment to transfer an anti-freeze protein from cold-water flounder to enhance the tolerance to cold of field to-matoes was only attempted once in 1991 and was unsuccessful (see www.plant.uoguelph.ca/safefood/gmo/gmo-index.htm).

Another evocative example is the purported risk to Monarch but-terflies posed by genetically engineered Bt-corn. And, despite the con-tinual accumulation of evidence that Monarch butterflies are indeed safe from such crops, media and activist groups continually cite grow-ing evidence of risk. This is simply not true.

One of the first products of biotechnology to make a significant commercial impact in Canada has been insect-resistant corn, contain-ing the d-endotoxin produced by *Bacillus thuringiensis* and generally re-ferred to as "Bt-corn." *Bacillus thuringiensis* (Bt) is a gram-positive soil bacterium that produces an insecticidal protein in the form of a crystal. The insecticidal proteins are commonly designated as *cry* proteins and the genes encoding the proteins are known as *cry* genes (Lambert and Peferoen 1992). The Bt toxin is regarded as an environmentally friendly insecticide because of its target specificity and its decomposition to non-toxic compounds when exposed to environmental factors (Gould 1995). *Bacillus thuringiensis Berliner* is the most commonly used biopes-ticide (Wearing and Hokkanen 1995). Bt has been widely used in both

Figure 3 Responses to the survey question: "Which foods produced through biotechnology are currently in the supermarket?" (*n* = 331; multiple answers accepted)

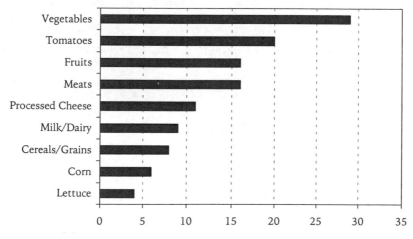

Source   IFIC 1999.

conventional and organic farming operations as an insecticidal spray with some drawbacks. In order for the Bt endotoxin to be effective, the insect must ingest it before it is broken down by environmental factors such as ultraviolet light or drought conditions (Webber 1995). One advantage of genetically engineered Bt-corn is that the insecticidal protein has been incorporated into the plant, limiting environmental exposure. Insecticidal properties of Bt can vary in activity against insects within a single insect order. The toxins encoded by the *cryI* genes are toxic to *Lepidopterans* such as the European corn borer (ECB), *Ostrinia nubilalis*. Various specific Bt-toxins have also been genetically engineered into potatoes and cotton, both of which have been approved for consumption in Canada.

Ostrinia nubilalis, the European corn borer, is a common pest in corn fields across Ontario, as well as other areas of concentrated corn production such as the American states of Minnesota and Iowa. There are risks associated with genetically engineered corn, predominantly the acceleration of the development of resistance in the target pest. Recognizing this, scientists in universities and industry have worked for years to develop management strategies to delay the development of resistance in the European corn borer.

The most frequently recommended management strategy is the use of *refugia*: when Bt crops are planted, a small section of the field is sown with non-transgenic crops to provide a "refuge" for susceptible insects to breed. Since these insects would not be in contact with the toxin, the selection pressure for rare resistant individuals would be removed. The constant supply of susceptible insects would then interbreed with the resistant insects flying amongst the transgenic crops, thereby diluting the number of resistant individuals in the population. The *refugia* strategy is combined with a "high-dose" strategy, yielding a "high-dose-plus-*refugia*" management scheme. The dose refers to the level of expression of Bt in the plants: a high dose refers to toxin expression at 25 times the dose required to kill 99 percent of insects under normal conditions (LD99) and will kill most insects while a mid-range or low dose will only kill some insects, thereby selecting for those that are resistant. A paper in March 2000 (Shelton, Tang, Roush, Metz, and Earle 2000) provided the first field evidence to validate predictions made by computer and by field-test that *refugia* appear to work at managing the development of resistance in the target pest.

Other management strategies have also been proposed. Among these schemes are rotation of plantings between transgenic and non-transgenic crops (in the years when non-transgenic crops are planted, use of other insecticides would be required); mixing seeds so that each field contains a variety of crops, each carrying different toxin genes;

engineering two or more toxin genes into a single plant (the two latter strategies assume other toxin genes have been identified and are effective); modifying the transgene such that the toxin is only produced in certain plant parts or at certain times during plant development.

The study by Losey et al. (1999) on possible impacts on Monarch butterflies attracted widespread media coverage as well as rebuttals and criticisms in the scientific press (Beringer 1999; Fumento 1999; Hodgson 1999). According to Shelton and Roush (1999), a previous and more relevant and realistic field study (Hansen and Obrycki 1999) had been largely overlooked. Further, the results of Losey et al. (1999) were far from unexpected, contrary to media assertions. When Bt-corn was approved in the United States and Canada, regulators and scientists reasoned that the impact of Bt-corn—or, more correctly, the pollen from Bt-corn containing active toxin—on Monarch populations would be minimal, given that milkweed, the desired food of Monarch larvae, is rarely found in corn fields but in adjacent fields, that the toxin is rapidly inactivated by ultraviolet light and drought conditions, and that non-discriminate spraying for other corn pests may present a significantly higher risk to the Monarch population through chemical drift.

In response to the report from Cornell, a consortium of biotechnology and pesticide companies—the Agricultural Biotechnology Stewardship Working Group (ABSWG)—funded 17 studies to quantify the risk of Bt-corn to Monarchs (Weiss 1999; Currie 1999). The research was conducted during the summer of 1999 at universities in corn-producing regions of North America (BIO 1999). Data presented at a meeting in November 1999 indicated that not all strains of Bt-corn are equally toxic (Brower and Zalucki 1999); some varieties of Bt-corn may, in a theoretical or laboratory setting, harm the butterfly while other types may not (Currie 1999). Furthermore, it was suggested that the amount of pollen migrating to milkweeds was "likely to be dangerous to only those monarchs feeding on milkweeds within or close to the edges of the cornfields" (Brower and Zalucki 1999). Although researchers have much to learn about the ecological consequences of Bt-corn on Monarch butterflies, the findings of the meeting were, according to media accounts and discussions with some participants, generally positive.

Stuart Weiss, a Stanford University expert in ecological modeling, was quoted as saying: "the worst-case scenario of this toxic cloud of pollen saturating the corn belt is clearly not the case." Mark Sears, chair of the department of environmental biology at the University of Guelph and chair of the Ontario Corn Borer Coalition, reported that virtually all pollen grains land within 10 yards from the field, 90 per cent of which travel less than five yards (Weiss 1999). Sears postulated that

the risk of the hazard to Monarch larvae is minimal, especially after dis-
covering that at least 500 grains of pollen per square centimeter of
milkweed leaf was necessary to sicken caterpillars. After three days of
accumulation during pollination season, Sears found this concentra-
tion was barely attained on nearby milkweed leaves.

Iowa State University's John Pleasants found that wind direction,
rainfall and other factors significantly affect pollen concentrations on
milkweed. Pleasants found that "88 per cent of milkweed within one
meter of a corn field would fall below the level where they could hurt
the caterpillars and 100 per cent of the milkweed just two meters from
a Bt field would be monarch-safe" (Kendall, 1999). Such findings on
pollen dispersion are especially significant when coupled with planting
preferences. Powell et al. (1999) found that planting the borders of a
corn field to non-Bt-corn was the second most prevalent implementation of Bt-*refugia* guidelines among 400 Ontario corn producers who
planted Bt-corn in 1999 and the most common practice among those
with more than 100 acres of corn (figure 4).

Further, a more recent study from scientists at the University of
Illinois suggests that non-target effects of genetically engineered Bt-
corn may be less severe than previously reported. Among the other insects at potential risk of exposure to pollen from Bt-corn is the black
swallowtail butterfly, *Papilio polyxenes*, whose host plants in the mid-

---

**Figure 4   Ontario farmers' choice of seven planting patterns for
seeding Bt and non-Bt-corn (*n* = 400)**

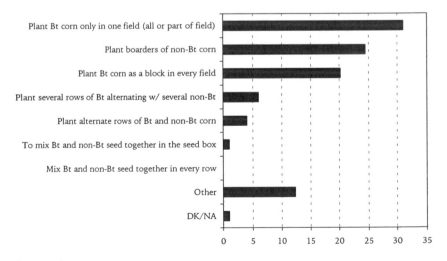

Source   Bt-corn survey.

western United States are located mostly in narrow strips near crop fields. Results of a field study investigating the affect of Bt-corn pollen on the mortality of the black swallowtails was published in the June 6, 2000 issue of the *Proceedings of the National Academy of Science* (PNAS). The researchers concluded that Bt-corn pollen from the variety tested is unlikely to harm wild populations of black swallowtail butterflies.

Such findings rarely make it into mainstream media, despite aggressive efforts by some farm groups and others; further, these findings are rarely, if ever, acknowledged by critics of agricultural biotechnology. Instead, groups like Greenpeace insist that "farmers are being duped." The basis of this assertion is apparently anecdotal evidence. Powell, Grant, and Lastovic (1999) found that when 400 Ontario growers of Bt-corn were asked in 1999 why they invested in the more expensive seed, the number-one reason was higher yield, followed by a desire to evaluate personally the technology (the latter had been the number-one reason in 1998). In short, farmers, knowing that all new technology is oversold, wanted to evaluate what worked on their farms and in the conditions on their land, hardly the attributes of someone being "duped" (figure 5).

Entomologists estimate that losses resulting from damage by the European corn borer (ECB)and the costs of controlling the pest exceed $1 billion each year (Ostlie, Hutchison, and Hellmich 1997; Dekalb 1998; Andow and Hutchison 1998; Haag 1999). ECB typically go through two life-cycles during the corn-growing season, and the second generation usually causes the most damage. In 18 tests over the last six years, researchers from Iowa State University found losses due to ECB of

---

Figure 5 Ontario farmers' reasons for planting Bt-corn hybrids, 1999 ($n = 400$)

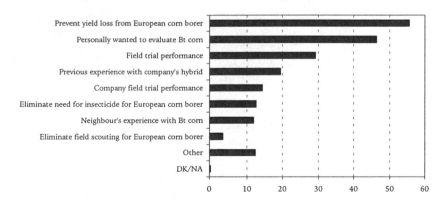

Source   Bt-corn survey.

4 bushels or more per acre from 94 percent of the fields they examined (Dekalb 1998). Very conservative estimates place the value of Bt-corn at $7 million to $10 million annually in improved corn yields in Ontario in 1998, when about 20 percent of the crop was planted to Bt varieties.

A report released on June 25, 1999 by the United States Department of Agriculture's Economic Research Service (ERS) indicated increased yields of up to 30 percent for Bt-maize versus its non-engineered counterpart (USDA 1999). Increased yields were shown in most applications of Bt-cotton. In July 1999, the National Center for Food and Agricultural Policy in Washington, DC (BIO 1999) released the first study aimed at assessing whether Bt-corn, Bt-cotton, and Bt-potatoes actually yielded benefits. For Bt-corn, the study found that in 1997, when ECB infestation was high, total yields were increased in the United States by 47 million bushels, boosting profits by US$72 million. That year, however, only 4 million acres of Bt-corn were planted. In 1998, when 14 million acres of Bt-corn were planted, though infestation by the corn borer was extremely light, farmers still saw an increase of 60 million bushels.

However, this did not translate into higher profits. While acreage of Bt-corn was three times higher in 1998 over the previous year, growers lost an estimated $26 million because pest-infestation levels had declined and the price of corn dropped well below average. Crops of Bt-cotton accounted for 17 percent of the total cotton crop in the United States in 1998 and it boosted total yields by 85 million pounds (see www.bio.org/food&ag/bioins01.html).

Benefits to human health

Feeding on maize kernels by ECB often leads to infection by fungi in the genus *Fusarium*, including the fumonisin-producing species (Munkvold et al. 1999). Fumonisins are a class of mycotoxins and esophageal cancer in humans has been associated with consumption of maize with high concentrations of the fumonisins (Munkvold et al. 1999). Recent research by the United States Department of Agriculture (2000) shows a reduction in mycotoxins of 30 to 40 times in Bt-field-corn compared to non-Bt-corn.

Such a discussion of risk and benefit can be developed for all technical questions about genetically engineered foods. Space constraints limit the examples but further elaborations can be found at www.plant. uoguelph.ca/safefood.

As technologies mature, the public discussion also matures from one of all benefit and all risk to one of managed risk. The current state of risk management and communication research suggests that those responsible with food-safety risk management must be seen to be reducing, mitigating, or minimizing a particular risk. Those responsible must be able to communicate their efforts effectively and they must be able to prove they are actually reducing levels of risk. As Slovic has noted:

> We live in a world in which information, acting in concert with the vagaries of human perception and cognition, has reduced our vulnerability to pandemics of disease at the cost of increasing our vulnerability to social and economic catastrophes of unprecedented scale. The challenge before us is to learn how to manage stigma and reduce the vulnerability of important products, industries, and institutions to its effects, without suppressing the proper communication of risk information to the public. (Slovic 1997)

Stigma is a powerful shortcut consumers may use to evaluate food-borne risks. Gregory, Slovic, and Flynn (1995) have characterized stigma as:

- the source is a hazard;
- a standard of what is right and natural is violated or overturned;
- impacts are perceived to be inequitably distributed across groups;
- possible outcomes are unbounded (scientific uncertainty); and,
- management of the hazard is brought into question.

These factors of stigmatization certainly apply to the products of agricultural biotechnology. Stigmatization is becoming the norm for food and water linked to human illness or even death. The challenge, then, is to reduce stigma. The components for managing the stigma associated with any food safety issue involve the following factors:

- effective and rapid surveillance systems;
- effective communication about the nature of risk;
- a credible, open and responsive regulatory system;
- demonstrable efforts to reduce levels of uncertainty and risk; and,
- evidence that actions match words.

Appropriate levels of risk management coupled with sound science and excellent communication about the nature of risk are required to garner further benefits of any technology, including agricultural biotechnology.

References

Androw, D.A., and W.D. Hutchinson (1998). Now or Never: Serious New Plans to Save a Natural Pest Control. Chapter 3: Bt-Corn Resistance Management. Union of Concerned Scientists. Anonymous. December 15, 1998. Bt-Corn for Control of European Corn Borer. Insect Pest Management for Field and Forage Crops. Digital document: www.aces.uiuc.edu/ipm/field/iapmh/ipmffcbtecb.html.

Ball, Norman R. (1992). Essential Connections: Past and Future; Technology and Society. In *Proceedings, Beyond the Printed Page: Online Documentation. Second Conference on Quality in Documentation.* Waterloo, ON: The Center for Professional Writing, University of Waterloo: 11–28.

Betsch, D.F., and G.D. Webber (1994). *DNA Fingerprinting in Agricultural Genetics Programs.* North Central Regional Publication (November1). Columbia, MU: Office of Biotechnology, University of Missouri. Digital document: muextension.missouri.edu/xplor/regpubs/ncr554.htm.

Beringer, J.E. (1999). Cautionary Tale on Safety of GM Crops. *Nature* 399: 405.

Biotechnology Industry Organization (BIO) (1999). Scientific Symposium to Show No Harm to Monarch Butterfly. Press release (November 2). Washington, DC: Biotechnology Industry Organization.

Brower, L.P., and M.P. Zalucki (1999). Bt-corn and Its Effect on Monarch Butterflies: A Note of Caution. November 11. E-mail listserve.

Bud, R. (1993). *The Uses of Life: A History of Biotechnology.* Cambridge: Cambridge University Press.

Cantley, M. (1999). Letters. *International Herald Tribune* (August 20).

Cornell University (1999). *Engineered Corn Can Kill Monarch Butterflies.* Press release (May 19).

Currie, B.M. (1999). Altered Corn-Butterflies. *Associated Press* (November 3).

Davis B. (1991). *The Genetic Revolution: Scientific Prospects and Public Perceptions.* Baltimore, MD: Johns Hopkins University Press.

Dekalb (1998). Corn Borers and Bt-corn. December 15. Digital document: www.dekalb.com/dktraits/Btcorn.htm.

Fumento, M. (1999). *The Wall Street Journal* (June 25): 4.

Gould, F. (1995). The Empirical and Theoretical Basis for Bt Resistance Management. *Information Systems for Biotechnology/NBIAP [National Biological Impact Assessment Program] News Report: Special Issue on Bt.* (December). Digital document: www.nbiap.vt.edu.

Greenpeace and Council of Canadians (1999). Press release (September 29). Canada Newswire.

Gregory, R., P. Slovic, and J. Flynn (1995). Risk perceptions, Stigma, and Health Policy. *Health and Place* 2, 4: 213–20.

Groote, J., C.B. Feldbaum, and A. Arke (1999). Letters. *International Herald Tribune* (August 18).

Haag, E. (1999). Is Bt-Corn Right for Silage? *Farm Journal—Daily Today* (March).

Hansen, L., and J. Obrycki 1999. *Non-Target Effects of Bt Corn on the Monarch Butterfly (Lepidoptera: Danaidae).* Digital document: www.ent.iastate.edu/entsoc/ncb99/prog/abs/D81.html.

Hodgson, J. 1999. Monarch Bt-Corn Paper Questioned. *Nature Biotechnology* 17: 627.

Kelley, J. (1995). *Public Perceptions of Genetic Engineering: Australia 1994.* Canberra: Australian Department of Industry, Science and Technology. Digital document: www.isr.gov.au/pubs/reports/genengin/content.html.

Kendall, P. (1999). Monarch Butterfly So Far Not Imperiled: Gene-altered Corn Gets an Early OK in Studies. *Chicago Tribune* (November 2): 4.

Krimsky, S. (1991). *Biotechnics and Society: The Rise of Industrial Genetics.* New York: Praeger.

Lambert, B., and M. Peferoen (1992). Insecticidal Promise of *Bacillus thuringiensis.* 112–22.

Losey, J.J, L. Raynor, and M.E. Carter (1999). Transgenic Pollen Harms Monarch Butterfly. *Nature* 399: 214.

May, K. (2000). Majority Immune to Biotech Health Scare: Poll—Willing to Take Risks. *National Post* (July 24): A1.

Munkfold, G.P., R.L. Hellmich, and L.G. Rice (1999). Comparison of Fumonisin Concentrations in Kernels of Transgenic Bt Maize Hybrids and Nontransgenic Hybrids. *Plant Disease* 83: 130–38.

Organisation for Economic Cooperation and Development (OECD) (1993). *Safety Evaluation of Foods Derived by Modern Biotechnology: Concepts and Principles.* Paris: OECD.

Ostlie, K.R., W.D. Hutchison, and R.L. Hellmich, Eds. (1997). *Bt Corn and European Corn Borer: Long-Term Success through Resistance Management.* University of Minnesota. Digital document: www.extension.umn.edu/distribution/cropsystems/DC7055.html.

Powell, D., K. Thomas (2000). *A Fish Gene in a Tomato.* Digital document: www.plant.uoguelph.ca/safefood/gmo/dp-thomas-flavrsavr.htm.

Powell, D.A., M.W. Griffiths (1994). Public Perceptions of Agricultural Biotechnology in Canada. Unpublished paper given at the annual meeting of the Institute of Food Technologists, Atlanta (June 25–29).

Powell, D. 1999. *Cauliflower Mosaic Virus Promoter: Potential Risks.* Digital document: www.plant.uoguelph.ca/safefood/gmo/camv35s/camv35s.htm

Powell, D.A., S.E. Grant, and S. Lastovic (1999). *A Survey of Ontario Corn Producers to Assess Compliance with Refugia Recommendations to Manage Development of Resistance to Genetically Engineered Bt-Corn in the European Corn Borer, 1999.* Agrifood Risk Management and Communication Tech. Report 10. Digital document: www.plant.uoguelph.ca/safefood/gmo/bt-survey/bt-survey.html.

Royal Society (1999). GMOs and Pusztai: The Royal Society Reviews the Evidence. Press Release (May 18). Digital document: www.royalsoc.ac.uk/press/pr_15_99.htm.

Shelton, A.M., and R.T. Roush (1999). False Reports and the Ears of Men. *Nature Biotechnology* 17, 9: 832.

Shelton, A.M., J.D. Tang, R.T. Roush, T.D. Metz, and E.D. Earle (2000). Field Tests on Managing Resistance to Bt-Engineered Plants. *Nature Biotechnology* 18: 339–42.

Slovic, P. (1997). Perceived Risk, Stigma, and the Vulnerable Society. Unpublished paper presented at the One-Day Conference on Risk (June 13, 1997), City University, London.

Wearing, C.H., and H.M.T. Hokkanen (1995). Pest Resistance to *Bacillus thuringiensis*: Ecological Crop Assessment for Bt Gene Incorporation and Strategies for Management. In H.M.T. Hokkanen, J.M. Lynch, (eds.), *Biological Control: Benefits and Risks*. Plant and Microbial Biotechnology Research Series. Cambridge: Cambridge University Press: 236–52.

Webber, G.D. 1995. *Insect Resistant Crops through Genetic Engineering*. Biotechnology Information Series (Bio-9). North Central Regional Extension Publication, Iowa State University. Digital document: www.nalusda.gov/bic/Education_res/iastate.info/bio9.html (July 10, 1997).

Weiss, R. 1999. Gene-altered Corn's Impact Reassessed: Studies Funded by Biotech Consortium Find Little Risk to Monarch Butterflies. *The Washington Post* (November 3): A3.

United States National Academy of Sciences (2000). US Regulatory System Needs Adjustment as Volume and Mix of Transgenic Plants Increase in Marketplace. Washington, DC (April 5).

United States Department of Agriculture (Economic Research Service) (1999). *Genetically Engineered Crops for Pest Management*. Digital document: www.econ.ag.gov/wahtsnew/issues/biotech (June 25).

United States Department of Agriculture (2000). *Bt Corn: Less Insect Damage, Lower Mycotoxin Levels, Healthier Corn*. USDA-ARS News Service (April 26).

3   Too Safe?

Progress at Risk
Using the Precautionary Principle as a Standard for Regulatory Policy

H. Sterling Burnett

Environmentalists in Europe and America have a new weapon in their arsenal that is aimed at innovative technologies being developed for the betterment of humankind: the Precautionary Principle (PP). There is, in fact, no single formulation of the precautionary principle in universal use but, in short, it means: "No human technology should be used or introduced into the environment until it is shown to pose no threat of harm to humans or the environment" (Graham 1999). Proponents of the precautionary principle argue that using it to frame policy is common sense like the old adage "better safe than sorry."

In one form or another, the precautionary principle has been incorporated both in domestic legislation in Europe and America and in more than 12 international treaties, beginning in 1987 with the Ministerial Declaration of the Second Conference on the Protection of the North Sea, and in domestic legislation and regulations throughout Europe and North America (VanderZwaag 1999). Each of the 12 treaties defines the precautionary principle differently with variations due to the scope of activities covered and the strictness and specificity of the

Note will be found on page 163.

control measures demanded. Other treaties and declarations that have adopted the precautionary principle include: the 1987 Montreal Protocol on Substances that Deplete the Ozone Layer; the 1992 Convention on Biological Diversity; the 1992 Climate Change Convention; the 1992 Treaty on European Union; the 1992 Convention for the Protection of the Marine Environment of the North-East Atlantic; the 1992 Helsinki Convention dealing with protection of the marine environment of the Baltic; the 1990 Bergen Declaration issued by ministerial representatives from European countries (as well as Canada); and the 1992 Rio Declaration on Environment and Development.

Proponents of the precautionary principle propose using it to frame regulations for numerous sectors of the economy, including the chemical, plastics, medical technology, and agricultural industries. Citing the precautionary principle, environmentalists have begun a sustained assault on the continued creation and widespread use of "artificial" or human-created chemicals in goods ranging from pesticides to industrial lubricants and from refrigerants to plastic softeners. They are also attacking the burgeoning fields of genetic engineering and biotechnology for medical and agricultural use.

While the precautionary principle may sound reasonable in theory, it would be disastrous if practised. One cannot prove a negative. Every food (including organic foods), product, and tool poses some risk of harm. Without the use of fire, automobiles, antibiotics, coffee, water, salt, and chlorine—to name just a few natural and human-created foods, applications, and tools—human life, in the words of the philosopher Thomas Hobbes, "would be nasty, poor, brutish, and short." Yet none of these would pass the standard set by the precautionary principle.

Among the flaws in the reasoning of the proponents of the precautionary principle, three stand out. First, the distinction between artificial and natural is an artifact of language having no basis in science. It harkens back to a pre-Darwinian view of humankind and their actions as separate from the "natural" world.

Second, proponents of the precautionary principle seem to cling to Barry Commoner's third law of ecology: "nature knows best" (Commoner 1971). This is not a metaphysical claim concerning nature as a conscious entity, though a few environmentalists may hold such a view, but rather a normative claim representing the view common among many environmentalists that the works and workings of nature absent human technological interventions are to be preferred or are "right" when compared to the world as shaped or affected by human actions. This view is subjective, having no basis in science, and, in reality, is rejected as a guide for living by all but perhaps the most extreme environmental radicals in their own lives. Few if any proponents of the precautionary principle live in caves or refuse lifesaving medical interventions for themselves or their families. "Back to the Pleistocene," as one tee-shirt fashionable in some environmental circles proclaims, may make a nice slogan but it is not a popular political platform or a common lifestyle choice.

These errors lead to a third. Because human actions are artificial interventions that can interfere with nature's evolutionary processes, supporters of the precautionary principle focus their regulatory efforts on preventing type-II errors (i.e., the error of concluding that there is no effect—in this case a negative effect on human health or the environment—where an effect exists) to the exclusion of preventing type-I errors (i.e., the error of concluding that there is an effect where one does not exist).[1] On this view, preventing hypothetical or minuscule threats of future harm should take precedence in regulatory policy over actions to reduce existing dangers with known catastrophic consequences in the present.

How do these flaws play out in practice? Many environmental organizations, including Greenpeace and the Natural Resources Defense Council, citing the precautionary principle for support, argue that the government should end the use of chlorine in plastics, pesticides, and as a disinfectant in water. They argue that chlorine's use increases, even if only by one chance in a million over a lifetime, a person's risk of contracting cancer or of being born with birth defects. In calling for a ban on chlorine use, these groups ignore or heavily discount several important facts.

- Chlorine is an ubiquitous natural element found in more than 1,500 organic and inorganic compounds including plants, animals, salt, and human blood and saliva.

- Chlorine is used to disinfect 98 percent of the world's potable water and is a key ingredient in 85 percent of the medicines and pharmaceuticals.

- Phasing out the use of chlorine would cost more than $91 million in the United States alone and likely lead to millions of deaths worldwide from water-borne diseases like cholera and typhus.

No credible scientific research has shown an increased risk of cancer, developmental disorders, or other illnesses attributable to background levels of chlorine or chlorinated compounds and the largest study of the potential dangers of chlorine to date found the mere presence of chlorine in a compound does not necessarily make it uniquely toxic (Heartland Institute 2000).

Since chlorine is critical to many medicines and to water disinfection, it is doubtful that the proponents of the precautionary principle will be successful in banning its use, at least in the near future. However, another chemical compound in widespread use is already being withdrawn from the market. On December 31, 1999, the European Commission banned phthalates, a family of six chemical compounds used as softeners in making vinyl flexible. They have been used with no ill effects for more than 40 years in numerous goods including toys, pacifiers, polyvinyl chloride pipes, electronic goods, siding, flooring, packaging, automotive parts, clothing, footwear, and blood bags and tubes.

Greenpeace International seized upon two sets of scientific studies to argue that phthalates could pose a threat of harm and thus ought to be removed from the marketplace as a precaution (Buckley 1999). Phthalates cause tumours in laboratory rats and mice when fed to the animals at extremely high doses for long periods of time. In addition, small amounts of phthalates leach from plastics and vinyl and are thus consumed by teething infants and small children when they place toys in their mouths and absorbed by patients on intravenous drips. In reaction to Greenpeace's publicity campaign and pressure tactics, almost immediately the European Commission banned the sale of certain toys, toy manufacturers stopped using phthalates in toys and pacifiers, and American toy stores pulled toys and pacifiers from their shelves.

Was this reaction justified by the evidence? Not at all. Forced feedings of high doses of phthalates over extended periods to animals with body chemistries more closely related to humans than rats and mice, including hamsters, guinea pigs and monkeys, did not cause tumours to form. Furthermore, despite 40 years of use, phthalates have never been linked to a single human illness, much less a death. Indeed, no recent studies on the issue found a risk of danger from phthalates. Rather:

- The United States Consumer Product Safety Commission reported in a study released in December 1998: "Generally, the amount [of phthalates] ingested does not even come close to a harmful level" (Dawson 2000: 4).

- The American Council on Science and Health, in a study chaired by former Surgeon General C. Everett Koop, found that the phthalate DINP "is not harmful for children in the normal use of these toys" (Dawson 2000: 4).

- A study by a Dutch Consensus Group stated that the possibility of a child's exposure exceeding the acceptable daily intake is "so rare that the statistical likelihood cannot be estimated on the basis of current data" and further found that the risk from phthalates was too small to justify a ban (Dawson 2000: 4).

- A study published in October 1999 by the journal Regulatory Toxicology and Pharmacology states that "the use of DINP in soft vinyl PVC toys and other children's products does not present a significant risk to children." (Dawson 2000:4)

Another factor dismissed by the European Commission when deciding to ban phthalates as a precaution is their usefulness, and their virtues in relation to possible substitutes or replacements. Phthalates are integral to polyvinyl chloride products. These products are durable, moldable, easy to keep clean, resistant to cracks or breaking, recyclable and relatively inexpensive. Medical professionals credit vinyl blood bags for keeping donated blood good for longer periods of time than other containers and this and other medical products have greatly reduced infection rates and the spread of diseases in hospitals. In contrast, alternative softeners to phthalates are more expensive and all contain additives, the toxicology of which has not been studied to the extent that that of phthalates has.

The facts concerning the value of phthalates and the lack of evidence of harm did not deter proponents of the precautionary principle from calling for a ban on their use in Europe and America because, after all, that is just what the precautionary principle is about: ending the use of products until they are proven harmless—technology is guilty until it proves itself innocent.

The proponents of the precautionary principle have focused even more attention on the agricultural industry than they have on the chemical industry. In particular, they have targeted the use of genetic engineering and biotechnology to produce hardier, disease-resistant and pest-resistant crops. They most recently demonstrated this at the United Nation's "Extraordinary Meeting of the Conference of the Parties," held to negotiate the terms of the Biosafety Protocol in Montreal in January 2000. At the behest of the supporters of the precautionary principle the draft language of the protocol stated: "Lack of full scientific certainty or scientific consensus regarding the potential adverse effects of a living modified organism shall not prevent the Party of import from prohibiting the import of the living modified organism in question ..." (United Nations Environmental Program 2000: 32).

At the present time there is very little evidence to show that bioengineered crops pose a threat to human health or the environment. The United States is the world's leader in genetic engineering and the biomodification of crops. Biotechnological modifications have made tomatoes more resistant to cold, and soybeans, cotton, and corn immune to selected herbicides used to control weeds. More than 50 percent of the American soybean crop—parts of which end up in more than 60 percent of processed foods—has been genetically modified since 1995 (Jenkins 1999).

Though all genetically modified foods rate criticism from the supporters of the precautionary principle, corn genetically modified to carry the Bacillus Thuringiensis bacteria (Bt-corn) stands out among biotechnological crops for raising an alarm among scientists not aligned specifically with environmental organizations. Bt-corn was developed as a way of controlling the European corn borer, an insect that causes millions of dollars of losses to corn growers each year. Bt-corn effectively prevents corn borer infestation, reducing the need for costly pesticide applications. These characteristics gave it growing popularity among corn growers. However, in 1999, laboratory studies showed that should Bt-corn pollen drift out of the fields in sufficient amounts and fall onto milkweed plants on which Monarch Butterflies lay their eggs and upon which newly hatched Monarch caterpillars feed, the caterpillars die at a rate far above average (Milius 1999: 391).

This was enough evidence for environmentalists to call for an end to the use of Bt-corn. Several organizations threatened to call for a consumer boycott of companies that used Bt-corn in their processed foods. The reaction from the food industry was quick and affected more genetically modified foods than Bt-corn. In a preemptive move to avoid negative publicity from a boycott and a publicity campaign threatened by the Sierra Club and the United States Public Interest Research Group, baby food manufacturers Gerber and Heinz announced that they would stop using genetically modified crops in their products. Frito-Lay told its farmers that it does not want Bt-corn for use in its chips. Seagram said that its wines and spirits would be free of biotechnological crops (Ritter 2000). And, food processing and shipping giant Archer-Daniels Midland (ADM) instructed its farmers to segregate biotechnological crops from conventional crops.

However, the lead scientist involved in the research that found the link between Bt-corn and mortality among Monarch caterpillars indicated that it was far too soon to say whether Bt-corn posed a real threat to butterflies or other beneficial insects, much less humans. He stated, "Our study was conducted in a laboratory and, while it raises an important issue, it would be inappropriate to draw any conclusions about the risk to Monarch populations in the field based solely on these initial results" (Milloy 1999: 21). His caution had merit. Further research confirmed his laboratory findings but found little evidence that Monarchs faced a threat outside of the lab. Monarchs avoid laying eggs on milkweed plants surrounded by corn and, on milkweed plants in areas adjoining corn fields, they prefer to lay eggs on the upper leaves of plants rather than the lower leaves where corn pollen builds up. In addition, corn pollen found on milkweeds along the immediate edge of corn fields (50 grains/cm^2) was found at levels less than those used to produce caterpillar deaths in the laboratory (135 grains/cm^2) and this level fell to between 1 grain/cm^2 and 15 grains/cm^2 10 meters from the cornfield edge (Milius 1999). While more research is merited, when all the evidence is weighed it seems unlikely that Bt-corn affects Monarch caterpillar mortality outside in the field and there is no evidence that it poses any harm to humans. In light of these and other findings, ADM subsequently dropped its requirement that farmers segregate GM grain from non-GM grain (Fumento 2000: A24).

Because the absence of substantial evidence of harm has not stemmed the call for preemptive regulation of biotechnology and genetic engineering, more than 600 scientists signed a letter presented in Montreal to the Biosafety Protocol negotiators in which they argued that the precautionary approach "which demands that new technologies be proved absolutely safe before they can be used" necessarily ignores the very real dangers of doing without the new technologies (Consumer Alert 2000). A more progressive approach would balance the risk of introducing new biotechnologies against the much more pressing risks of hunger and poverty.

The scientists argued that genetically modified crops are the best hope for feeding the world's growing population. They went on to point out that there is no scientific reason to believe that the use of recombinant DNA techniques or other advanced biotechnologies inherently poses new or more dangerous threats to biodiversity, to other aspects of environmental quality, or to human health, than do traditional methods of plant breeding or cell culture. Their views were reinforced on April 5, 2000, when the National Research Council (NRC) issued its comprehensive report on genetically modified foods. The NRC researchers found that "there is no evidence suggesting [genetically modified food] is unsafe to eat." They went on to report that there is "no strict distinction between the health and environmental risks posed by plants genetically engineered through modern molecular techniques and those modified by conventional breeding practices" Associated Press 2000: 5A). As Holman Jenkins wrote recently, "biotechnology might go awry in 105 unexpected ways, but the result would be a nuisance rather than a catastrophe" (Jenkins 1999: A23). At least for the present, the concerns raised by the 600 scientists who protested the inclusion of the precautionary principle in the draft Biosafety Protocol convinced negotiators to strip that particular provision from the final version of the interim Protocol.

Why is all of this important? Approximately 800 million people do not currently get nutritionally adequate diets. Four hundred million people currently suffer from Vitamin A deficiency, including millions of children who go blind each year. The human population is growing, especially in countries where people are already malnourished, and will probably plateau sometime in this century at between eight and nine billion people.

With approximately six million square miles under cultivation— an amount of land equal in size to the United States and Europe—the world currently produces more than enough food to feed the earth's six billion people. Malnutrition and the most famous instances of mass famine and starvation occur due to distribution systems that break down primarily during wars (civil and otherwise) or when starvation is used as a political tool under totalitarian regimes.

Most countries are becoming more open and democratic. And, in democratic countries, no longer fearing the iron boot of oppression, people demand higher standards of living. They look to the West and in many regards they want to live as well off as people in the developed world—this is natural. However, feeding nine billion people (and their pets) diets similar to those enjoyed by people in industrialized countries will require the production of approximately three times more food by 2050.

If all of the world's farmers adopted the best modern farming practices with high inputs of fertilizers and pesticides, it might be possible to double current crop yields on the same amount of land—but we need to triple yields to feed the coming generations.

Alternatively, if we went totally "organic," eschewing the use of "artificial" fertilizers, pesticides, and biotechnologies, we would have to double the amount of land under active cultivation. This would be disastrous for wildlife and native plants, as the lands most likely to be converted to agriculture are forests, rangelands, and other wildlands. Massive losses of biodiversity from land conversion for organic food production is especially likely since the relatively undeveloped tropics, the most biodiverse region on earth, is also where population growth is occurring and where hunger and malnutrition are most prominent.

There is a third option: the judicious use of biotechnology; being quick to regulate or end the use of products that are shown to cause harm.

Agricultural biotechnology is already improving lives. For instance, Dennis Avery of the Center for Global Food Issues at the Hudson Institute points to the success of the Rockefeller Foundation's "golden rice" project (Avery 1999). This genetically altered rice was modified to contain beta-carotene (which readily converts to Vitamin A) and new genes to overcome iron deficiency. The Rockefeller Foundation reports that golden rice is preventing thousands of cases of childhood blindness and reducing the amount of anemia suffered by more than 2 billion women in rice-dependent countries.

Technologies being tested include a biotechnological rodent contraceptive. Rodents consume substantial portions of the world's cereals and grains so reducing rodents' reproduction rates would increase the amount of food available for human consumption without increasing crop yields or land under cultivation.

Avery estimates that using bioengineered agricultural products already in existence, those currently being developed or tested, and those that are likely to be discovered, we could increase food production the three-fold needed for nine billion people to eat well—and all without increasing the amount of acreage in production. In addition, in its report on genetically modified foods the NRC concluded that any negative impact on non-target species, such as beneficial insects, is likely to be smaller than that from chemical pesticides. Indeed, the NRC found that using bio-engineered pest-protected crops in place of conventional crops with chemical pesticides could lead to greater biodiversity in some geographical areas.

Using biotechnology we can provide the world's future population with enjoyable, nutritionally adequate diets. Otherwise we cannot, at least not without arguably unacceptable environmental consequences. In the United States, biotechnological foods undergo careful review by three federal agencies before they are approved for use: the Food and Drug Administration, the Department of Agriculture and the Environmental Protection Agency. Turning our back on lifesaving, welfare-enhancing, thoroughly tested bioengineered products when there is ample evidence of the ills they can prevent and little or no evidence that they threaten any harm would irresponsibly condemn millions of people to unnecessary suffering and early deaths—that would be playing God with a vengeance.

Does this mean the precautionary principle has no utility whatsoever? Not at all. In the words of the Social Issues Research Center (1999), in Oxford, England, "If we apply the precautionary principle to itself—ask what are the possible dangers of using this principle—we would be forced to abandon it very quickly."

Note

1 Tickner 1997. For critical comments concerning the regulatory bias of the proponents of the precautionary principle in relation to type-I and type-II errors, see Cross 1996.

References

Associated Press (2000). Study Says Bio-engineered Foods Safe, but More Tests, Monitoring Urged. *The Dallas Morning News* (April 6): 5A.

Avery, Dennis (1999). Biotechnology: Trade Crisis or Path to Future. *Global Food Quarterly* (Summer): 1, 3.

Buckley, Neil (1999). Toymakers' Softener Falls Foul of Brussels' Hardline on Safety: EU "Precautionary Principle" Has Prompted a Ban on Some Phthalates Used in PVC Toys and Dummies. *Financial Times* (December 16). Digital document available at www.globalarchive.ft.com.

Commoner, Barry (1971). *The Closing Circle*. New York: Knopf.

Consumer Alert (2000). Free-Market NGOs Distribute Letter; Scientists' Declaration to Delegates. *News from Montreal: Bits and Bites on Biosafety Special Bulletins from International Consumers for Civil Society and Its NGOs in Montreal (Gregory Conko, Competitive Enterprise Institute, Barbara Rippel, Consumer Alert, Frances B. Smith, ICCS and Consumer Alert)* (January 24). Digital document: www.consumeralert.org/monday.html.

Cross, Frank B. (1996). Paradoxical Perils of the Precautionary Principle. *Washington & Lee Law Review* 53, 3: 851. Abstract available as digital document at http://www.wlu.edu/~lawrev/abs/bradshaw.htm.

Dawson, Carol (2000). EC Bans Toys with Phthalates: White House Told US Government Not to Intervene in "Precautionary" Policy in the EU. *Issue Brief* (January 17) Washington, DC: Consumer Alert: 1–7.

Fumento, Michael (2000). Biotech Food Fights May Be Over Soon as Facts Frustrate Fearmongers' Case. *Investor's Business Daily* (March 14): A24.

Graham, John D. (1999). Making Sense of the Precautionary Principle. *Risk in Perspective* 7, 6 (September): 1–6.

Heartland Institute (2000). *Facts about Chlorine and Dioxins*. Instant Expert Guide.

Jenkins, Holman W., Jr. (1999). Fun Facts to Know and Tell about Biotechnology. *The Wall Street Journal* (November 17): A23.

Milius, Susan (1999). New Studies Clarify Monarch Worries. *Science News* 156, (December 18 & 25): 391.

Milloy, Steven J. (1999). The Greens' Ear-ie Ad. *The Washington Times* (December 10: 21.

Ritter, Jim (2000). Genetic Food Fallout. *Associated Press Wire* (February 28.

Social Issues Research Centre (1999). Beware the Precautionary Principle. Digital document: www.sirc.org/articles/beware.html.

Tickner, Joel (1997). Precautionary Principle. *The Networker: The Newsletter of the Science and Environmental Health Net* (May). Digital document: www.safe2use.com/data/precaut1.htm.

United Nations Environmental Program, Conference on Biodiversity (2000). ExCOP/1/L.2/Rev.1 (January): 32.

VanderZwaag, David (1999). The Canadian Environmental Protection Act and the Precautionary Approach. Digital document: www.ec.gc.ca/cepa/ip18/e18_01.html.

Dying Too Soon
How Cost-Effectiveness
Analysis Can Save Lives

Tammy O. Tengs

For every one of us, death is inevitable. Premature death, however, is not. Through some reasonable mix of public and private strategies, we can substantially reduce the chance that we will die before our time. We can exercise and eat right, avoid tobacco, wear our seat belts and make sure our smoke alarms have working batteries. When more collective action is warranted, the federal government can regulate industry so as to protect us from such hazards as exposure to certain carcinogens in the air we breathe and the water we drink. As a society, we can adopt policies to immunize our children, pass laws setting speed limits and requiring motorcycle helmets and adopt uniform building codes so that structures will not collapse on us in the event of natural disasters.

All risk-reduction policies have two things in common: they have economic consequences and they save lives. Thus, it makes sense to compare life-saving interventions according to their "value for the money."

Notes will be found on page 186. This chapter was originally published by the National Center for Policy Analysis (Dallas TX) as NCPA Policy Report No. 204 (May 1997).

Determining the value of a health promotion intervention requires estimating the costs as well as the benefits of that intervention. Costs are usually defined as the dollar value of the resources consumed. For example, when a physician takes the time to counsel a patient to stop smoking, the physician's time represents a resource that is consumed and a dollar value can be attached to that resource. From a societal perspective, all costs should be considered, regardless of who bears those costs.[1]

The survival benefits of a health promotion intervention can be captured in any number of ways but the most common measures are "lives saved" and "years of life saved." The latter measure has the advantage of taking into account the prevention of a premature death. For example, avoiding the premature death of a 40-year-old who then lives to be 78 would imply that 38 years of life are saved.

However, the benefits of a health promotion intervention are generally not limited to an extension of years of life. Seat belts, for example, reduce the risk of dying in serious automobile accidents but they also prevent nonfatal injuries. Environmental regulations reduce human exposure to certain carcinogens but they also protect the ecosystem. Medical therapy can improve patients' survival prospects and also affect their quality of life.

Thus, decisions about public health investment inevitably require making trade-offs between cost, increased life expectancy and other benefits. The technique of cost-benefit analysis (as opposed to cost-effectiveness analysis) handles these trade-offs not only by measuring the cost of the resources consumed but also by placing a dollar value on the years of life saved and on other benefits as well. The implication is that if the monetary benefits exceed the costs, the program should be implemented. While cost-benefit analysis is theoretically sound, offering a way to trade off all of the effects of an intervention using a single metric, techniques for monetizing health and other benefits are in their infancy. Thus, in this report we refer not to cost-benefit analysis, but to cost-effectiveness analysis. This technique defines costs in a similar manner but "effectiveness" is defined simply as "life-years saved." Of course, this has the disadvantage of ignoring any other benefits of health promotion interventions. The advantage is that it temporarily sidesteps the need to place a dollar value on a year of life.[2]

Cost-effectiveness of common interventions

Not all health and safety measures are equally cost-effective (see figure 1):

- By spending $182,000 every year for sickle cell screening and treatment for black newborns, we add 769 years collectively to their lives at a cost of only $236 for each year of life saved.

Figure 1 Cost of Gaining an Additional Year of Life

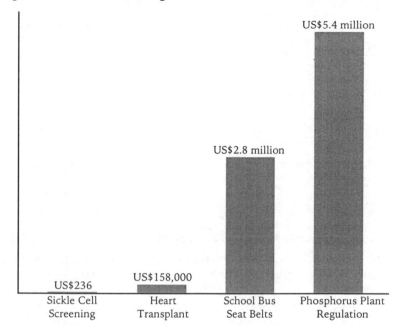

- By spending about $253 million per year on heart transplants, we add about 1,600 years to the lives of heart patients at a cost of $158,000 per year of life saved.

- Equipping just 3 percent of school buses with seat belts costs about $1.6 million per year; but since this effort saves only one child's life every year, the cost is about $2.8 million per year of life saved.

- We spend $2.8 million every year on radionuclide emission control at elemental phosphorus plants (which refine mined phosphorus before it goes to other uses); but since this effort saves at most one life every decade, the cost is $5.4 million per year of life saved.

Cost-effectiveness of government regulation

Specific policies resulting from proposed government regulations vary widely in their cost-effectiveness, depending on the agency involved. For example, as table 1 shows, the median proposed EPA regulation costs 100 times more per year of life saved than the median proposed highway safety or consumer product safety standard (Tengs et al. 1995).

Table 1   Cost Effectiveness of Proposed Regulations

Regulator	Median Cost per Life-Year Saved
Consumer Product Safety Commission (CPSC)	$68,000
National Highway Traffic Safety Administration (NHTSA)	$78,000
Occupational Safety and Health Administration (OSHA)	$88,000
Environmental Protection Agency (EPA)	$7,600,000
Source: Tengs et al. 1995	

How cost-effectiveness analysis can save lives

Because of the radical differences in cost-effectiveness that now exist, redirecting even relatively small amounts from less cost-effective to more cost-effective areas could have a noticeable impact. For example, suppose we took away $45,000 per year from the money we spend regulating emissions at phosphorus plants and used it instead to screen the 20 percent of black newborns who are not now screened for sickle cell anemia. The effect on life expectancy of phosphorus plant workers would be negligible. However, black children would gain an additional 192 years of collective life expectancy every year.

Cost-effectiveness as a guide for public policy

This chapter explores how the use of cost-effectiveness information to guide health policy decisions can improve our survival prospects. The chapter begins by clearing up a number of misconceptions about cost-effectiveness analysis. Next, it compares the use of cost-effectiveness as a guide to other strategies for making survival investment decisions. Finally, it considers how our present failure to make policy decisions based on economic efficiency results in the loss of life.

Misconceptions about cost-effectiveness analysis

Confusion often surrounds discussions of cost-effectiveness analysis. Some people wrongly believe that a health promotion intervention that is "cost-effective" actually saves money or is, at least, quite inexpensive. Others use the phrase "cost-effective" when they want to convey that an intervention is very effective or benefits a large number of people. Each of these mistaken uses can result in bad health policy decisions.

The discussion below exposes four misconceptions related to cost-effectiveness analysis. It explains why cost-effective interventions do not necessarily affect large numbers of people, why they do not necessarily offer important survival benefits and why they are not necessarily low in cost. Further, it explains that, contrary to what common sense would suggest, we do not necessarily gravitate to the most cost-effective interventions. Some of the interventions referred to are summarized in table 2 (Tengs and Graham 1996).

Misconception #1
Cost-effective interventions affect large numbers of people

An intervention is not always more cost-effective simply because it affects large numbers of people. For example, compare the current practice of banning asbestos in brake blocks (the braking mechanism inside vehicle wheels) to protect exposed workers with the proposed policy of installing seat belts on school buses to protect children. Banning asbestos benefits only those few people exposed in the workplace while school buses are ridden by millions of children each year. Yet, at approximately $29,000 per life-year saved, banning asbestos in brake blocks is far more cost-effective than installing seat belts at $2.8 million per life-year saved (see Appendix 1). This is, in part, because asbestos exposure is always hazardous but fatal school bus accidents are quite rare.

Misconception #2
Cost-effective interventions are very effective

Cost-effective interventions are not necessarily those interventions that are most effective. For example, tripling the wind-resistance capabilities of new buildings to protect the occupants in the event of a hurricane would save an average of 4,616 life-years annually. Thus, it could be said to be highly effective. However, because the $12 billion annual cost would be exorbitant, the cost per year of life saved would be $1.3 million. On the other hand, although sickle cell screening for black newborns saves fewer years of life—961 annually—this intervention, at $236 per year of life saved, is much less costly and, therefore, relatively more cost-effective.

Misconception #3
Cost-effective interventions are low cost

Just as cost-effectiveness does not always imply that the benefits are high, it also does not always imply that the costs are low. For example, screening women for breast cancer every three years from the age of 50 to 65 and treating any cases discovered would consume $26.1 million

Table 2   Ten Life-Saving Interventions

		Full Implementation		
		People Affected	Total Annual Cost	Total Annual Life-Years Saved
1	Smoking cessation advice for pregnant women who smoke	Many	–$72,237,187	6,568.0
2	Sickle cell screening for black newborns	Many	$226,876	961.0
3	Ban asbestos in brake blocks	Few	$311,781	10.8
4	Heart transplants	Some	$460,048,544	2,915.0
5	Arsenic emission control at glass manufacturing plants	Few	$4,785,532	3.563
6	Seat belts, auto center back seat	Few	$101,602,435	52.0
7	Seat belts for school buses	Many	$52,995,773	19.2
8	Radionuclide emission control at surface uranium mines	Few	$940,645	0.23976
9	Radionuclide emission control at elemental phosphorus plants	Few	$2,821,935	0.5184
10	Ban asbestos in automatic transmission components	Few	$22,112	0.000333
	Total			

in resources annually. Yet, because mammography is relatively accurate in older women and treatment is effective when breast cancer is caught early, this intervention would save 9,764 years of life annually. Thus, it is quite cost-effective at approximately $2,700 per year of life saved. In contrast, the cost of radionuclide emission control at surface uranium mines is much less at about $1 million annually. Yet, the benefits are minuscule: only 0.24 years of life saved annually (or 1 year of life saved every 4 years). Thus the cost-effectiveness ratio is high at $3.9 million per year of life saved.

Misconception #4
Cost-effective interventions are more likely to be implemented

It seems reasonable to suppose that decision makers would implement those health promotion measures that yield the biggest bang for the

Cost / Life-Years Saved	Actual Implementation		
	Percent Implementation	Annual Cost	Annual Life-Years Saved
≤$0	80%	−$57,789,750	5,254
$236	80%	$181,501	769
$28,869	100%	$311,781	11
$157,821	55%	$253,026,699	1,603
$1,343,119	100%	$4,785,532	4
$1,943,893	5%	$5,080,122	3
$2,760,197	3%	$1,589,873	<1
$3,923,277	0%	$0	0
$5,443,547	100%	$2,821,935	<1
$66,402,402	100%	$22,112	<1
		$210,029,805	7,645

buck. Yet, for the ten interventions in Appendix 1, there appears to be no relationship between cost-effectiveness and implementation. Although the interventions in this table are arranged in order according to cost-effectiveness, the percent of people in the target population who actually receive the intervention (shown in the column, "Percent Implementation") reveals that there is no relationship. For example, when doctors counsel pregnant women to give up smoking, the counseling saves more money than it costs and improves the short-term and long-term survival prospects of both mother and child. Of course, a physician's time is expensive and many smokers ignore their physicians' advice. But, even taking these factors into account, cost savings occur because the lower cost of medical treatment for mother and child for those women who do quit successfully more than offsets the cost of physicians' time. Although this counseling saves money and has important health benefits, experts estimate that only 80 percent of pregnant women who smoke receive advice to stop smoking. In contrast, radionuclide emission control at elemental phosphorus plants has a cost-effectiveness ratio of $5.4 million per year of life saved. Despite the high cost-effectiveness ratio, this regulation is fully implemented.

Clearly, health promotion decisions are not currently based on cost-effectiveness. If they were, we could achieve a more economically efficient allocation of our limited health promotion resources.

Strategies for health policy

When policy analysts advocate "economic efficiency," they are suggesting that a reasonable goal of health policy is to choose the portfolio of health promotion interventions that simultaneously

- maximizes health benefits given the resources consumed

- minimizes the resources consumed for the health benefits achieved

- makes trade-offs between health benefits and money at a rate that reflects our true values.

Thus economic efficiency is simply getting the biggest bang for the buck, spending the fewest bucks possible for a bang and not spending more on any single bang than it is worth.

How can we achieve economic efficiency? Let us consider four strategies that are routinely advocated, implicitly or explicitly, by those charged with making decisions that affect public health:

(1) invest in the interventions affecting the most people;

(2) invest in the most effective interventions;

(3) invest in the least costly interventions;

(4) invest in the most cost-effective interventions.

We can evaluate the wisdom of each of these four strategies by referring to the ten interventions in Appendix 1. Holding constant the total amount that we are currently investing annually in these interventions, we can explore the ramifications of hypothetically investing this sum using each strategy. Which strategy yields the most years of life saved given the resources consumed?

Before performing this hypothetical analysis, we first need to calculate what we are currently investing in these ten interventions and what survival benefits we are currently realizing. We can develop a rough estimate of the level of investment in each intervention by multiplying its cost by the extent of its implementation. For example, sickle cell screening would consume $226,876 annually if all black infants received it. Since only 80 percent of infants are currently screened, it consumes roughly $181,501 annually (calculated as $226,876 x 0.8).

If we estimate investments in each of the ten interventions and add them up, we find that the set consumes $210,029,805 in annual resources and saves 7,645 life-years annually. Now, let us hold resources constant at $210,029,805 and consider each strategy.

Strategy #1
Invest in the interventions affecting the most people

Public health professionals routinely advocate investing in the most important public health problems or the problems affecting the most people. To explore the wisdom of this strategy, we begin by ranking interventions 1 to 10 according to the number of people affected. This ranking appears in table 3. The number of children who ride school buses probably exceeds the number of black infants born in any given year, so seat belts in school buses and sickle cell screening for black infants are ranked first and second, respectively. Further, the number of black infants probably exceeds the number of women who are pregnant and smoke, and the number of these women probably exceeds the number of people who need heart transplants in any given year.

If we invest the same $210,029,805 according to the number of people affected, we would be able to implement fully programs 7, 2 and 1. With the leftover resources, we could ensure heart transplants for 50 percent of those who need one. In total, we would save approximately 8,999 years of life.

Strategy #2
Invest in interventions that save the most lives

We could, instead, take the same $210,029,805 and invest it first in those interventions yielding the greatest number of years of life saved, ignoring other considerations. To follow this strategy, we rank interventions as they appear in table 4. We would first make sure that physicians advise pregnant women to stop smoking, saving 6,568 years of life annually. Next, we would pay for heart transplants for everyone who needs them because doing so yields 2,915 years of life. At the bottom of the list would be banning asbestos in automatic transmission components, which saves only 0.000333 years of life annually.

If we worked our way through the list from top to bottom, investing the same $210,029,805 until it ran out, we would find that we could afford the smoking cessation program for all pregnant women, and heart transplants for 61 percent of those who needed them. Following this strategy, we would save 8,357 years of life annually.

Table 3   Strategy #1: Invest in the Interventions Affecting the

		Full Implementation		
		People Affected	Total Annual Cost	Total Annual Life-Years Saved
7	Seat belts for school buses	Many	$52,995,773	19.2
2	Sickle cell screening for black newborns	Many	$226,876	961.0
1	Smoking cessation advice for pregnant women who smoke	Many	–$72,237,187	6,568.0
4	Heart transplants	Some	$460,048,544	2,915.0
3	Ban asbestos in brake blocks	Few	$311,781	10.8
5	Arsenic emission control at glass manufacturing plants	Few	$4,785,532	3.563
6	Seat belts, auto center back seat	Few	$101,602,435	52.0
8	Radionuclide emission control at surface uranium mines	Few	$940,645	0.23976
9	Radionuclide emission control at elemental phosphorus plants	Few	$2,821,935	0.5184
10	Ban asbestos in automatic transmission components	Few	$22,112	0.000333
	Total			

Strategy #3
Invest in the least costly interventions

Some advocate investing in those interventions that consume the fewest resources. In table 5 the ten interventions are ranked from low to high according the total annual cost of the program. Smoking advice for pregnant women actually saves more money that it costs, taking into account the avoided cost of treating smoking-related illnesses. Thus, smoking cessation advice is ranked first. Next, banning asbestos in automatic transmission components consumes few societal resources at $22,112. Ranked last, heart transplants would consume more than $460 million if everyone who needed one received one.

If we invest the same $210,029,805 in the least costly interventions first, we could fund 100 percent of every program except heart transplants, with enough left over for 26 percent of those who need transplants. The result would be 8,367 years of life saved.

Most People

Cost / Life-Years Saved	Actual Implementation		
	Percent Implementation	Annual Cost	Annual Life-Years Saved
$2,760,197	100%	$52,995,773	19
$236	100%	$226,876	961
≤$0	100%	–$72,237,187	6,568
$157,821	50%	$229,044,343	1,451
$28,869	0%	$0	0
$1,343,119	0%	$0	0
$1,943,893	0%	$0	0
$3,923,277	0%	$0	0
$5,443,547	0%	$0	0
$66,402,402	0%	$0	0
		$210,029,805	8,999

Strategy #4
Invest in the most cost-effective interventions

Finally, suppose that we made investment decisions based on cost-effectiveness. Table 6 ranks the ten interventions according to cost per life-year saved. If we followed this strategy, we would begin by making sure that physicians advised their pregnant patients to stop smoking because the ratio of cost to life-year is < $0. Next, we would make sure that all black newborns were screened for sickle cell because the ratio of cost to life-year is $236. Our last priority would be banning asbestos in automatic transmission components at a ratio of cost to life-year of more than $66 million.

Using this strategy, we find that we could spend the same $210,029,805 by funding the first three programs and heart transplants for 61 percent of those who need them. If we did so, we would save 9,325 years of life.

Table 4   Strategy #2: Invest in Interventions that Save the Most

		Full Implementation		
		People Affected	Total Annual Cost	Total Annual Life-Years Saved
1	Smoking cessation advice for pregnant women who smoke	Many	−$72,237,187	6,568.0
4	Heart transplants	Some	$460,048,544	2,915.0
2	Sickle cell screening for black newborns	Many	$226,876	961.0
6	Seat belts, auto center back seat	Few	$101,602,435	52.0
7	Seat belts for school buses	Many	$52,995,773	19.2
3	Ban asbestos in brake blocks	Few	$311,781	10.8
5	Arsenic emission control at glass manufacturing plants	Few	$4,785,532	3.563
9	Radionuclide emission control at elemental phosphorus plants	Few	$2,821,935	0.5184
8	Radionuclide emission control at surface uranium mines	Few	$940,645	0.23976
10	Ban asbestos in automatic transmission components	Few	$22,112	0.000333
	Total			

As shown in table 7, funding the most cost-effective interventions first saves more years of life than any other strategy. Further, if we had performed a different experiment, in which we specified a number of life-years to be saved and sought the strategy that would minimize costs, cost-effectiveness would again have proven superior. Finally, using cost-effectiveness information strategically allows us to make tradeoffs between small improvements in survival (i.e., quantity of life) and costs (i.e., all other goods and services).

These results are not due to chance and the superiority of the cost-effectiveness strategy is not specific to the interventions chosen for this example. Basing welfare decisions on some measure of the relationship between costs and benefits will always prove superior to any other strategy, when the goal is to maximize benefits given the resources consumed.

Years of Life

Cost / Life-Years Saved	Actual Implementation		
	Percent Implementation	Annual Cost	Annual Life-Years Saved
≤$0	100%	−$72,237,187	6,568
$157,821	61%	$282,266,992	1,789
$236	0%	$0	0
$1,943,893	0%	$0	0
$2,760,197	0%	$0	0
$28,869	0%	$0	0
$1,343,119	0%	$0	0
$5,443,547	0%	$0	0
$3,923,277	0%	$0	0
$66,402,402	0%	$0	0
		$210,029,805	8,357

The Harvard Life-Saving Study

The lifesaving interventions referred to above represent just a fraction of those surveyed by the Harvard Life-Saving Team. Funded by that National Science Foundation, my colleagues and I amassed cost-effectiveness information for hundreds of different interventions.

Although the full data set contains cost-effectiveness estimates for 587 interventions, national annual cost and effectiveness estimates were available for only 185 of these interventions. For each, we supplemented cost-effectiveness data with information on the degree to which that intervention was implemented. (See Appendix, pages 185–86 for the Methodology of the Harvard Life-Saving Study.)

To learn more about the economic efficiency of societal investments, we contrasted the current pattern of investment in these 185 interventions with the hypothetical "optimal" pattern of investment

Table 5   Strategy #3: Invest in the Least Costly Interventions

	Full Implementation		
	People Affected	Total Annual Cost	Total Annual Life-Years Saved
1 Smoking cessation advice for pregnant women who smoke	Many	–$72,237,187	6,568.0
10 Ban asbestos in automatic transmission components	Few	$22,112	0.000333
2 Sickle cell screening for black newborns	Many	$226,876	961.0
3 Ban asbestos in brake blocks	Few	$311,781	10.8
8 Radionuclide emission control at surface uranium mines	Few	$940,645	0.23976
9 Radionuclide emission control at elemental phosphorus plants	Few	$2,821,935	0.5184
5 Arsenic emission control at glass manufacturing plants	Few	$4,785,532	3.563
7 Seat belts for school buses	Many	$52,995,773	19.2
6 Seat belts, auto center back seat	Few	$101,602,435	52.0
4 Heart transplants	Some	$460,048,544	2,915.0
Total			

that cost-effectiveness would dictate. Like the interventions in table 2, some of the 185 were implemented fully, some partially and some not at all. Further, as figure 2 illustrates, there was no relationship between implementation and cost-effectiveness. We estimated the resources currently consumed by these interventions at $21.4 billion and the life-years currently saved at 592,000.

Our research revealed that if the entire $21.4 billion were spent on the most cost-effective interventions, and none on the cost-ineffective interventions, we could save 1,230,000 years of life annually. That is 636,000 more than the 592,000 we are currently saving. Roughly, we could double the survival benefits of our investments at no additional cost!

The efficient frontier

This phenomenon can be understood by referring to the diagram in figure 3. The curve represents the maximum number of life-years that

Cost / Life-Years Saved	Actual Implementation		
	Percent Implementation	Annual Cost	Annual Life-Years Saved
≤$0	100%	–$72,237,187	6,568
$66,402,402	100%	$22,112	<0
$236	100%	$226,876	961
$28,869	100%	$311,781	11
$3,923,277	100%	$940,645	<0
$5,443,547	100%	$2,821,935	<0
$1,343,119	100%	$4,785,532	4
$2,760,197	100%	$52,995,773	19
$1,943,893	100%	$101,602,435	52
$157,821	26%	$119,013,655	752
		$210,029,805	8,367

could be saved for a given level of resources consumed. This curve is called a "cost curve" or "efficient frontier" because it represents an efficient use of resources. It would be impossible to be above the curve because the maximum survival benefits for each level of resource consumption is plotted. However, it is possible to be inside the curve—by failing to maximize survival benefits for a given level of expenditures. Notice that the curve increases at a decreasing rate. This reflects "decreasing marginal returns." That is, the first few interventions cost very little relative to the survival benefits they achieve but, as we spend more money, although we realize more survival benefits, the amount we gain with each added dollar declines.

It is clear that the efficient frontier is a good place to be. But, it is not clear where we should be on the frontier. That choice depends upon the maximum we are willing to spend to save one year of life. If that value is approximately $600,000, then we would want to be at point *B*

Table 6   Strategy #4: Invest in the Most Cost-Effective

		Full Implementation		
		People Affected	Total Annual Cost	Total Annual Life-Years Saved
1	Smoking cessation advice for pregnant women who smoke	Many	−$72,237,187	6,568.0
2	Sickle cell screening for black newborns	Many	$226,876	961.0
3	Ban asbestos in brake blocks	Few	$311,781	10.8
4	Heart transplants	Some	$460,048,544	2,915.0
5	Arsenic emission control at glass manufacturing plants	Few	$4,785,532	3.563
6	Seat belts, auto center back seat	Few	$101,602,435	52.0
7	Seat belts for school buses	Many	$52,995,773	19.2
8	Radionuclide emission control at surface uranium mines	Few	$940,645	0.23976
9	Radionuclide emission control at elemental phosphorus plants	Few	$2,821,935	0.5184
10	Ban asbestos in automatic transmission components	Few	$22,112	0.000333
	Total			

because the slope of the curve at that point is 1/600,000. That is, *B* represents the point where the last and least cost-effective lifesaving intervention funded costs $600,000 per year of life saved. *B* would be the right choice if our willingness to pay was $600,000. If we were not willing to spend as much as $600,000 per life-year, then we might choose something like point *C*, where the cost per year of life saved is, say, $100,000. If our willingness to pay were even lower than that, we might choose point *D*, where the cost per year of life saved is $10,000. Economists have estimated that people tend to make trade-offs between survival and money at the rate of $3 million to $7 million per life saved (Viscusi 1993). A figure of $5 million per life saved would translate into a few hundred thousand per year of life saved, assuming ten to 20 discounted years of life saved when a premature death is averted. Thus some point between *B* and *C* might be a reasonable choice.

Interventions

Cost / Life-Years Saved	Actual Implementation		
	Percent Implementation	Annual Cost	Annual Life-Years Saved
≤$0	100%	–$72,237,187	6,568
$236	100%	$226,876	961
$28,869	100%	$311,781	11
$157,821	61%	$281,728,335	1,785
$1,343,119	0%	$0	0
$1,943,893	0%	$0	0
$2,760,197	0%	$0	0
$3,923,277	0%	$0	0
$5,443,547	0%	$0	0
$66,402,402	0%	$0	0
		$210,029,805	9,325

Unfortunately, our current pattern of investment puts us at point *A*, reflecting our current expenditures of $21.4 billion and saving of 582,000 years of life. If we divide $21.4 billion by 582,000 years of life we obtain an average of $37,000 per life-year. This result may appear attractive but, in fact, we can do much better. If our current lifesaving portfolio did not ignore many cost-effective investment opportunities and contain many cost-ineffective interventions, we could be at point *B*, saving 1.2 million years of life. The portfolio at point *B* could be achieved by holding expenditures constant at $21.4 billion, investing in all interventions with marginal cost-effectiveness ratios less than $600,000 per life-year and none of the interventions with higher marginal cost-effectiveness ratios. The vertical distance between points *A* and *B* represents the 636,000 years of life lost annually due to our failure to invest wisely in life-saving interventions.

Table 7   Summary of the Performance of Each Strategy

	Annual Cost	Annual Life-Years Saved
Current Investment Pattern	$210,029,805	7,645
Strategy #1: Invest in the Interventions Affecting the Most People	$210,029,805	8,999
Strategy #2: Invest in the Most Effective Interventions	$210,029,805	8,357
Strategy #3: Invest in the Least Costly Interventions	$210,029,805	8,367
Strategy #4: Invest in the Most Cost-Effective Interventions	$210,029,805	*9,325

(*Maximum survival benefits)

Figure 2   Relationship between Implementation and Cost-Effectiveness

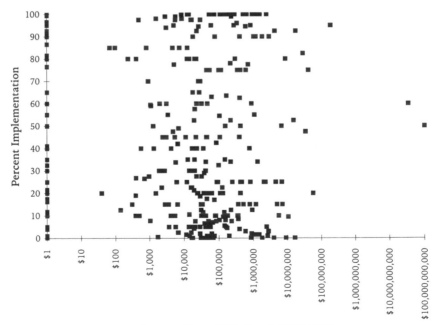

Cost per Year of Life Saved (1993 US$)

Figure 3 Inefficiency in Life-Saving Investments

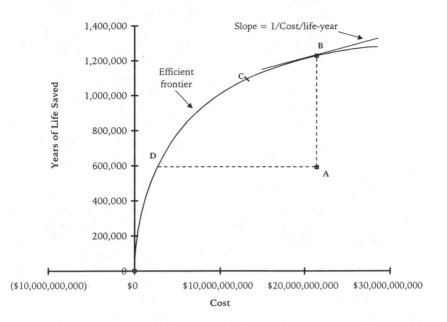

If we preferred to spend less than $21.4 billion on promoting survival because, for example, we valued life-years at only $100,000 each, we could be at point *C*. If this were our choice, we would spend less, yet gain survival benefits relative to the status quo.

Government regulations and economic efficiency

Just as the Harvard Life-Saving Study found no relationship between cost-effectiveness and implementation of lifesaving interventions overall, it found no correlation between cost-effectiveness and implementation when it comes to government regulations.

Table 1 reports the median cost-effectiveness of regulations considered by several agencies. Large differences exist. Some highly cost-effective regulations have been implemented, such as the Consumer Product Safety Commission's ban on three-wheeled all-terrain vehicles. By avoiding the costs of treating injuries, this ban saves more than it costs. But, other highly cost-effective regulations were considered by federal agencies and not implemented: for example, the Occupational Safety and Health Administration's workplace practice standard for electric power generation operation at $59,000 per life-year saved. Perhaps more worrisome, a number of very cost-ineffective regulations have been implemented, such as the Environmental Protection Agency's regulation controlling benzene emissions during waste operations at $19 million per life-year saved. Wisely, other cost-ineffective regulations considered have not been implemented, including benzene emission control at chemical manufacturing process vents at $530 million per year of life saved.

Because of this haphazard pattern of investment, government regulations save fewer lives than they might, given the resources consumed, and consume more resources than necessary, given the survival benefits offered. The solution is to base regulatory decisions on whether they are economically efficient. But, just how important are the losses due to inefficiency? How many more years of life could be saved? How much money could be saved?

To answer these questions, we performed the same kind of hypothetical reallocation described above but restricted our investigation to the 139 government regulations for which we had data. Results indicated that the 139 regulations consume $4.11 billion annually and save 94,000 years of life. Thus, if we divide resources consumed by years of life saved, we find an average cost of about $44,000 per year of life saved. If we had invested the same $4.11 billion in the most cost-effective regulations, we would be saving more than twice as many years of life—211,000 annually or 117,000 more than the status quo (see figure 4).

Figure 4   Applying Cost-Effectiveness to 139 Regulations

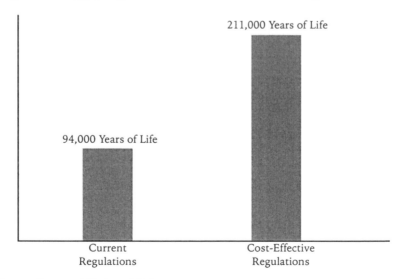

Source: Tengs and Graham 1996.

Conclusion—cost-effectiveness can save lives

This paper has demonstrated why the simple ratio of the cost of a health promotion intervention to the health benefits accrued can be very helpful in making public health decisions. It shows that cost-effective interventions can benefit few or many; can be very effective or not very effective; can be expensive or inexpensive. When maximizing survival is the goal, the use of cost-effectiveness information for selecting investments out-performs other strategies, such as considering only the number of people affected, considering only the effectiveness or considering only the cost.

Because we fail to base public health decisions on cost-effectiveness, we sacrifice many lives every year. Allowing cost-effectiveness to inform those decisions will improve the allocation of scarce life-saving resources.

Appendix
Methodology of the Harvard Life-Saving Study

To identify cost-effectiveness information for the 587 interventions studied, a comprehensive search for publicly available economic analyses was performed. Two trained reviewers (from a total of 11 reviewers) read each document and independently recorded the nature of the life-saving intervention, the base case intervention to which it was compared, the target population, the resources consumed by the intervention, total lives saved, total life-years saved, cost per life saved and cost per life-year saved. After working independently, the two reviewers came to a consensus on the content of the document.

To increase the comparability of cost-effectiveness estimates drawn from different economic analyses, nine definitional goals were established. When an estimate failed to comply with a goal, reviewers attempted to revise the estimate to improve compliance. The nine definitional goals were:

(1) Cost-effectiveness estimates should be in the form of "cost per year of life saved." Estimates of cost per life saved should be transformed to cost per life-year by considering the average number of years of life saved when a premature death is averted.

(2) Costs and effectiveness should be evaluated from the societal perspective.

(3) Costs should be "direct." Indirect costs such as forgone earnings should be excluded to avoid double-counting effectiveness measures.

(4) Costs and effectiveness should be "net." Any resource savings or mortality risks induced by the intervention should be subtracted out.

(5) Future costs, lives and life-years saved should all be discounted to their present value at a rate of 5 percent.

(6) Cost-effectiveness ratios should be marginal or "incremental." Both costs and effectiveness should be evaluated with respect to a well-defined baseline alternative, usually the next best intervention.

(7) Costs should be expressed in 1993 dollars using the general consumer price index.

(8) Total costs, total lives saved and total life-years saved should be annual, annualized over a meaningful time horizon suggested by the author of the economic analysis or annualized over a 10-year time horizon if no time horizon was suggested. Costs, lives and life-years should reflect the total consequences of implementing the intervention nationwide.

(9) Total costs, total lives saved and total life-years saved should be measured with respect to the "do nothing" alternative that involves no additional expenditure and results in no additional survival benefits relative to the status quo.

Notes

1 Further, costs should not be confused with prices, which, due to imperfections in the economy, may or may not reflect the actual value of the resources consumed.
2 This report also takes the "societal" perspective and thus does not differentiate between public expenditures and private, voluntary spending.

References

Tengs, T.O., et al. (1995). Five Hundred Life-Saving Interventions and Their Cost-Effectiveness. *Risk Analysis* 15, 3 (June): 369–90.

Tengs, T.O., and J.D. Graham (1996). The Opportunity Costs of Haphazard Societal Investments in Life-Saving. In R. Hahn (ed.), *Risks, Costs, and Lives Saved: Getting Better Results from Regulation* (New York: Oxford University Press).

Viscusi, W.K. (1993). The Value of Risks to Life and Health. *Journal of Economic Literature* 31: 1912–46.

The Reluctance to Use Cost-Effectiveness Analysis in Regulatory Decision-Making

PETER J. NEUMANN

Despite the tremendous growth in the performance and publication of cost-effectiveness analyses (CEA) and other forms of economic evaluation in health and medicine, some policy makers, especially in the United States, have shied away from its use. Moreover, in some cases regulatory policy has discouraged its use. This paper explores reasons for this situation.

Cost-effectiveness analysis in health and medicine

The rise in the number of economic evaluations of health and medical interventions has been well-documented (Elixhauser et al. 1993; Elixhauser et al. 1998). One recent review of the literature found over 3,500 cost-benefit and cost-effectiveness analyses published from 1991 through 1996 (Elixhauser et al. 1998). An international database that maintains information on health economic evaluations contains over 11,000 entries (OHE-IFPMA 1998).

Cost-effectiveness analysis (CEA) has emerged as the dominant approach to economic evaluation in health and medicine (Office of Technology Assessment 1994; Gold, Siegel, Russell, and Weinstein

1996), though other forms of analyses such as cost-benefit analysis (CBA), cost-minimization analysis, and cost-consequences analysis have also been used.

The appeal of CEA is that it yields a ratio—costs per unit of health effect achieved—that is relatively straightforward to interpret and that allows for comparisons across a broad spectrum of interventions. Cost-effectiveness analyses show the relationship between the resources used (costs) and the health benefits achieved (effects) for an intervention compared to an alternative strategy. The cost per effect (C/E) ratio reflects the difference in the interventions' costs divided by the difference in their health effectiveness (Gold et al. 1996). If ratios are estimated in similar terms, they can be compared to illustrate the most efficient ways to maximize health benefits in the allocation of limited resources.

In contrast, CBA requires the monetary valuation of health benefits, which presents measurement difficulties and raises ethical issues (i.e., placing a dollar value on life). Other approaches also have limitations. Cost-consequence analyses (in which components of incremental costs and consequences of alternative interventions are computed and listed without any attempt to aggregate the results) may offer advantages in terms of their understandability but lack standards for methodological practices and do not produce results that can be easily compared across studies. The performance of cost-minimization analyses, which are used to compare the net costs of programs that achieve the same outcome, are less common because of the stringency of the requirement that competing programs yield similar effects.

Uses of cost-effectiveness analysis

In some cases, cost-effectiveness analysis has been used explicitly by policy makers. In Canada, for example, guidelines for performing economic evaluations of pharmaceuticals have been published (Menon, Schubert, and Torrance 1996; Baladi, Menon, and Otten 1998). The purpose of the guidelines is to "achieve sustainable pharmaceutical resource allocation, effective pricing policies, and equitable drug coverage" (Menon et al. 1996). The guidelines process is managed by the Canadian Coordinating Office for Health Technology Assessment (CCOHTA), a corporation created by federal, provincial, and territorial governments in Canada.

The guidelines stipulate that economic evaluation should not be part of the federal regulatory review process but rather should be used to demonstrate the value and cost-effectiveness of products being considered for reimbursement. Over the past few years, CCOHTA has assessed some four to six pharmaceuticals per month and has conducted evaluations in numerous areas, including cervical cancer screening and the use of new medications for the management of major depression and acute migraine.

In the United States, some private managed-care plans have developed and used similar guidelines (Integrated Pharmaceutical Services 1997; Regence 1997). In general, however, policy makers have been reluctant to use cost-effectiveness analyses explicitly. For example, the Canadian federal Medicare program, which provides health coverage to elderly and disabled individuals, has been unable to enact a regulation that would add cost-effectiveness to the criteria used in coverage decisions for new medical technologies. Policy makers in the state of Oregon encountered difficulties when they attempted to follow the cost-effectiveness paradigm too closely for use in their Medicaid program, which provides health care to low-income individuals.

Barriers to using cost-effectiveness analysis

There are a number of barriers to the explicit use of cost-effectiveness analysis. Results from a handful of surveys conducted over the past few years shed some light on the issue (Lax and Moench 1995; Zellmer 1995; Drummond 1995; Luce and Brown 1995; Luce, Lyles, and Rentz 1996; Steiner et al. 1996a; Steiner et al. 1996b; Sloan, Whetten-Goldstein, and Wilson 1997). While the surveys differ in their scopes, methodologies, and sample sizes, several main conclusions emerge.

Many decision-makers feel ill-equipped to evaluate the information

One barrier to greater use of CEA is a feeling among decision makers that they do not possess adequate knowledge or training. Zellmer (1995), for example, reported that almost 40 percent of health-care managers said that they were ill-equipped to analyze and compare pharmacoeconomic claims critically. In another survey (Sloan et al. 1997), 15 percent of respondents listed lack of knowledge as a reason that cost-effectiveness analysis is not used more often. A similar percentage stated that a better explanation of methods was needed if CEAs were to be more useful to hospital managers.

Decision-makers remain skeptical of the information because they fear bias on the part of the study sponsors

The credibility and reliability of studies is also perceived as a problem. Zellmer found that fewer than 20 percent of respondents agreed with the statement "the comparative pharmacoeconomic claims made by drug manufacturers generally meet high standards for reliability." Moreover, only 51 percent of respondents agreed with the statement "my managed care plan is in a position to put pressure on manufacturers to conduct scientifically rigorous pharmacoeconomic studies." In interviews with 43 managed-care providers, Lax and Moench (1995) found that the top concern expressed was "bias" followed by "freedom to control the study" and the "validity of the study." In a study of 446 medical professionals in the United Kingdom, Drummond (1995) reported that the greatest barrier stated was that "industry funded studies are not credible," reported by almost 60 percent of respondents. In the study by Sloan et al., over 20 percent of respondents said that a way to make CEA more useful to hospitals was to sponsor independent research. Almost 40 percent of respondents in the survey by Drummond et al. said that an external reviewer was needed to critically review studies for decision makers.

Decision makers emphasize the need for more timely information

In a survey of 231 managers of private health plans, Steiner et al. (1996) found that the greatest reported barriers to decision makers were "no timely effectiveness data," expressed by 90 percent, followed by "no timely cost-effectiveness data (70 percent) and "no timely safety data" (60 percent). Among the barriers to use of cost-effectiveness analysis reported by Sloan et al. (1997) was the fact that studies were published too late. Almost 30 percent of these respondents replied that one way to make CEA more useful to hospitals was to make studies available sooner.

Decision makers want targeted information
that is more relevant to their own decisions

Sloan et al. (1997) reported that the two greatest barriers to the use of cost-effectiveness analysis among hospital pharmacists were that the analyses were not targeted at drugs of interest (34 percent) or that the analyses did not apply to hospitals (28 percent). When asked how cost-effectiveness analysis could be made more useful to hospitals, the most frequent response was that studies should be made "generalizable to the hospital setting." Drummond (1995) found that among the barriers reported by respondents were that "savings are anticipated, not real," that the Department of Health in the United Kingdom is only interested in cost containment, not cost-effectiveness, and that they "couldn't take the long-term view."

Cost-effectiveness remains a secondary
consideration after clinical factors

It is also important to keep in mind that cost-effectiveness remains a secondary consideration after clinical factors. Luce and colleagues

(1996) interviewed 51 managers of managed care plans and asked about the usefulness of information on clinical effectiveness, safety, cost of treatment, and cost-effectiveness. Rated on a scale from 1 (most useful) to 6 (least useful), clinical effectiveness (1.6) was thought to be most useful followed by information on cost-effectiveness (2.6) safety (2.7), and cost of treatment (4.0). Luce et al. (1996) also found that respondents gave higher ratings to information from clinical trials as opposed to information from retrospective reviews and models. On a scale of 1 (excellent) to 4 (poor), clinical trials rated highest (1.8) followed by retrospective reviews (2.1) and models (2.6).

Regulatory barriers

A final barrier to the use of cost-effectiveness information is regulatory. In the United States, the Food and Drug Administration has traditionally concerned itself with matters of safety and effectiveness and not cost-effectiveness. But the Agency has long held authority to ensure that information disseminated by drug manufacturers is not inaccurate or misleading. The emergence of cost-effectiveness analysis has thus confronted the Agency with a new dilemma: how does it regulate promotional materials containing claims about a drug's cost-effectiveness?

In 1995, the FDA's Division of Drug Marketing and Communications (DDMAC) issued draft guidelines on the issue (FDA-DDMAC 1995). The guidelines stipulated that pharmacoeconomic studies would be required to produce "an adequate level of precision, scientific rigor, and validity (both internal and external) to support the resulting claims" (FDA-DDMAC 1995). All comparative claims would be required to provide "substantial evidence" typically demonstrated "by two adequate and well-controlled studies ... Computer and mathematical models would be acceptable only when well-controlled trials could be performed; intermediate health outcomes and quality-of-life measurements can be employed only with evidence of the scientific association" (FDA-DDMAC 1995).

The draft guidelines were problematic because they were overly prescriptive, because they put too much stock in randomized controlled trials (RCTs) for economic endpoints, and because they gave short shrift to modeling exercises, which lie at the heart of cost-effectiveness analyses. The guidelines were also limited in that they did not show sufficient appreciation for the growing sophistication of purchasers—particular managed care plans—in using pharmacoeconomic information (Neumann, Zinner, and Paltiel 1996). In addition, cost-effectiveness should not be held to the same standard as safety and efficacy because the danger to consumers is an economic risk—paying too much for the benefits conferred—and not a health or safety risk.

Staff at the United States Federal Trade Commission (FTC) put forward many of these concerns, arguing that strict adherence to RCTs could result in the prohibition of truthful, non-deceptive claims of cost-effectiveness. They suggested a more flexible substantiation for economic claims based on "competent and reliable evidence" without an *a priori* specification for well-controlled trials (Neumann et al. 1996). "Competent and reliable evidence," they noted, might include epidemiologic or administrative claims, as long as adequate disclosure was provided (Neumann et al. 1996).

Legislation on the matter was addressed in the FDA Modernization Act of 1997. The provision states that "health care economic information provided to a formulary committee, or other similar entity . . . with respect to the selection of drugs for managed care or similar organizations . . . is based on competent and reliable evidence (US Congress 1997). While this legislation might offer some relief, it remains unclear how the "competent and reliable" evidence standard will be interpreted. Moreover, the FDA has yet to offer interpretive policy. A key issue in the debate is how well the FDA believes consumers are able to understand the information and separate "good" from "bad" information. In the meantime, pharmaceutical companies will likely remain reluctant to make claims about the cost-effectiveness of their products, despite a demand for such information on the part of health-care payers.

The road ahead

Considerations of cost will always play an important role in health-care decisions, whether they lurk in the shadows or are appraised openly. The real question is how explicit we are in using such information. Since cost-effectiveness analysis can help to illustrate how to improve health with society's limited resources, more efforts should be undertaken to make such information available.

To date, public-policy officials have shied away from using cost-effectiveness analysis as an explicit tool of policy making. Part of the problem is a lingering perception that the field lacks standards, making it difficult to compare cost-effectiveness ratios across studies. Some observers have also been troubled by the fact that many analyses are sponsored by drug companies with an interest in obtaining favorable results.

In recent years, progress has been made in addressing these concerns, including the publication of guidelines covering both methodological practices and the independence of researchers. To enhance the comparability of analyses, leaders in the field now suggest that cost-effective researchers undertake a "reference case" analysis, which involves a standard set of methodologic practices (Gold et al. 1996). New guidelines suggest that analyses consider the societal perspective for the reference case and that they add other perspectives if they are important to the decision at hand.

The government can improve upon these efforts by sponsoring more research in the field, ensuring that this research adheres to the high standards recommended by leaders in the field, and allowing its dissemination to the public. The private sector can help by establishing mechanisms for independent, third-party review of cost-effectiveness claims. Editors of peer-reviewed journals would enhance these efforts by establishing more rigorous protocols for reviewing cost-effectiveness analyses prior to publication.

A more difficult hurdle for cost-effectiveness analysis is that its candid use raises the specter that health care is being "rationed." Here too, public-policy makers can help by leading efforts to educate the medical and health-policy communities about the usefulness of cost-effectiveness analysis in helping to maximize a nation's health tools under constrained health budgets.

References

Baladi, J.F., D. Menon, and N. Otten (1998). Use of Economic Evaluation Guidelines: 2 Years' Experience in Canada. *Health Economics* 7: 221–27.

Brown, M.L., and L. Fintor (1993). Cost-Effectiveness of Breast Cancer Screening: Preliminary Results of a Systematic Review of the Literature. *Breast Cancer Res Treatment* 25: 113–18.

Drummond, M. (1995). Economic Evaluation in Health Care. Presentation at Duke University (November).

Elixhauser, A., B.R. Luce, W.R. Taylor et al. (1993). Health Care CBA/CEA: An Update on the Growth and Composition of the Literature. *Medical Care* 31: JS1.

Elixhauser, A., M. Halpern, J. Schmier, and B.R. Luce (1998). Health Care CBA and CEA from 1991 to 1996: An Updated Bibliography. *Medical Care* 36: MS1–MS9.

Food and Drug Administration, Division of Drug Marketing, Advertising, and Communication [FDA-DDMAC] (1995). *Principles for the Review of Pharmacoeconomic Promotion: Draft Guidelines.*

Gold, M.R., J.E. Siegel, L.B. Russell, M.C. Weinstein (1996). *Cost-Effectiveness in Health and Medicine.* Oxford: Oxford University Press.

Integrated Pharmaceutical Services and Foundation Health Corporation (1996). *Guidelines for Formulary Submissions.* Rancho Cordova (CA): Integrated Pharmaceutical Services and Foundation Health Corporation.

Lax, J., and E. Moench (1995). Pharmacoeconomics and Managed Care: Understanding the Issues, Concerns, and the Environment. Presentation at the Food and Drug Administration Hearing, *Pharmaceutical Marketing and Information Exchange in Managed Care Environments*, Silver Spring, Maryland (October 19).

Luce, B.R., and R.E. Brown (1995). The Use of Technology Assessment by Hospitals, Health Maintenance Organizations, and Third-Party Payers in the United States. *International Journal of Technology Assessment in Health Care* 11: 79–82.

Luce, B.R., A.C. Lyles, and A.M. Rentz (1996). The View from Managed Care Pharmacy. *Health Affairs* 4: 168–76.

Menon, D., F. Schubert, G.W. Torrance (1996). Canada's New Guidelines for the Economic Evaluation of Pharmaceuticals. *Medical Care* 34: DS77–DS86.

Neumann, P.J., D.E. Zinner, and A.D. Paltiel (1996). The FDA's Regulation of Cost-Effectiveness Claims. *Health Affairs* (Fall): 54–71.

Neumann, P.J., D.E. Zinner, and J.C. Wright (1997). Are Methods for Estimating QALYs in Cost-Effectiveness Analyses Improving? *Medical Decision Making* 17: 402–08.

Office of Technology Assessment (1994). *Identifying Health Technologies that Work: Searching for Evidence*. Washington, DC.

OHE-IFPMA Database Ltd. (1998). *The Health Economic Evaluations Database*. Company brochure.

Regence Washington Health Pharmacy Service (1997). *Guidelines for Submission of Clinical and Economic Data Supporting Formulary Considerations, Version 1.2* (September). Regence Washington Health, University of Washington, Seattle, WA.

Sloan, F.A., K. Whetten-Goldstein, and A. Wilson (1997). Hospital Pharmacy Decisions, Cost-Containment, and the Use of Cost-Effectiveness Analysis. *Social Science and Medicine* 45, 4: 525–33.

Steiner, C., et al. (1996a). The Review Process Used by Health Care Plans to Evaluate New Medical Technology for Coverage. *J Gen Internal Medicine* 11: 294–302.

Steiner, C., et al. (1996b). Coverage Decisions for Medical Technology: Relationship to Organizational and Physician Payment Characteristics. *American Journal of Managed Care* 2: 1321–331.

Udvarhelyi, I.S., G.A. Colditz, A. Rai, et al. (1992). Cost-Effectiveness and Cost-Benefit Analyses in the Medical Literature. *Ann Intern Med* 116, 3: 238–44.

United States Congress (1997). Prescription Drug User Fee Act (US House Bill 1141 and US Senate Bill 830). Washington, DC.

Zellmer, W. (1995). Comments of the American Society of Health-System Pharmacists. Presentation at the Food and Drug Administration Hearing, *Pharmaceutical Marketing and Information Exchange in Managed Care Environments*, Silver Spring, MD (October 19).

Reforming
Risk Regulation in Canada
The Next Policy Frontier?

W.T. STANBURY

1 Introduction

(a) Contradictions and paradoxes

We live in an age in which attitudes toward risk[1] are a strange bundle of paradoxes, if not contradictions. Consider just the following:

(1) Governments often mandate the expenditure of over $100 million per "life saved" to comply with a new regulation expected to save a handful of lives each year—all while ignoring other opportunities to save many more lives at a cost to society of far less than $1 million each (see Hahn 1996; Tengs and Graham 1996). Graham (1996: 184) has described this as "a syndrome of paranoia and neglect." (See also Mac-Queen 1999.)

(2) "A growing body of evidence ... shows that many recent expenditures on risk reduction have done very little to actually reduce risks. Indeed, in some cases, those investments are likely to have increased risks to human health" (Hahn 1996: vii).

Notes will be found on pages 245–53.

(3) Life expectancy reached a record high in 1999: 75.1 years for men and 81.4 years for women (McIlroy 1999b: A1). In other words, the effects of all risks has declined—most people die of old age.[2] Yet, at the same time, there are increasing demands for government to create a "risk-free society."

(4) We have "created entire economies around activating this fear system under safe conditions in the form of theme-park rides and Stephen King novels and films that have us on the edge of our seats. It is as if an archival survival circuit in our brains has become a cathartic button that gets pushed at great profit" (Hall 1999: 45).

(5) Between February 1993 and January 1994, some two million residents of the Los Angeles area were directly touched by disaster-related death, injury, or damage to homes and businesses by an earthquake, floods, firestorms, and a riot. The earthquake in January 1994 alone caused some US$42 billion in damage. According to a comprehensive account of these and other hazards, "cataclysm has become virtually routine" in the area of Los Angeles (Davies 1998: 7). Most notable is the idea that "Los Angeles has deliberately put itself in harm's way ... it has transgressed environmental common sense" and the result has been a long series of avoidable tragedies (Davies 1998: 9).

(6) The number of participants in "extreme sports"[3] has increased markedly in Canada, the United States, and other western industrialized countries.

(7) It could reasonably be argued that *much* government activity is aimed at dealing with a wide variety of risks to physical and economic security—rather than responding to traditional market failures.[4]

(b) Classifying risks

A surprising amount of government activity can reasonably be described as actions aimed at managing risks. This includes efforts to reduce risks, ameliorating the consequence of adverse events for certain people, providing information to assist individuals in better coping with risks, and providing some form of insurance with respect to certain risks. Appendix 1 (page 239) provides a classification of the risks that are subject to some form of action by the Canadian federal government.[5] While the categories are not mutually exclusive and exhaustive, they seem useful in highlighting several points.

(1) A wide range of *types* of risks are subject to government action within the metacategories of risks to life, limb, (i.e., accidents), health, and wallet (risks to income or wealth). Most relate to *physical* rather than economic risks, i.e., harm to one's body including the risk of death.

(2) There are many types of safety regulation reflecting (albeit imperfectly) the large range of hazards we face in everyday life. (This is not to suggest we live in a risky world, certainly not by the standards of history or of people currently living in developing countries.)

(3) Some of the risks subject to government action include those that go to the *raison d'être* of government itself, namely the protection of persons and property from villains within the nation and outside it.

While economic regulation (focusing on price and entry control) has declined dramatically since the 1980s, "social regulation" has increased substantially. Much social regulation is risk regulation and most risk regulation focuses on harms to human health and safety. While some forms of health and safety regulation have their roots deep in the past (e.g., mine safety, railroad safety, pure food and drugs laws), much of the current large stock of health and safety regulation was put in place in the past three decades. The biggest component is called "environmental protection regulation" but most of it is concerned, directly or indirectly, with the well-being of people rather than plants, animals, and ecosystems.[6] Risk regulation is important not only because it constitutes a major part of government activity (particularly when major income transfers are interpreted as a means of addressing risks to income flows) but also because by far the largest costs relating to risk regulation occur *outside* of government, i.e., in the private sector. This fact makes it easy for those who would reduce risk through government regulation to underestimate the social costs of such intervention.

(c) Categories of government actions in dealing with risks

If we consider all the risks that are subject to action by the federal government in Canada, we can identify the following categories of government actions in dealing with risks. First, government can implement regulation with the objective of *directly* reducing the probability or size of the hazard, or of reducing the risk of some citizens' exposure to the hazard. In some cases, government may prohibit certain forms of behaviour by individuals or certain actions by firms. Regulation may involve the *mandatory* disclosure of information about hazards, e.g., warnings on cigarette packages; and prospect for securities to be sold to the public. Here the objective is to reduce risks *indirectly* by giving individuals information that permits them to avoid or reduce their exposure to certain risks.

Second, government can create liability rules; establish courts; and enforce judgments of those courts. All the actions are designed to facilitate efficient *private* legal actions. Third, government can act as the last-resort bearer of risks, e.g., pay some compensation in the face of natural disasters. This is often done on an *ad hoc* basis after politicians see which way the wind is blowing. In some cases, government acts as a re-insurer for private insurers for truly catastrophic risks or the very small chance that a number of very large losses cluster in a few years and overwhelm the company's reserves, i.e., the government provides compensation for losses beyond those covered by private insurance.

Fourth, government generates and provides information to the public to predict risks and facilitate actions to reduce losses, e.g., weather forecasting, provision of information to consumers to aid in purchasing decisions such as product labelling, and trade-mark laws. This category also includes monitoring and surveillance activities that may have effects on private-sector behaviour. Fifth, government creates and operates insurance scheme(s)—particularly where private insurance is not available. In many cases, however, public schemes are not true insurance schemes at all but devices to subsidize and redistribute income, e.g. so-called unemployment insurance and flood insurance. Four provinces in Canada operate automobile insurance schemes that pursue a number of "social" policy objectives besides providing liability insurance.

(d) Purpose and structure of this chapter

The main purpose of this chapter is to propose ways of improving the way the federal government in Canada manages risks.[7] Improvements in risk management,[8] however, depend upon a reasonably accurate diagnosis of the problems that currently beset the government's risk-management activities. This term is taken to include risk analyses, risk assessment, the generation of alternative policy actions (including not intervening) and the implementation of policies.[9] In short, the focus of this paper is on government decision-making relating to efforts to control, reduce and cope with risks to life, limb and wallets.

The main body of the paper is organized as follows. Section 2 examines some aspects of risks that are important to risk-management activities of governments. Section 3 describes a number of "pathologies" of the federal government's management of risks. Section 4 sets out my proposals for improving risk management by the federal government in Canada. In particular, government must greatly improve its risk communication as a means of addressing the large gap in risk perceptions. Finally, the conclusions are in section 5.

2   Background: Aspects of risk relevant to risk management by government

Risk is a complex, multi-faceted phenomenon. There is a large literature devoted to the issue, including the academic and professional journal, *Risk Analysis.*[10] In this context, it is necessary to be highly selective and to focus on matters that appear to be most relevant to risk management by government.

(a) Fear and risk

Fear is an important part of the way people characterize risks. Indeed, the essence of risk is some probability of *adverse* consequences for people. Fear can be both rational and irrational. Irrational fears are those that have no basis in objective reality. Rather they are the creation of our imagination. Irrational fears lead to irrational behaviour—this is the problem created by severe anxiety disorders[11] (Hall 1999: 44).

Humans are made fearful, even when the "cause" of such fears is patently irrational, because of our prodigious imaginative capacity, which stirs the amygdala and so creates fear and anxiety. Our imagination often enhances—and possibly greatly exaggerates—risky situations. Even very remote harms (in probabilistic terms) can seem to be both immediate and large. We can psychologically simulate disasters easily. (On the other hand, it appears that testosterone-poisoned teenaged males have too little imagination when it comes to dealing with risk situations involving driving, extreme sports, addictive drugs, and criminal activity.)

Research by neuroscientists shows that fear can be generated in the brain not only by direct experience but also by learning, hearsay, rumour, suggestion, word of mouth, subliminal suggestion. The amygdala is activated even when one hears about a fearful situation (Hall 1999: 70). Hall suggests that "fear, and its fellow traveler anxiety, in some ways represent a hard-wired alarm system in the brain in search of [or at least ready for] genuine life-threatening dangers" (1999: 45). He argues that physical dangers (e.g., large predators) have been replaced by "social predators and situations—the boss at work, the intolerant mate, the teacher, the bully." To this list we might add the dangers of the technological age: man-made carcinogens, computer failures that destroy a hard drive holding a huge amount of information central to one's work, teethers that are said to leach toxic chemicals and, of course, the risk of a nuclear "event."[12]

Fear generated by the perception of a risky situation cannot be so easily labelled as "irrational" for several reasons: (a) the degree of risk aversion varies from individual to individual; (b) there is no optimal degree of risk aversion—it is a matter of preference; and (c) citizens do not characterize risks simply in terms of the variance or probability (of death or injury)—at least several other attributes are relevant, as we shall see.

Human imagination is a double-edged sword. The negative side is our ability to imagine possibilities that are extremely remote or not even possible at all and to paint them in vivid colours with depth and shading so that they seem real.[13] Anxiety is caused by the negative anticipation of future events, a capability that is possessed by humans but apparently not by other animals. A prominent neuroscientist has said: "A rat can't worry about the stock market crashing. But we can" (quoted in Hall 1999: 45).

Real fear induces two primary atavistic responses in humans: fight or flight. Ancient programming tells us that spending time on analysis, gathering more information, and engaging in dialogue could be very hazardous to our health or even continued existence. Such programming was helpful for our ancestors living among sabre-toothed tigers and other plentiful, hungry carnivores but it is positively unhelpful in dealing with most of the "new risks" today (e.g., mad-cow disease, bovine growth hormone additions to feed, and scores of manmade carcinogens).[14]

(b)   *Disparities in the perception or characterization of risks*[15]

Policy analysts have long emphasized the importance of problem definition for policy analysis and the choice of policy actions by government. Part of the task of problem definition is determining whether there is a problem at all or, if there is a problem, whether it is of sufficient importance to merit analysis of alternative possible "solutions."

Risk management by government is often made very difficult by the fact that many risk issues are characterized so differently by citizens and experts. What is seen by experts as a tiny risk to which very few people are exposed and so unworthy of any government action may be seen by at least some citizens as a serious risk for which government should impose new regulations regardless of the cost. If these citizens are represented by a vocal interest group, government may respond to the citizens' fears and ignore the experts' advice.

At the outset of this section, a few preliminary observations are in order. First, the perception of risk is inherently subjective, even if different observers agree about all of the objective characteristics of a risky situation. Among the most important are the probabilities of various types of harms and the number of persons exposed to the hazard. But, other characteristics are often deemed important by lay-persons: for instance, the extent to which exposure to the hazard is voluntary and the extent to which the risk can be controlled. Paul Slovic (1992), the father of the analyses of risk perceptions, notes that "there is no such thing as 'real risk' or 'objective risk.'"[16] The way we view risks is a "social construction." People use different frameworks for the way they describe (characterize) and relate to risks. Second, in this context, the perception of a risk really refers to the utility or disutility related to the risky situation in question. Third, there is no optimal degree of risk aversion. A person's propensity to take or accept risks is essentially a "taste" variable. People have different tastes for risk as they do for all goods and services.

"Experts typically define risk in a narrow, technical way. The public has a richer, more complex view" (Chociolko 1995: 21). It is fairly common for experts to define risks very simply as the probability or likelihood that certain harm(s) will occur. Often, the focus is on the probability of death. A slightly more comprehensive characterization by experts usually includes the following attributes:

- types of harm that may occur;

- likelihood that each type of harm will occur;

- exposure to harm (i.e., how many people are subject to the risk);

- some description of the quality of the information relating to the first three variables.[17]

In the United States, the Presidential/Congressional Commission on Risk Assessment (1997) proposed the following questions to characterize risks in a much broader fashion than has been common by experts:

- Considering the hazard and the exposure, what is the nature and likelihood of the health risk?

- Which individuals or groups are at risk? Are some people more likely to be at risk than others?

- How severe are the anticipated adverse impacts or effects?

- Are the effects reversible?

- What scientific evidence supports the conclusions about risk? How strong is the evidence?

- What is uncertain about the nature or magnitude of the risk?

- What is the range of informed views about the nature and probability of the risk?

- How confident are the risk analysts about their predictions of risk?

- What other sources cause the same type of effects or risks?

- What contribution does the particular source make to the overall risk of this kind of effect in the affected community? To the overall health of the community?

- How is the risk distributed in relation to other risks to the community?

- Does the risk have impacts besides those on health or the environment, such as social or cultural consequences?

Citizens (collectively, if not individually) generally have a more complex characterization of risk. Much of this has been captured by Y.I. Vertzberger in what he calls "the texture of risk." The components as he describes them are as follows:

(1) *Risk transparency.* How ambiguous or well understood are the risky consequences of a decision? Debates among experts and policy advisors are likely to increase doubts among the decision-makers regarding whether the risks of a particular policy are really understood . . . [18]

(2) *Risk severity.* How serious and damaging are the perceived consequences of a decision or situation?

(3) *Risk certainty.* How certain is any particular adverse outcome to materialize? If risks cannot even be guessed at, the level of perceived risk will be much higher because of the possibility of surprise and the possible lack of resources to cope with whatever risk emerges . . .

(4) *Risk horizon.* How close in time are the adverse consequences? The closer in time they are, the more vivid and salient they will seem and the more weight they will be given. Distant negative consequences are underweighed and perceived as less likely to occur; they therefore have only a minor impact on decisions . . .

(5) *Risk complexity* . . . can be assessed using four criteria:

  (a) Measurability of risk, with risk dimensions being more elusive and difficult to assess the less quantifiable they are.

  (b) Variability of issue dimensions, that is, the range of issue-areas affected by risk dimensions (e.g., economic, military, political).

  (c) Multiplicity of time dimensions, that is, whether or not all risky effects are expected to occur within the same time frame (i.e., whether they are all short-term or long-term consequences, or both).

  (d) Interactivity of risk dimensions, that is, whether change in one risk dimension affects the level of risk in other dimensions, with the risk calculus becoming more complex with greater interaction among the risk dimensions.

(6) *Risk reversibility.* Are risky decisions reversible once they are made, and at what cost?

(7) *Risk controllability and containability.* Are the risks generated by the decisions controllable and containable? The answer matters even when risk decisions are irreversible.

(8) *Risk accountability.* Will decision-makers be held responsible by the public for adverse consequences? If so, what is the magnitude of the personal political cost that they will have to bear? "As a general rule, the more directly accountable a decision-maker is to the public, the more likely it is that public perceptions will receive consideration in priority setting" [reference omitted].

(Vertzberger 1998: 26–27)

But even this characterization of risks fails to capture some attributes that research has shown to be important to citizens. A very important one is the extent to which exposure to the risk is *involuntary*. In general, involuntary risks have a disutility up to 1000 times that of voluntary risks, e.g., mountain climbing, hang gliding, amateur automobile racing. Another is the extent to which citizens believe they can trust the estimates of the risk provided by government (rather than other actors, e.g., an interest group).

Slovic et al. (1987), in their factor analysis of citizens' risk perceptions, identified three dimensions: (a) dread risk (lack of controllability, threat, catastrophic potential, fatal, unfair distributional consequences); (b) unknown risk (risks seen as unknown, not perceivable, new, delayed negative consequences); and (c) scale (number of people exposed to the risk). Slovic concluded that there is hardly any systematic relation that seems to exist between the perceived risks of an activity or technology and its benefits.

(c) Is the gap the result of differences in framing?

"Persistent disagreements about risk appear to have their origin in different belief and value systems" (Vaughan and Seifert 1992: 120). These shape the way people define, weigh, and frame dimensions of risk. The framing of a risk issue (indeed, any issue) is how a problem is conceptualized and, therefore, how it is interpreted to a large extent.[19] A frame seeks to define what an issue is "really about." Frames are based on broadly shared beliefs and values and people use them in order "to give meaning, sense, and normative direction to their thinking and action in policy matters" (Schon and Rein 1994: viii). "Framing not only defines the issue, but it also suggests the solution" (Menashe and Siegel 1998: 310).[20]

Vaughan and Seifert (1992: 123) suggest that three ways in which risk problems are framed "particularly seem to intensify conflicts."

These are (a) the scientific or economic frame versus the equity and fairness frame; (b) risks to the population as a whole versus the frame in which the risk population is highlighted, particularly those who are the most vulnerable; and (c) the frame that focuses on potential gains versus the frame that focuses on potential losses (i.e., Kahneman and Tversky's prospect theory).

While experts often speak of statistical risk estimates for the population as a whole or for the entire population, citizens often frame the issue in terms of *personal* risk (including personal susceptibility). This often leads to a consideration of who in the community bears the risk and which are the most vulnerable persons (e.g., children). It has been argued that the public's apparent high degree of risk aversion for even minute amounts of a potential carcinogen is "associated with a normative expectation for a reference point of zero risk, and an overemphasis on certainty" (Vaughan and Seifert 1992: 130).

"When dissimilar frames are adopted, information, regardless of its quality, may do little to narrow differences because information compatible with one framework is judged to be of little use from another perspective" (Vaughan and Seifert 1992: 124). Yet one of the main tasks of risk communication[21] aimed at "closing the gap" is to get groups that have different frames "to see and understand the legitimacy of alternative ways of defining policy issues." This may involve negotiating a more widely shared perceptual framework (Vaughan and Seifert 1992: 131).

(d)   Other possible explanations

Experts commonly observe that citizens want and expect government to provide a risk-free or zero-risk world. A 1992 survey of 1,506 Canadians found that over 60 percent believed that "a risk-free environment is an attainable goal in Canada" (Strauss 1995: A1). Experts frequently point out that this goal is not attainable even in theory, let alone in practice. Zero risk is an illusion. The same survey found that women ranked all but one of the 38 hazards as riskier than men. In most cases, the difference was over ten percentage points.[22]

Experts tend to focus on saving lives (preventing pre-mature deaths) in general in the most cost-effective fashion.[23] On the other hand, citizens seem to want government to address the most fearful risks[24] of which they are aware. Citizens do not address risk issues in a synoptic fashion (as do many experts). Rather, they respond to information about those risks that come to their attention (often by the actions of an interest group). The way citizens deal with risk is an example of Lindblom's (1959) idea of policy-making as disjointed incrementalism.

Experts have more formal education in risk issues. They are used to the idea of trying to use reason and logic to address what in the first instance are visceral fears. At the same time, studies of expert judgment indicate that disagreement among experts is common and is often the result of legitimate differences in interests and perspectives (Chociolko 1995: 19). When dealing with risk, expert judgment, research shows, is subject to a number of biases: (a) unstated assumptions and mind-sets based on experience and conventional wisdom in their field; (b) structural biases, notably the way the problem is presented (or framed) and the organization and presentation of data; (c) motivational biases, notably one's ego or self interest; and (d) cognitive biases (overconfidence, anchoring, availability).[25]

Experts, to understand a risk, implicitly (if not explicitly) compare it to other risks. Comparisons are much easier if only few attributes are used and these attributes can be described in numerical terms.[26] It appears that most citizens instinctively translate information on a risk into personal or family terms. Deaths are not statistics on paper; rather they mean the agony of attending the funeral of a child or a friend or a neighbour. Thus they tend to "frame" risk issues differently than do experts.

Citizens feel little obligation to explain or defend their responses to various types of risk: "That's just the way I see it." Experts have to explain their assessments of risks and methods of reasoning. Efforts by officials to confront citizens outraged by a risk (or prospective risk) in the sense of asking them to justify highly expensive (and usually restrictive) actions by government in the face of minute risks to a few people is likely to increase citizens' frustration. With few exceptions, citizens seem to care little about the costs to society of reducing risks.

Moreover, we are living in an era in which purely subjective feelings have been given extraordinary respect. The cry of Descartes, "I think, therefore I am," has given way to "I feel very strongly about this, so nobody should question me on it." On the other hand, it has been suggested by a scientist that "there is unquestionably a tendency among scientists to ignore or minimize dangers growing out of scientific activity" (Rollin 1995: 70). Further, he suggests that "We lack the ability to predict everything that can possibly go wrong" (72). Murphy's Law is always with us.

(e) Nature of the gap

The gap between experts and citizens in the perception of risks appears to be of two types. The first gap is between experts' and citizens' estimation of the probability (or rank-ordering by probability) of a wide range of hazards. Research indicates that citizens usually overestimate rare causes of death and underestimate more common causes of death (see Slovic, Fischhoff and Lichtenstein 1979). When estimating the number of deaths each year from a collection of hazards, low frequencies were overestimated and high ones were underestimated (with a few exceptions). On the other hand, experts' judgments corresponded closely to statistical frequencies of death.

The second gap relates to what actions government should take (if any) to reduce risks. Some experts describe some of the federal government's actual policies—largely reflecting citizens' priorities—as "haphazard," "idiosyncratic," "inefficient," or characterized by both "paranoia and neglect." The pathologies associated with the federal government's risk-management policies are the subject of section 3.

Today, experts often characterize risk issues on more comprehensive terms (e.g., Presidential/Congressional Commission on Risk Assessment 1997) than they once did and many of the attributes they use are similar to those used by citizens. However, when providing policy advice, it appears that experts tend to focus on what they believe to be the more *objective* attributes of a risk, namely the type(s) of harm, the probability of each type, and the number of people exposed to the harms. In addition, they add what is necessarily a subjective element: an assessment of the quality of their estimates.

It *is* possible to distinguish the more objective characteristics of a hazard from its more subjective characteristics. The *meaning* of a hazard (or risky situation), even when each person agrees on the facts, can vary greatly across individuals. The meaning of a risk is what economists are trying to capture when they speak of the utility (or disutility) of a risk. That is why research indicates that citizens are particularly fearful of hazards that they perceive as being imposed upon them (involuntary risks), not controllable, have the possibility of being a catastrophe, and generated by new exotic technologies.

To summarize, there are notable differences in the way most experts or specialists talk about risk and the way citizens do so. A number of important differences are summarized in figure 1.

It appears that the gap between experts and citizens in the perception of the more subjective attributes is an important explanatory factor in some of the pathologies of government's management of risks.

3   What's wrong with risk management?
Routine pathologies

While the primary objective of this chapter is to propose ways to improve risk management, particularly risk regulation, by the federal government, the effectiveness of the remedies depend upon the quality of the diagnosis. This axiom applies as much to policy analysis as

Figure 1 Comparing the perceptions of experts and ordinary citizens about risk

Experts and Specialists	Ordinary Citizens
There is no such thing as zero risk or perfect safety.	I want to be perfectly safe. I expect there to be zero risk.
We live in a stochastic world—there are no certainties (except death).	I expect the world to be deterministic ("is or is not; no grey areas").
As a practical matter, we have to define "acceptable levels of risk" in making public policy.	The objective of public policy should be the safety of the public. Period.
Policy makers necessarily have to focus on "statistical deaths" since they consider risks in probabilistic terms.	Statistical deaths are an abstraction. It is specific people who die—they have a family and friends who care about them. Policy must recognize this fact.
In general, a death is a death but a person's age at death matters, so government should use loss of years of life expectancy as a measure of the harm created by a wide range of hazards.	When one person dies it matters. My child's death means the world to me. Accidental deaths ought to be prevented at all costs.
Useful comparisons of risk can be made across a wide variety of risks using only the number of deaths (or other standardized harms such as accidents or illnesses) and the probability that they will occur (per unit of time).	The most acceptable comparisons of different types of risks are (a) same type of risk at different times, (b) risks versus a well accepted standard, and (c) different estimates of the same risk.
Risks are seen as hazards of various kinds. Comparisons are instinctive in order to appreciate the hazard under study.	Risk is an outrage, particularly when it is involuntary, hard to detect, could result in catastrophic consequences, or attributable to new and exotic technologies.

to persons with an illness. Thus, the purpose of this section is to offer a diagnosis by describing the routine pathologies of the federal government's risk-management activities.

Pathology #1   Insufficient or poor economic analysis

Risk regulators in Canada rarely conduct a cost-benefit analysis[27] of proposed new regulations aimed at reducing risks.[28] Consider the following recent important example. The federal government devoted nine years to the study of the physical consequences of permitting the use of recombinant bovine growth hormone (rbST) for the purpose of increasing a cow's production of milk.[29] On January 14, 1999, Health Canada announced that it would not approve rbST for sale in Canada[30] even though the scientific panel found no risk to human safety through ingestion of products from rbST-injected animals (Royal College of Physicians and Surgeons of Canada 1999).[31] The rationale for rejection: rbST causes certain health problems in cows (although there was no suggestion that these are passed on and adversely affect humans).[32] The Department's statement (two pages) was notable for its brevity. None of the vast amount of work done by or for the Department assessing the risks of rbST involved a cost-benefit analysis. Yet, the whole point of using the hormone is to increase milk production—an economic benefit. If there is no harm to humans, surely it makes sense to ask if the social benefits (an increase in milk production of about 15 percent)[33] exceed the social costs (greater frequency of certain illnesses in cows; the costs of rbST itself; the costs of treatment for cows; etc.). The result is that Canadians have no idea of the (likely) opportunity cost of banning rbST.[34] How is the failure to use this tool of rationality (cost-benefit analysis) to be explained to our children?

More generally, the Federal Regulatory Policy of November 1995 spells out six "policy requirements" that all federal regulatory authorities must meet barring "exceptional circumstances," in which case they "must justify and document the exception" (Regulatory Affairs Directorate 1995). Efficiency is the subject of two requirements.[35] How can one assess the efficiency of new regulations without cost-benefit analysis or at least cost-effectiveness analysis? It appears that the federal government understands this point but fails to put it into practice.

Since 1986, Treasury Board policy has specified that a Regulatory Impact Analysis Statement be prepared for all new regulations and spelled out what it must contain (Stanbury 1992). For new "major"[36] regulations, departments and agencies are to prepare a cost-benefit analysis.[37] Yet research by Fazil Mihlar (1997: 11–13) on new regulations created in 1995 and 1996 indicates that this policy requirement is seldom met. While over 80 percent of the Regulatory Impact Analysis

Statements (or other analyses) identified who would benefit from the new regulation, only in 17 percent (1995) and 34 percent (1996) of the cases did the analyses quantify the benefits.[38] The cost was quantified in about the same percentage of analyses, 11 percent (1995) and 37 percent (1996). In only a small percentage of cases did the estimate of costs include the cost of compliance to industry or the public (11 percent in 1995; 25 percent in 1996) and in an even smaller percentage was the cost to government included (4 percent in 1995; 12 percent in 1996).

One reason why so few cost-benefit analysis are done for regulations aimed at reducing risks is that it would that require the analyst put an economic value on human life (i.e., the average value to society of premature deaths averted). This raises difficult issues for the government of the day and that probably explains Pathology #2.

Pathology #2   No guidance on the economic value of life

A large amount of risk regulation is aimed at preventing premature death. Therefore, to estimate the economic benefits of such regulation it is necessary to use an estimate for the economic value of life. The federal Treasury Board has failed to provide any guidance on this matter. In some of its studies of proposed new safety regulations in the 1980s, the Department of Transport used a value based on the costs of fatal accidents ($325,000 in 1985 dollars). This is not a satisfactory measure because it does not reflect people's willingness to pay to reduce the probability of a life-threatening risk. More recently, Transport Canada (1994: 43) states that it uses the figure of $1.5 million (1991 dollars) as the value of a fatality avoided in all modes of transport. This figure is said to be "based on a review of international studies and practices." Transport Canada proposes that a sensitivity analysis be performed using $500,000 and $2.5 million for the economic value of a life saved.

More generally, the federal government places no maximum on the amount it will require Canadians to pay for each statistical premature death averted by means of regulation or other form of government action.[39] The absence of a maximum on the "value of life" makes it easier for the government to adopt regulations that have an implicit cost far beyond estimates of the economic value of life derived from individual's observed willingness to pay for reductions in the risk of losing their own life (see Viscusi 1992). From a score of studies, Viscusi concludes that "most of the reasonable estimates of the value of life are clustered in the [US1990] $3 million to $7 million range" (1992: 73).[40] Note that the low point on Viscusi's range is over twice the figure used by Transport Canada (CDN$1.5 million in 1991 dollars).

One of the effects of not placing an upper bound on the cost of lives saved by regulation is that government regulators adopt some regulations that have a very high cost indeed. Consider the following examples:[41] Viscusi's (1992: 264) review of 21 proposed federal regulations in the United States in the period form 1980 to 1989 found that the implicit cost per life saved exceeded $100 million in 12 cases; four of these regulations were adopted. Another compilation of health and safety regulations, in the *Regulation Program of the United States Government, 1991/92,* found that the implicit cost of 14 of 53 regulations created between 1967 and 1991 exceeded $50 million per life saved. Hahn (1996b) reviewed 37 health, safety, and environmental regulations created by the American government between 1984 and mid-1995. The implicit cost per life saved exceeded $100 million for eight regulations. Hahn (1996) and others suggest that a larger fraction of *recent* risk reduction regulations in the United States have imposed costs on society of over $100 million per premature death averted.

The principal benefit of using a consistent quantitative measure for the economic value of a premature death averted by government initiatives that reduce risks is to achieve efficiency in the total portfolio of regulatory and other programs whose objective is to reduce the number of deaths.[42] In practical terms, it seems reasonable to use a figure of (say) $10 million for the general *limit* on the costs mandated by government to save a statistical life. Ministers would be free to override this limit provided they gave a reasoned explanation for doing so.[43] (Of course, it is very difficult to get cabinet ministers to reduce the vast amount of discretion they have.)

Pathology #3   *Idiosyncratic selection of risks for government action*

Government targeting of risks for regulation or other action seems idiosyncratic[44] or "haphazard," [45] and is undoubtedly inefficient in terms of the number of lives saved for the current level of resources used to reduce risks to human health and safety. It must be understood, however, that the ways in which ordinary citizens characterize and perceive risks makes this statement of little import to them. The difference in the way expert policy analysts and citizens perceive risk has been discussed in section 2 above.

Stephen Breyer (1993) describes this pathology as "random agenda selection." He notes that often much regulatory effort is focused on what experts or objective information suggests is a low risk or a hazard with modest harm, usually the former. Also government risk agendas are often driven by pressure from interest groups (often reinforced by extensive coverage in the media). More important risks are ignored or have a much lower priority. It appears that cancer risks are over emphasized in the United States.[46] There has been a mismatch between funding priorities (set by Congress) and those of particular agencies.

Both in Canada and in the United States, it is estimated that cigarettes cause 30 percent of all avoidable deaths from cancer, while 2 percent to 3 percent of all cancers are associated with environment pollution, and 3 percent to 6 percent associated with radiation. Yet a very great deal of regulation focuses on cancers caused by pollution.[47] The whole vastly expensive panoply of environmental regulations might prevent one-quarter of one percent of cancer deaths.[48]

The billions of dollars spent on health and safety regulation or risk regulation more generally have almost nothing to do with the leading causes of death. Heart disease, the number-one cause of death, carries off eight times as many Canadians as do all types of accidents. Yet most accidents occur in contexts that are unregulated or only lightly regulated, i.e., in one's house. The most intensive forms of health and safety regulation occur in areas where the number of lives lost are small relative to the other causes of death.

Pathology #3 takes several forms. I consider three. First, there are many government interventions (e.g., risk-reduction regulation) that focus on risks that, in fact, currently result in relatively *few* deaths each year.[49] (Note that about 228,000 Canadians died in 1999.) Thus the potential gains from additional regulation are not large, even if the intervention is perfectly successful. For example, about 5,000 women die from breast cancer each year but only about 40 die in commercial air travel accidents (Statistics Canada 1996). Thus a reduction of one percent in the deaths due to breast cancer will save more lives than a 100 percent reduction in deaths due to commercial air travel. *A priori*, does it make sense to add more air-travel safety regulations? Would it not be better to apply the additional resources to a much "richer" target like breast cancer?

An enormous amount of government regulation in Canada is devoted to reducing risks associated with transportation—from airlines[50] to motor vehicles to railways to maritime traffic (including small pleasure craft). Such regulation appears to have been successful in that, despite our vast amount of travel in Canada, only about 1.7 percent of all deaths are attributed to transport-related accidents (3,425 in 1994). Further, if accidents involving motor vehicles are excluded, only 237 people died in accidents in all other modes of transport in 1994.

To use a mining metaphor, transport safety regulators, particularly those not dealing with motor vehicle and highway safety, are continuing to dig in mines that are—frankly—almost played out. In 1997, for example, only 107 people died in railroad accidents in Canada, 76 in aviation accidents, 24 in water-related accidents and 3,064 in road-related accidents.[51] There is very little additional gold to be found in the sense of more lives to be saved aside from road-related accidents—

compared to other areas. But, even the number of road-related deaths has been declining. The estimate for 1998 (2,672) is only 40 percent of the number of road-related deaths 25 years ago when motor-vehicle traffic was one-half the level of 1998.[52] Thus, the death rate for road accidents in Canada is now far lower than what it was 25 years ago.

There would appear, then, to be a strong case against further government action unless there is clear evidence that the number of deaths is increasing much faster than the population.[53] Note that the present low number of deaths in a specific area may be partly due to the existing stock of government regulation or other programs designed to reduce risks. The idea is not to eliminate existing risk-reduction regulations but to avoid adding inefficient new ones. The point is that zero deaths is the obvious limit on risk-reduction activities. Further, when the number (or the rate) is close to zero, it is unlikely that further government actions to reduce fatalities will be justified in terms of benefit-cost analysis. Over the past two decades, an average of 2.3 persons died each year in tug-and-barge accidents. Yet, the federal government persists in making more regulations to improve safety—and do so without doing a cost-benefit analysis (see Stanbury 2000).

Second, the federal government in Canada focuses extensive resources on some risks while it virtually ignores other risks—even though the number of deaths associated with the risks to which it pays less attention is far greater.[54] Even casual observation will confirm Canadians do not, in fact, express the same concern in rhetorical and tangible ways about all causes of death. A most obvious current example is the reaction to two diseases: AIDS[55] and breast cancer.[56] Breast-cancer activists know that the millions of dollars directed into AIDS research by governments in industrialized countries eventually resulted in not one but two scientists claiming to have found the cause. In 1992, Health Canada pledged $25 million over five years to the Breast Cancer Initiative. At the same time, it allocated $203.5 million for a five-year national AIDS strategy.[57] And yet, since 1982, just over 9,500 Canadians have died of AIDS,[58] while more than 60,000 died of breast cancer (Mallet 1996: D3). In 1994, 1,628 people died of AIDS[59] or about one-third the number who died of breast cancer.[60]

The disparity in the support for research into breast cancer and AIDS research continues. On May 28, 1998, the federal Minister of Health announced that $42.2 million would be spent on AIDS research annually with no requirement that the program be reviewed for the renewal of the funds (Canadian Press Newswire May 28, 1998). On June 19, 1998, the federal Minister of Health announced that $45 million would be spent on breast-cancer research over the next five years (including $10 million by the Medical Research Council)—an increase from $25 million over the previous five years. No wonder that Reform MP Grant Hill is quoted as saying: "I was shocked when I came to Ottawa to discover that the government has no objective formula to decide which diseases will get what proportion of their health budget. Apparently, they just give the most money to whoever shouts the loudest" (*Alberta Report*, June 8, 1998).[61]

The third form of Pathology #3 consists of government interventions that may have a moderate (or high) cost per statistical life saved (premature death averted) but have a very high cost per additional *year* of life saved. This occurs when we spend the same amount to save the life of a person over age 65 as we do for a teenager. Obviously, the latter has many more years to live.

Before looking at the details, it is useful to look at the big picture. The data for 1994 indicate that at the time of their death 70 percent of men and 81 percent of women in Canada were age 65 or older.[62] At the other end of the distribution, only 5.62 percent of males and 2.56 percent of females died before they reach the age of 30. Thus, the gains in number of lives saved is fairly modest (n = 10,271), but the number of additional years of life would be considerable if they live a "normal life span," i.e., about 73 for men and 79 for women.

Among the ten leading causes of potential years of life lost (PYLL) before age 75 in Canada in 1993,[63] only one (motor-vehicle accidents) is the object of intensive risk regulation though it ranks number 3 for men and number 4 for women (Wilkins 1995). This is because it is the leading cause of death among young males (Wilkins 1995). The three leading causes of PYLL among males were ischaemic heart disease (13 percent of total PYLL), suicide (9 percent) and motor-vehicle accidents (9 percent). For women, the leading causes of PYLL were breast cancer (9 percent), lung cancer (7 percent) and ischaemic heart disease (7 percent).[64] If the central goal of a risk-reduction strategy is to reduce the number of years of life lost due to premature death, then the focus of such strategies should be on (a) the absolute number of years of life now lost to various causes, and (b) the cost to society of saving each additional year of life.

It should be noted that Canada, unlike the United States, has never tried to rank order, even roughly, its priorities for government actions aimed at reducing risks to human health and safety.[65] The failure to do so is symptomatic of the "silo management" approach to risk reduction policy.

Pathology #4 *"Silo management"*

Risk-reduction activities (notably by means of regulation) of the federal government are conducted within a host of different departments or agencies essentially independent of each other. Risk regulators operate in a system that effectively encourages "institutional myopia" in the sense that their mandate is to focus on a comparatively narrow range of problems and eliminate or reduce them to insignificance. The big risk regulators (e.g., Transport Canada, Health Canada,[66] Agriculture Canada, Environment Canada) each may deal with a range of types of risks but none is forced to look outside its own relatively narrow domain. Thus, officials responsible for maritime safety are very unlikely to tell their minister that it would be better to not add more safety regulations in their area because the "return" would be much lower than it would be by investing society's scarce resources elsewhere.

Of course, it is desirable to exploit Adam Smith's principles of specialization and division of labour. Given the exotic nature of some of the risks addressed by government, specialization is absolutely necessary. The problem is that we have in Canada too much of a good thing. The result is that government forces citizens to invest in risk reduction activities beyond the point where the additional benefits exceed the additional costs. (One reason for this may be the fact that the federal government does not have a *general* policy for risk reduction or risk management. It has scores of both—and most are very difficult to find.)

Stephen Breyer (1993) describes this pathology as "Tunnel-Vision (or the last 10 percent)." It involves the single-minded pursuit of a single goal that goes too far. Policy-makers fail to recognize diminishing returns within a department and fail to consider other risks across government ("silo thinking"). Removing the last 10 percent of harm can be hugely expensive (because the function is non-linear).

Efforts to regulate the transportation of dangerous goods by the federal Department of Transport provide a good example of "silo management." The average number of reportable accidents involving dangerous goods declined from an average of 520 in the period from 1987 to 1989 to 311 in the period from 1994 to 1996.[67] The average number of *deaths* due to dangerous goods for the same periods fell from three to 0.33. Yet the Department states that the number of such deaths "obviously remain a cause for concern." The stated goal is "to reduce, and possibly eliminate all potential danger through activities such as improving standards related to road cargo tanks, rail tank cars and intermodal containers."[68]

The key point is that there is no *centralized* effort by the federal government in Canada or the United States to identify and measure the costs and benefits of reducing a wide variety of risks to life and limb and to rank priorities given scarce resources (Sub-Committee on Regulations and Competitiveness 1993).[69] Each proposal to reduce risks appears to be considered on its own merits (as noted above) against department-specific criteria that are rarely in the public domain (the Health Protection Branch is an exception). The autonomy of individual departments is increased because the federal government refuses to provide a reference-point value of life above which the minister responsible would have to explain publicly why it makes sense to spend far more than the reference value to save lives using this particular new regulation.

The federal government does have a regulatory policy (see Regulatory Affairs Directorate 1995) but it is very general and focuses on regulations (subordinate legislation) rather than regulation as a governing instrument.[70] The federal government has no general risk reduction policy that is overseen by a central agency. Nor, does it have a standardized risk-management protocol[71] for dealing with crisis situations or normal ones. The present situation could be likened to handling government expenditures (a) without a central budget to control expenditures at both the departmental and government-wide level and (b) not having a Treasury Board to assess, monitor, and control expenditure plans. Yet, risk regulation alone certainly imposes huge costs on society if not on government itself.[72]

The issue here is the same raised by a number of students of government regulation generally when they have advocated that the federal government adopt a "regulatory budget" (see Litan and Nordhaus 1983; Stanbury 1992: chap. 8). Such a budget brings an element of "horizontality" to what is now a host of separate "silos." [73] Also, a "risk-reduction budget" would force government to incorporate into its decision-making, and to economize on, the private-sector costs of reducing risks per government action, rather than considering only the government's administrative costs, which are only a small fraction of the former.

Silo management can mean that even if additional risk reduction in area X meets the $B > C$ test, the net benefits of a comparable investment in area Y may yield far higher benefits. Effective risk-management techniques developed in department A may not be transferred to other departments that employ less effective ones. Further, it is likely that specialists in area D can benefit from the perspective of those with a reasonable level of knowledge of risk issues in areas E, F, G, H, I and so on.

Along the lines of this pathology, Breyer (1993) notes that there are in the United States a variety of "inconsistencies" within and among both programs and agencies that focus on risks:

- they use different methods of estimating risks of death;

- they apply different economic values of life in doing risk management;

- agencies ignore interdependencies among risk regulation programs; and

- regulation of small risks can cause more harm to health than is prevented (atrogenic regulation) and the "income effect" of regulation is ignored.

All of these can fairly be attributed to the problem of "silo management."

Pathology #5   *Government actions are too often based on the preferences of the most fearful*

A major policy (and ethical) problem arises when government action to deal with risk is based on the risk preferences of the most fearful in society.[74] Stephen Strauss, a reporter for the *Globe and Mail* has suggested: "People are not reasoning machines, they are fearing machines and, when there's a scare, politicians and scientists better tremble" (quoted in Powell and Leiss 1997: 21). (Recall the discussion in section 2[a] above.)

It must be emphasized again that public policy toward risks does not exhibit any consistent pattern in the sense of (a) focusing on larger risks, (b) focusing on risks that generate large numbers of deaths, (c) focusing on risks where the difference between the benefits and costs of action is the greatest. I suggest that to the extent government actions focus on very remote risks, where only a minute percentage of the population is expected to benefit and where the costs per life saved are huge, it is reasonable to describe such actions as serving the interests of the most fearful in society.

Government actions to deal with risks based on the preferences of the most fearful is largely the result of interest groups that are able to create and then exploit the public's fear for their own organizational purposes, e.g., to obtain publicity in the news media or to raise money.[75] In this effort, groups are aided by the news media's strong preference for "bad news" stories. It is front-page news when a terrorist threatens to blow up a single airline flight. It is not news if several million people around the world arrive safely from many thousands of flights every day for months on end. In general, the federal government has made little effort to engage in a risk communication process that "counters" the claims of interest groups with facts, comparison of risks, and explanations of the trade-offs involved (see Powell and Leiss 1997).

To a surprising degree, a few zealots drive the activities of interest groups.[76] Their fears (which may be highly idiosyncratic) can shape public policy by creating fears in others through the adroit use of the media (see Fumento 1999). One strategy is to focus on (new) absolute risks and ignore the fact that relative to other more familiar risks, the risk is low. Interest groups in this context often focus on a single issue and do not want to recognize the need for trade-offs among various types of risks. Nor do they want to make trade-offs between additional costs to society and additional benefits of risk reduction.

Efforts to regulate risks are driven by crises and disasters that get extensive coverage in the news media. In such crises, the abstract is made real, identifiable individuals die (or their life is threatened), latent fears and insecurities are tapped, and news coverage generates I-told-you-so responses. "Disasters" (such as the crash of TWA flight 800 off Long Island on July 17, 1996) have both advantages and disadvantages in influencing public policy concerning risk reduction:

- they get people's attention and create a receptive audience;

- they may induce panic "solutions" that may be very costly to society;

- they often prompt a more general examination of the problem though this may occur *after* government has taken some action;

- they may focus limited political energy on what is, in fact, a less significant risk when one looks at the larger picture.

In some cases, a "crisis" can be "manufactured" by interest groups, e.g., the "Alar" pesticide scare in 1989 was the creation of the Natural Resources Defense Council. It was helped by actress Meryl Streep, who testified before a United States congressional committee and received extensive coverage in the media. Greenpeace made a great effort to pressure governments in Europe and North America into banning the use of phthalates as a softener in children's toys and teethers made of PVC (see Stanbury et al. 2000).

What are the consequences of making public policy based on the preferences of the most fearful? First, society (rather than simply the most fearful) pays a large risk premium (often to reduce very tiny probabilities of death to very few people).[77] Second, there is a redistribution of income from the less to the more fearful. Unlike private insurance, the redistribution resulting from government regulation is involuntary (all buyers have to pay higher prices for the regulated product, not just the most fearful). Third, the freedom of individuals is reduced, perhaps needlessly. This is true where the provision of more or better information by government would permit individuals to act to reduce the risks they face in such a way as to maximize their utility. Fourth, for any given size of social budget for reducing risks, devoting more resources to the risks most feared by the most fearful citizens means that fewer lives can be saved than could be if amounts in the budget were reallocated on the basis of saving lives at least cost first, then gradually working one's way up the list to more costly actions (Breyer 1993; Stanbury 1992).

Pathology #6   One-size-fits-all types of government action

To date, Canada's public policy toward risks (such as it is) has suffered from the one-size-fits-all syndrome. Put another way, we have "over socialized" many risks when it was possible and practicable to adopt strategies that would help individuals (families) to bear the amount (types) of risk that maximizes *their* utility. Consider the following example. The province of British Columbia is considering imposing a "thrill tax" of 0.5 percent on a wide range of adventure-sport products and services including ski-lift tickets. The expected revenue of $2 million per year is to help pay for the rising costs of rescuing errant adventurers (Cheney 1999: A1). In 1989/1990 there were 350 rescues; in 1994/1995 there were 684. By 2000, the number may hit 1400. In addition, a fine of $500 might be imposed on persons who ski or snowboard in prohibited areas. It should be noted that British Columbia's 77 search-and-rescue teams are staffed largely by volunteers. The Attorney General said that the proposal was based on the user-pay idea.

My colleague Paul Kedrovsky (1999) has described the proposed tax as a "wonky bit of policy making." Why? "Instead of making the people who need to be rescued pay, [the Attorney General] proposes making everyone pay." He notes that while the tax would bring in about $1000 per rescue, the estimated cost (based on American figures) is in the range of $8,000 to $12,000 per "hapless hiker—considerably more if the hiker is seriously injured." Kedrovsky points out the obvious problem of moral hazard[78] as well as the unfairness of taxing the vast majority of persons who never need to be rescued. Why not spend a modest amount of government money advertising the fact that a "rescued-person pays" policy is in force and that the average estimated cost is $10,000. Further, persons who ski or hike in prohibited areas will pay a civil monetary penalty equal to the actual cost of the rescue, i.e., they will pay double. Apparently, hikers in the Grand Canyon already "face the sobering thought that they will be financially responsible for their own rescue" (*National Post* editorial, March 9, 1999: A19).[79]

The one-size-fits-all approach to risk regulation is undesirable for several reasons. (1) It can result in the moral hazard problem as noted in the example above and so may not deter the behaviour of those most prone to take risks. (2) It results in a misallocation of scarce resources. (3) It results in unfairness: people are forced to buy insurance for amounts far above the actuarial value of the risks to which they are exposed.

The case for allowing the greatest (practical) degree of individuation in the response to risks is based on two main propositions: (a) the utility of the same objectively defined risk varies greatly across individuals and (b) greater individuation in responding to risks is often both more efficient and respectful of individuals' freedom. Exposure to specific hazards varies greatly: non-skiers do not bear the risk from skiing; people who live in small cities with no heavy industry do not breathe in the harmful substances in smog. Individuals can reduce the risks to which they are exposed, e.g., they can drive a larger, heavier car (at the expense of higher fuel consumption) and practise defensive driving. They can avoid travelling with a "testosterone-poisoned" young male. They can avoid "extreme sports" and stay within the designated areas on ski hills. Recently two teenaged female snow-boarders were killed when they went into an area clearly marked out of bounds (see Hume 2000).

People often believe that the risks to the category do *not* apply to them. This may be true in the sense that the individual can or does take actions that reduce the odds for him, e.g., an 18-year-old male can (a) drive less, (b) drive more carefully, (c) limit driving at night, (d) drive a larger and heavier car, (e) never drink and drive, or (f) let his girl-friend do half the driving. All of these reduce the risk that *this* person will be involved in a fatal auto accident, even though he cannot change his sex or age.

The strategies governments can use to facilitate beneficial individuated responses to risks are described in section 4 below.

Pathology #7   *Potential misuse of the precautionary principle*

Here I address a pathology in the making, one that—if environmental and other activists get their way—will have large adverse effects on the well-being of Canadians.

In about two decades, the precautionary principle has come to have a major influence on public policy, partly because it so evocatively links us to the "folk wisdom" embedded in the aphorisms "It is better to be safe than sorry" and "An ounce of prevention is worth more than a pound of cure."

There are numerous versions of the precautionary principle.[80] In general terms, they state that where an activity raises the threat of harm to the environment or human health, precautionary measures should be taken even if certain cause-and-effect relationships are not established scientifically. For example, Principle 15 of the Rio Declaration of 1992 (signed by Canada) is that "where there are threats of serious or irreversible damage, lack of full scientific certainty shall not be used as a reason for postponing cost-effective measures to prevent environmental degradation."

VanderZwaag (1996) notes that Canada has shown support for the precautionary principle in a number of policy actions: Canada has signed international agreements that incorporate some version of the precautionary principle; the federal government adopted "reverse listing" approach in the Pest Control Products Act; pollution-control provisions in the Fisheries Act are consistent with the precautionary principle; it can be found in the 1993 Comprehensive Air Quality Management Framework for Canada and in the growing number of statutes that embrace sustainable development (of which the precautionary principle is a subsidiary principle).

One of the 13 "guiding principles" in the development of the federal government's health-protection legislation is to "inscribe in law the principle that Health Canada should take remedial action in cases where there is evidence of a potential health risk to Canadians, even though the risk cannot be proven or measured with certainty" (Health Canada 1999b: 1). This glittering generality begs a few hard questions: How much evidence? Of what kind? How great a health risk? To how many Canadians? Known with what degree of certainty? At what cost? How could the action be reversed if the perceived danger proves to be far less than initially believed? In summary terms, this looks like an excellent example of the misuse of the precautionary principle. Even worse, it is to be embedded in law.

Steven Milloy argues: "The precautionary principle is now simply an excuse, rather than a reason to take action against politically unpopular technologies, chemicals and products" (Milloy 2000: C7). He notes that Greenpeace insists that the use of the principle should not rely on a risk assessment, the scientific process for measuring potential harms. The ADM Working Group on Risk Management (2000: 5) indicates that the precautionary principle is one of the four common elements in the federal government's framework of public risk management. This could be a serious problem.

Use of the precautionary principle makes a great deal of sense in dealing with risky situations characterized by large potential harms that are *also* irreversible (or at least very difficult, costly or slow to remedy or reverse). Note that sometimes even "catastrophic" harms are reversible with the application of sufficient resources (loved ones cannot be replaced, of course). Irreversibility implies not only can the *status quo ante* not be achieved but that the harm is of a very serious nature, i.e., there are no even reasonably close substitutes. Also, the precautionary principle encourages citizens and policy makers to anticipate the possible adverse consequences of new technologies, substances, production processes, and so on. It may be true that the costs of preventing harm may be far less than remediation after the harm has come to pass but this is not always the case. Further, using the precautionary principle as a general frame may well help society to deal better with changes where the potential benefits are large and nearly immediate while the adverse effects are subtle, delayed, and possibly imposed on the next generation.

The rub comes when the precautionary principle is applied on a broad basis, i.e., far beyond the few situations where there are even small risks of large potential harms that are also irreversible. Widespread adoption of the precautionary principle would put the onus on the proponents of, say, a new technology (particularly one expected to harm the environment) to prove that it is "safe" (so-called reverse-onus approach). Theoretically, it is impossible to prove that an action will cause no harm. Also, there is, in reality, no such thing as zero risk or perfect safety.[81] The *status quo* is not risk free—it is just that the risks are more familiar (or people are not aware of many risks).

According to Marlo Lewis the "fatal flaw" in the precautionary principle is its "complete one-sidedness." He continues, "Environmentalists demand assurances of no harm only with respect to actions that government might regulate, never with respect to government regulation itself. But government intervention often boomerangs, creating the very risks precautionists deem intolerable" (Lewis 1997). Elizabeth Whelan argues that widespread application of the precautionary principle is undesirable for several reasons.

> First, it always assumes worst-case scenarios. Second, it distracts consumers and policy makers alike from the known and proven threats to human health. And third, it assumes no health detriment from the proposed regulations and restrictions. By that I mean that the Precautionary Principle overlooks the possibility that real public health risks can be associated with eliminating minuscule, hypothetical risks. As an ancient philosopher said, "It is a serious disease to worry over what has not occurred. (Whelan 1996: 4)

Of course, environmental regulation entails physical risks of its own, including perverse side effects that undermine the intended benefits of the regulation. Alternatives to regulated activities can produce unanticipated physical risks.[82] Similarly, regulating a substance may result in the loss of the substantial benefits for public health or the environment that the substance provided. Risks of remediation are a third set of physical risks of environmental regulation that Cross identifies.

Finally, two of the proponents of the precautionary principle note that it "offers no guidance as to what precautionary measures should be taken ... [or] how many resources should be committed or which adverse outcomes are the most important" (Costanza and Cornwell 1992: 3). In the extreme application, all actions that pose risks for society are banned until the proponents can prove that they are "safe."

Pathology #8   Poor risk communication

As noted earlier, risk management is a broad term and it usually includes the following components: risk analysis (the identification, description, and measurement of risks); risk assessment (consideration of whether government should intervene, an examination of the options that are likely to be effective and politically feasible), and risk communication.

The United States National Research Council (1989) defined risk communication as the "interactive process of exchange of information and opinion among individuals, groups and institutions concerning a risk or potential risk to human health or the environment." After a review of several authors' definitions, Gutteling and Wiegman define risk communication as "the systematic planning of information transfer, based on scientific research, to prevent, solve or mitigate the risk problem with adjusted and customized information (risk messages) for specific target groups" (1996: 42). They also emphasize that risk communication, is "a social process in which different types of communication (i.e., one-way, two-sided, or multi-sided dialogues) will be applied depending on the circumstances and the phase of the planning process" (1996: 42–43).

A broader and, I believe, more useful definition is given by Powell and Leiss. They describe risk communication as "the process of exchanges about how best to assess and manage risks among academics, regulatory practitioners, interest groups, and the general public" (1997: 33). They go on to say that "exchanges can mean anything from a presentation of relatively straightforward information to arguments over contested data and interpretations, to sincere or disingenuous concern, to what is in the eyes of some just plain misinformation (inadvertently misleading data) or disinformation (deliberately misleading data)" (Powell and Leiss, 1997: 33–34).

Powell and Leiss have examined in detail a number of major risk controversies in Canada. They were critical of the federal government's risk communication efforts.

(1) In the case of "mad-cow disease," "leadership by abdication may be the Canadian way but, given both the public discussion of BSE [bovine spongiform encephalopathy] to date and the newest scientific findings, such a strategy must be regarded as irresponsible and archaic" (Powell and Leiss 1997: 22).

(2) On the dioxin issue:

> In Canada, so far as one can tell, those in government appear to believe that, in cases (like dioxins) where they throw huge amounts

of resources at scientific research and risk assessment programs, the *meaning* of the results of those efforts will somehow be diffused serendipitously throughout the public mind ... those in government who are in charge of environmental and health protection programs simply do not believe that constructing an effective risk communications dialogue with the public is part of their responsibilities. (Powell and Leiss 1997: 67).[83]

Referring to the Minister of the Environment's speech when tabling the new Canadian Environmental Protection Act in December 1996, Powell and Leiss continue, "the most recent Canadian federal government actions [were] pointless and indeed self-defeating" (1997: 72).

(3) With respect to the VTEC family of toxins generated by *E. coli* bacteria often found in hamburgers, regulatory agencies in the United States have been active participants in the evolving debate over changes in policy but, "once again, Canadian authorities are largely quiet" (1997: 98). The Auditor General (1999: ch. 15) has recently criticized the Canadian Food Inspection Agency's handling of one of the largest outbreaks of food-borne disease in Canada in 1998.

(4) "Health Canada engaged in no risk communications on rbST [bovine growth hormone], failed to explain risk assessment assumptions (let alone the entire risk assessment process), and utterly failed to take responsibility on the issue of rbST approval" (Powell and Leiss 1997: 148). It also failed to recognize that a variety of socioeconomic concerns surround the decision on rbST and not just the scientific issues that Health Canada had insisted be the sole basis of decision making.

(5) "It is Health Canada policy [in 1992] not to issue press releases on any product decisions; it is up to the companies to do so" (Powell and Leiss 1997: 148). Note that Health Canada did issue a brief news release announcing its decision on rbST on January 14, 1999.

(6) PCBs appear to share with dioxins the "dubious distinction of being stigmatized substances." The federal government provided no publicly understandable authoritative information to supplement the diet of stories in the news media about PCB-related incidents. "For more than two decades, neither Environment Canada nor Health Canada, the two regulatory agencies responsible for the risk assessment of PCBs, made a concerted attempt to challenge the characterization of PCBs in media stories as "cancer-causing" or to communicate the fact that at current levels of exposure, most people are very unlikely to be affected adversely by these compounds" (Powell and Leiss 1997: 195).[84]

Woody Allen once said: "Sixty per cent of life is just showing up." Federal departments and agencies—with few exceptions—have not learned this lesson when it comes to risk communication. It usually leaves the field to interest groups, individual activists, newspaper editorials of various types, junk science, and the usually defensive utterances of those businesses whose activities are under attack.

4 Prescription: Proposals for improving risk management

Having offered my diagnosis of what is wrong with the federal government's management of risk, I turn now to my prescription to remedy the pathologies identified in section 3. The federal government's risk-management policies need to be modified in several major ways.

Remedy #1 Take a longer-run perspective

The federal government needs to take a *longer-run* perspective. This means thinking in terms of a decade or more, not just until the next election.[85] This will involve, among other things, developing better co-ordination across government departments and agencies, perhaps through "horizontal mechanisms" (see Remedy #2 below). The government will have to recognize the role of emotion, fear, and possibly distorted perceptions play in political pressures on government (notably politicians) and modify their risk-management efforts accordingly. This means putting risk communication at the centre of its efforts (see Remedy #8 below). For this change to be put into practice, government will need to educate all of its regulators (including experts and scientists) on importance of risk communication.

Like any other major change, better risk management will require leadership by cabinet ministers—explaining, educating, exhorting, and making the institutional changes necessary. These will include ensuring that more and better analysis is done before committing the government to action (see Remedy #4 below) and routinely making more information about its risk management activities available to the public (see Remedy #3 below).

Better risk communications (Remedy #8 below) will include efforts by political leaders to encourage citizens to reflect upon the hard choices embodied in public policy—it is their lives and their resources and most of these choices involve *value* judgments. It will also require changing the future of risk regulation in Canada. The regulation of risk has expanded greatly in the past two decades in the name of saving lives and reducing the damage of accidents and illness although it appears that a large number of resources is being devoted to slight or even quite remote dangers while much more substantial and well-documented risks are all but ignored.

Political leadership (aside from that which consists of echoing the latest public opinion polls) is always in short supply. Innovations in public policy are usually seen as highly risky in political terms. Politicians tend to be quite risk averse when they believe that their future may be adversely affected by the inevitable objections to change.

Remedy #2   Create "horizontal mechanisms"

The federal government needs to make a number of changes to combat the problems flowing from the pathologies of "silo management" and so increase the "horizontality" of its policies relating to risk. "Silo management" amounts to excessive reliance on specialization and division of labour. Too much of a good thing can produce negative consequences and has done so in the case of risk management. Some types of risks are regulated beyond diminishing returns while other, greater, risks are (virtually) ignored (recall Pathology #4 in section 3 above).

Unlike other major areas of government intervention, the federal government has no *general* policy aimed at creating coherence among its risk-management activities. This defect must be remedied. To begin with, it is essential that the general policy statement specify the objectives of the government's risk-management efforts. These can be made more operational by spelling out the criteria to be applied to specific decisions. Here Fraiberg and Trebilcock (1998) have some useful suggestions. In general, government should adopt four cardinal rules in risk-management decision-making:[86] (a) maximize expected value, i.e., expected net benefits or social benefits minus social costs, both discounted to present value; (b) avoid catastrophes (i.e., apply the precautionary principle to risks involving very large amounts of harm or large harms that are also irreversible); (c) dismiss extremely remote possibilities, i.e., those that are less than one in one million; and (d) adopt equitable regulations, i.e., even those that fail to meet criterion (a) if they prevent inequitable treatment of certain groups. The general policy statement should spell out the following:

(1) the standardized risk assessment procedures (protocol) to be used by all departments/agencies;[87]

(2) the economic value of life to be used in cost-benefit analyses (CBAs);

(3) the discount rate to be used in CBAs or cost-effectiveness analyses;

(4) risk levels above which government will take action and below which it will not.

Items (2) and (4) are bound to be highly controversial. As I have discussed, the case for an "official" value of economic life above, I shall concentrate on the last item. In the United Kingdom, the Health and

Safety Executive (established in 1974) has proposed the following dividing lines for policy action in relation to risks.

(1) The government *will* act to reduce risks where (a) the annual risk of death for workers is greater than 1 in 1000, and (b) where the annual risk for members of the public that is imposed on them in the wider interest of society exceeds 1 in 10,000.

(2) In general, the government *will not* act where the annual risk of death for individual members of the public (including workers) is less than 1 in 1 million (see McQuaid and Le Guen 1998: 30).

I do not suggest that these are the right levels of risk for the two thresholds. Rather, I wish to encourage ministers, public servants, and citizens to engage in a debate that will derive appropriate probabilities.

Further, the general (i.e., government-wide) policy should specify (a) that regulatory agencies are to make use of the best available scientific information in conducting risk assessments and (b) that, when scientific knowledge about risk is imperfect (and it usually is), agencies are to employ probabilistic methods of uncertainty analyses.[88] Also, the policy should indicate the conditions under which the precautionary principle should be applied (preferably not beyond situations in which, although there may be a very low probability of harm, the potential harm is both huge and *irreversible*).

In general, similar techniques should be applied to risk management as have been applied to traditional expenditure programs by the Treasury Board, cabinet committees and sub-committees, and the budget process. The social costs of risk regulation are largely external to government. It is citizens as a whole who pay the freight for both expenditure programs and risk regulation. Both types of outlays come out of the same economy (scarce resources). It is inefficient to fail to weigh both together and to make necessary trade-off across both types of information.

There is a strong case for the federal government to adopt a "risk-reduction budget," which would be, in effect, a subset of a more general regulatory budget (see Litan and Nordhaus 1983; Stanbury 1992). Given the substantial reduction in economic regulation since the 1980s (see Ostry and Stanbury 1999), by far the largest expenditures relate to risk regulation and other actions by government designed to deal with risks. The key objectives of a "risk-reduction budget" are (a) to get regulators to take into account private sector-costs of compliance (so as to properly measure total costs to society), (b) to save more lives for whatever outlay on risk reduction ministers believe is desirable,[89] and (c) to force the ministers and officials to rationalize their proposed actions to reduce risks across all (competing) departments and agencies.

Finally (and this will be hard to do), the federal government's risk management policies must take into account the fact that the key policy makers in risk management are also at risk in terms of career prospects, status, and reputation. Risk to citizens create risks for cabinet ministers and, to a lesser extent, for the officials who advise them and implement policy.

Remedy #3   *Routine disclosure of more and better information*

It is hard to overemphasize the importance in Canada of getting vastly more information into the public domain about all governments' efforts to manage risks. The traditions of secrecy endemic in the Westminster model have severely handicapped independent analysts in Canada. That is why it has not been possible to provide documentation to support the arguments in this paper. The fact that so little information is publicly available is *prima facie* cause for alarm. If risk management was being well done by government, ministers would have an incentive to shout the good news. In general, their silence is deafening.

By comparison, there is much more information about how the United States federal government is going about risk regulation. For example, on the matter of the costs and benefits of new regulations, Hahn (1996: 213) reviewed 92 regulations created by five American agencies between 1990 and mid-1995. He found that for 80 the benefits were quantified but for only 23 were they monetized. The cost or savings were assessed for 91 of 92 new regulations. As noted in section 3, while cost-benefit analyses of proposed major regulations has been required of all regulatory agencies since 1986, Mihlar (1997) shows that this requirement is seldom being met.[90] But this type of information is only part of what needs to be disclosed routinely about risk management in the federal government.

While disclosure is far from perfect in the United States, there is vastly more information routinely available there than in Canada. That is one of the reasons why there is so much more analytic and commentary literature in the United States on risk management by government. To summarize: without much more information disclosure by the federal government about its risk-management activities, it will not be possible to offer better critiques and more closely targeted suggestion for improvement. Lack of information may serve the interests of ministers but it does *not* serve the interests of the citizens—and they are the ones who really bear the risks.

To help to establish a *baseline* for future government policy toward risks, it would be useful to conduct a careful review of the current stock of risk regulation (and other actions by government to manage risks). This would include the following:

- a compilation of all statutes, regulations, and policy guidelines classified into the major categories of risk regulation (and other actions by government to deal with risks)

- estimates of the government's outlays for the administration of risk regulation in each major category

- estimates of the costs to the private sector of complying with the laws, regulations, and guidelines for each major category of risk regulation

- estimates of the benefits of government action in each category, e.g., lives saved, injuries and illness avoided, property damage avoided, and so on.

Ideally, the cost-benefit analysis should be sufficiently detailed to provide estimates of *incremental* costs and benefits associated with each major component of regulation within each category.

Each department or agency that engages in risk regulation should make public the following:

- the risk assessment protocol it uses in both crisis and routine situations (the Health Protection Branch already does this; see Health Canada 1993)

- a statement of its main risk-management policies including its priorities for future action and risk assessments for the proposed regulations if not included in the Regulatory Impact Analysis Statement (RIAS) as presently required by the Treasury Board.[91]

Remedy #4   More and better analysis that is externally reviewed and enforceable

The federal cabinet should live up to the policy established in 1986 to require departments and agencies to conduct a cost-benefit analysis of proposed new major regulations. As noted in section 3, this requirement has not been enforced—largely because cabinet ministers do not like to regulate their own behaviour and they occupy the apex of political power in Canada.

The federal government should require all departments or agencies engaged in risk management to prepare and publish promptly a formal risk assessment where it proposes major regulations as part of its risk-management activities. Further, the risk assessment should be subject to a peer review by a panel of independent experts, to be paid for, and published promptly, by the federal government.[92]

The government should, as part of the CBA, require regulatory agencies to provide details on the distributional aspects of the risks to be regulated. I expect ministers will be more interested in this part of the analysis than the efficiency issue.

Further, affected citizens should be given the necessary standing to seek judicial review where government departments and agencies fail to conduct a cost-benefit analysis of a major regulation. For the courts to exercise judicial review, the requirement to do a CBA for major regulations must be embedded in subordinate legislation. From 1986 to 1998, it was part of the Treasury Board's Administrative Policy; now it is merely a policy statement of the Privy Council Office (PCO).

Remedy #5 *Try to anticipate risk controversies*

The federal government should put in place a carefully crafted management protocol and team to deal with crises relating to risk-regulation issues. The objective is to reduce the odds that risk controversy crises will lead to government actions (e.g, new regulations) that embody egregious errors because of intense pressure from interest groups reflected in extensive coverage in the news media.

The federal government should devote more effort to anticipating risk-management problems before they "blow up in our faces." Some are rooted in new technologies. Some are rooted in changing values. Some may be due to changing demographics.[93] Powell and Leiss emphasize that "some astute forecasting capacity is absolutely essential, for timeliness is everything in effective risk communication: overcoming entrenched perceptions that are broadly dispersed in the social environment is a thankless task with almost no chance of succeeding" (1997: 219).

Here is a list of issues "likely to engender long-term endemic public controversies over the next ten years . . . food safety generally,[94] endocrine disruptors (including dioxins); greenhouse gases and global climate change; biotechnology, especially agriculture applications; and health impacts of atmospheric pollutants" (Powell and Leiss 1997: 220). To this list, one might add the following: electromagnetic fields surrounding wireless communications devices (see Royal Society of Canada 1998); level of taxes paid to finance the government pension plans; and a range of risks to health attributable to lifestyle choices.[95]

Once future risk issues have been identified, it would be highly desirable to rank (even if very roughly) these prospective risks.[96] The goals are two-fold: to reduce the element of surprise and so be less subject to regulating under crisis conditions, and to avoid major errors such as committing large (huge!) amounts of scarce resources to obtain small reductions in very low probabilities of hazards to which only a tiny number of people are exposed.

Remedy #6   Rank risks and establish
priorities for government action

To counteract the "risk issue of the month" syndrome or "risk panics" created by interest groups, the federal government should commission an independent study (about every three years), which would rank order a wide range of risks on a multi-dimensional basis for the purpose of assisting ministers in setting priorities for government action.[97] The analysis should reflect the ranking priorities of both experts and panels of ordinary citizens. The methodology for doing this is quite well developed (e.g., see Davies 1996; Science Advisory Board 1991). The study should be widely distributed (e.g., perhaps available on the Treasury Board's website).

The ranking of environmental risks has been done twice in the United States by or for the EPA.[98] Both studies indicated that the priorities for government action suggested by experts and specialists were quite different from those of the most vocal environmental groups. Several states and cities in the United States have conducted a number of types of comparative-risk assessments (see Minard 1996). Note that most comparative-risk assessments (CRAs) distinguish (a) various risk issues in order of seriousness, (b) ranking of risk-issues problems in the order government should take action, (c) ranking the manageability of risk issues, e.g., in terms of existing public awareness, existing legal authority, existing control programs, and the costs related to government action. Of course, the rankings of risks can, albeit with more difficulty, reflect the richer characterization of risks often made by citizens (see, for example, Morgan et al. 1996).

Remedy #7   Adopt policies that facilitate
individuated responses to risks

Why do the perceptions of many risks held by ordinary citizens (often described as "irrational") constitute a public-policy problem? "Irrational" tastes for an enormous variety of goods and services are seen as an opportunity for business people and one of the virtues of a competitive market economy, which is able to do a remarkable job in satisfying highly diverse tastes (and budgets).

The great variability in the perception of the same risk across citizens is a strong argument for governments risk-management actions to consider first whether it can help to facilitate individuated responses to a given risk situation.

Government strategies to facilitate individual responses to risks would include the following:

(1) providing unbiased, accurate (as reasonably possible) information about risks (types of harms, probabilities, timing) so that individuals

can better decide what they want to do (this may include pressing the government for certain actions);

(2) providing similar information on the *exposure* of various groups in the population (e.g., by age, sex, location, occupation, etc.); and

(3) providing a list of possible actions individuals can take to reduce their *personal* exposure (hence risk), e.g.,

- using sunscreen to reduce the risk of skin cancer,

- buying insurance for houses, etc. on a flood plain,

- avoiding consumption of certain foods, drugs, etc.

- avoiding high crime areas, cities, etc. and purchasing products that have more safety precautions.[99]

The point is that if there are big differences in the utility of certain risks and there are reasonable actions the *individuals* can take, then the case for a one-size-fits-all strategy by government is very weak.

It must be remembered that the biggest health risks by far are what are very largely *voluntary* life-style choices. For example, to reduce the risk of cancer, individuals can reduce or eliminate smoking, increase their consumption of fruits and vegetables, control infections, avoid intense exposure to the sun, increase physical activity, and reduce the consumption of alcohol (Ames and Gold 1996: 4). Most of the risks that seem to provoke the most fear may involve involuntary exposure but they also reduce the odds of a normal life span by very, very little. In other words, the fault lies not in the stars, but in ourselves.

Remedy #8   Greatly improve risk communication

The federal government must devote far more time, money, and skill to what is called risk communication but is better thought of as consultation with citizens throughout the whole enterprise of risk management. Risk communication must be moved to the centre of the risk management process[100] (see figure 2). "There is simply no cheap solution [for governments to deal effectively with risk controversies], and in an era of declining overall budgets this entails the reallocation of resources toward public communication efforts" (Powell and Leiss 1997: 219).

Using better risk communications to bridge the gap between the risk perceptions of experts and those of citizens does not mean simply trying to move the citizen's characterization of risk closer to that of the experts.[101] It also means having the experts assess risks using attributes found to have been most important to citizens. Closing the gap will be

**Figure 2   Increasing the Role of Risk Communication
in Risk Management**

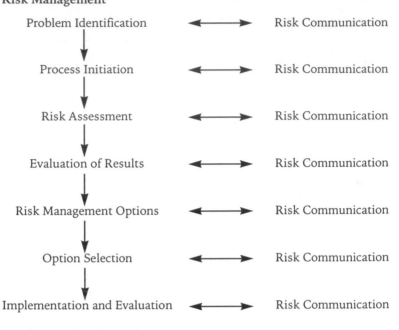

Source: Canadian Food Inspection Agency

difficult and may not even be possible. At the very least, it will involve an intensive, on-going dialogue (see Rollin 1995).

Better risk communications will not be a glamorous job. Each "victory" will be small and unlikely to be politically popular. Worse from the perspective of ministers, the benefits will usually be widely diffused. I believe that effective risk communication by government will involve, among other things, having cabinet ministers exercise leadership by actively engaging citizens and interest groups (notably the "danger lobby") to discuss, explain, listen to fears and to get citizens to confront the complex policy choices involved in regulating risks.

Powell and Leiss (1997) frequently refer to the "risk-communications vacuum" in their compendium of studies of risk-management controversies. In doing so, they fall into a trap that they describe in the book, namely the misleading use of a familiar metaphor. What their studies show is not a vacuum, i.e., the absence of risk communication, but rather extensive communications by some actors (most notably the opponents of new technologies such as rbST)[102] and a paucity of communications by government (most notably, the agency responsible for the regulation of the product in question.) It would be better to say that their very useful case studies were characterized by a large asymmetry in the communication flows where official government sources are far less visible (and audible) than other participants.

Risk communication activities must be centred upon policy and decisions. These activities are not about conducting a seminar on the risk issues in question. They must be conducted with a clear appreciation of their likely impact on trust and credibility (see Peters, Corello, and McCallum 1997; Jungerman 1997; Slovic 1993). These vital attributes are hard to achieve and easy to lose. There is no "silver bullet"—even if the budget were unconstrained—and searching for one is certain to delay the adoption of strategies likely to be useful in addressing the complexities of risk controversies. The need to settle in for the long haul and to stay the course with what seems to be a substantial commitment of resources is not the natural forte of cabinet ministers. Not only is the policy unglamorous, the time horizon is all wrong in terms of the political oestrous cycle.

Government regulators with the mandate to deal with the risk issue are also responsible for effective risk communication. Thus, they must confront "the issues as they are posed in society, not [only] how they appear in science-based risk assessments" (Powell and Leiss 1997: 224). Therefore, government will have to face up to the charge that its "attempting to manipulate the public." Countering misinformation, disinformation, illogical arguments, and schools of red herrings hardly qualifies as "manipulation." But, when an issue is highly contentious, some participants will use any weapon at hand. Advancing the public interest in the best sense of that term often requires government to be constructively engaged with the other actors in the political arena.

Leiss and Chociolko (1994) suggest that effective risk communication requires, at a minimum, that (a) the assumptions underlying the government's risk assessment be made clear, (b) the nature of the public's concerns be understood by government decision makers, and (c) a government agency take responsibility for the government's risk communications efforts and attempt to forge a consensus about what actions should be taken.

Powell and Leiss (1997: 30) argue that good risk-communication practices involve, among other things:

- "translating" the science into terms understandable by the general public;

- explaining the uncertainty ranges, knowledge gaps, and ongoing research programs that characterize a risk controversy;

- addressing the issue of credibility and trust;

- understanding the public as opposed to the expert "framing" of the risk issue;

- providing, as far as possible, answers to questions that arise in this domain; and

- establishing the kinds of interactions between the organization and the public appropriate to the issues at stake.

The United States Environmental Protection Agency's (EPA) rules for risk communication seem obvious and simple but they are often ignored. (1) Accept and involve the public (early) as a legitimate partner in risk management processes. (2) Plan carefully and evaluate the performance of risk-communication strategies. (3) Listen to your audience including the emotions and symbolic meanings. (4) Be honest, frank and open (information, trust, and credibility are the keys). (5) Coordinate and collaborate with other credible sources. (6) Meet the needs of the news media—they are the source of most of the information on risks obtained by citizens. Speak clearly and with compassion using language ordinary people can understand. Use comparisons to provide perspective, particularly those which respond to the distinctions the public usually makes.[103]

Improving the federal government's risk communication will be a difficult task. At least three factors are likely to limit efforts to improve risk communication: lack of knowledge of *how* to do it; citizens' lack of trust in government generally; and the idea that more risk communication could be perceived as another attempt by government to manage the news. See Appendix 2.

5   Conclusions

In this section, I will do three things: outline in skeletal terms the central argument in this paper, summarize my recommendations for the federal government to improve its management of risks, and sketch the federal government's most recent effort to improve risk management—in Health Canada. The key elements of my main argument are as follows.

(1) The management of a wide variety of risks is a very important part of the federal government's activities.

(2) The government's risk management activities, particularly those relating to risk regulation, are subject to a number of "routine pathologies." They are

- insufficient or poor economic analysis;

- no guidance (from the Treasury Board) on the economic value of life;

- idiosyncratic or haphazard selection of risks for government action;

- "silo management" or a lack of "horizontal mechanisms" to implement a general risk management policy across a score of specialized departments and agencies;

- government actions too often based on the preferences of the most fearful;

- one-size-fits-all types of government action to deal with risks;

- potential misuse of the precautionary principle; and

- poor risk communication.

(3) It appears that the most important causal factor underlying these pathologies is the well-documented gap between the perception of experts of a wide variety of risks and that of ordinary citizens. In general, citizens have a richer characterization of risk issues than do experts (but experts have conducted much useful research into the ways citizens perceive risks). In many (perhaps most) risk controversies, the government adopts a characterization closer to that of citizens (often shaped by aggressive interest groups).

(4) The gap presents a problem for governments primarily in those circumstances where government must take coercive action such as regulation aimed at reducing risks. Where government actions focus on helping individuals to respond more effectively to risks, for example, by providing useful information, there is no coercion.

(5) Efforts to improve the management of risks by the federal government should take two principal forms: (a) improvements in risk communication focusing on closing the gap and (b) actions to remedy directly the specific pathologies identified above.

(6) Improving the government's risk communication will be difficult for several reasons: lack of knowledge about the risk communication (despite a considerable and growing literature), lack of trust in government generally, and the possibility that better risk communication will be perceived more as an effort at news management by government than as genuine communication.

(7) Effort to address the pathologies of risk regulation will require government to take a long-run perspective (i.e., far beyond the current electoral circle) and require cabinet ministers to exercise leadership (often in short supply).

(8) Specifically, the following actions should be taken by the federal government to remedy the other routine pathologies of risk management:

(a) Create a number of "horizontal mechanisms" to combat "silo-management":

- establish a government-wide risk-management policy to guide the many departments and agencies which design and implement government actions on risk issues;

- apply to risk management activities the same sort of oversight as Treasury Board now applies to expenditures; and

- create a "risk-reduction budget," to rationalize society's mandated expenditures for risk reduction.

(b) Increase the amount of information routinely disclosed about risk-management activities (e.g., risk-assessment protocols, risk-management policies, and risk assessments).

(c) Mandate more and better analysis of risks e.g., risk assessments, and cost-benefit analysis, which is already required but not enforced. In addition, both types of analysis should be subject to independent peer review. Citizens should also be allowed to seek judicial review to enforce these provisions.

(d) Try to anticipate (and manage better) future risk controversies by forecasting.

(e) Make a systematic effort to rank risks in terms of their importance and establish priorities for government action.

(f) Adopt policies that facilitate individuated responses to risks.

Finally, citizens and experts should not be too sanguine that these apparently reasonable ideas will be adopted. But, stranger things have happened. That is why the study of the management of risks is so interesting and also so frustrating.

In mid-1998, the federal government launched a review of its extensive health-protection legislation, an enormous body of risk regulation. Extensive consultations were held in the fall of 1998 and a report on these was issued in April 1999 (Health Canada 1999b). In mid-1999, the government decided to slow down the proposed pace of change (Kennedy 1999). There is to be another discussion paper in the winter of 1999 or spring of 2000 before revised health-protection legislation is introduced. Thus, it could be several years before it passes Parliament.

The consultations indicate that Canadians have extraordinarily high expectations for the Health Protection Program. The dominant messages included the following: (a) health and safety must take precedence over economic and other considerations; (b) Health Canada should be more accountable to the people of Canada; (c) HPB's activities and decision-making processes need to be more transparent to the public; (d) Health Canada needs to explain better the methods it uses to manage health risks; (e) industry's goal is generally not deregulation but the updating of existing regulations to reflect contemporary conditions better (Health Canada 1999b: vi).

The federal government proposes to separate clearly risk assessment, which defines the nature and degree of risk based on scientific evidence, and risk management, which develops and implements appropriate government interventions. The latter "needs to take account of other things besides science, including gender, social, economic, cultural, political and policy considerations" (Health Canada 1999b: 3). The government indicates that "there is no universally acceptable level of risk" and that Health Canada should take into account "the different needs, values and perspectives of women, cultural minorities, seniors, children and other groups, each of which may be affected differently" (Health Canada 1999b: 3). Aside from a fulsome expression of political correctness, what does the last statement mean? Does it mean that where, say, women[104] rather than men are exposed to a certain risk, that policy will closely reflect their risk preferences? But what if—as one would expect—there are big variations in the degree of risk aversion across women? Which particular level will be chosen? What if a risk affects several of the named groups of particular concern to the federal government? Will Health Canada try to supply a differentiated policy— one that varies with each group's perceptions of the risk in question? How will it do this in a practical sense? Would the differentiated policy stand up to a challenge under the *Charter of Rights and Freedoms*.

It is good to hear that Health Canada (1999b: 5) "must be considerably more active in the area of risk communication." The paper suggests that the content of such communication will include the nature and extent of health risks, the methods used to assess such risks, the results of the assessment, the level of confidence in the assessment, the factors taken into account in the development of the risk strategy and the margin of safety afforded by government action. If implemented, this approach has much to commend it. But, I find it hard to believe that had the policy been in place in 1998, that Health Canada would tell Canadians frankly about the *political* calculus that underlay its decisions with respect to the allegedly toxic teethers and children's toys during the risk scare raised by Greenpeace (see Stanbury et al. 2000).

It is good to see that Health Canada recognizes that "effective communication is especially important in cases where the public perceives a risk to be high, although scientific assessment might show a moderate or low level of risk" (1999b: 5). Realistically, to deal with risk scares induced by interest groups, the federal government will have to take a far more active role in combatting information that is incomplete, distorted, or misinterpreted by activists. This will require a major change in policy—one that can only be effected by the cabinet. So we are back to the matter of political leadership, something that always appears to be in short supply. It appears that both ministers and senior officials in Ottawa have a growing interest in improving the government's extensive risk management efforts. As of April 2000, a number of initiatives were underway that may bear fruit in time (see ADM Working Group on Risk Management 2000).

Appendix 1   Classification of risks subject to government intervention

Transportation-related

- automobiles
- motorcycles
- trucks
- railroads
- ships and barges (including non-commercial
- watercraft or pleasure craft)
- pipelines (oil, gas, commodities)
- electricity (electromagnetic field around major power lines)

Environment-related

- climate change and global warming
- air, water, and land pollution
- timber harvesting practices
- toxic and hazardous chemicals (including pesticides)
- migratory birds
- wildlife habitat

Hazardous products

- automobiles and small trucks (seatbelts, bumpers, high rear-mounted stoplights, daylight running lights)
- drugs (for humans and animals)
- medical devices
- pesticides
- children's toys, clothing, cribs, car seats, teethers
- explosives
- pleasure boats (including personal water craft such as "Seadoos")
- tires

Plant and animal health

- harm to animals from growth hormones
- living conditions for animals
- infectious diseases

Financial or economic risks

(a) *Related to financial instruments and institutions*

- securities (debt and equity)

- banking and other financial institutions (which accept deposits)
- insurance companies
- pension plans
- deposit insurance

(b) Related to purchase of products

- product labelling (including trademarks)
- weights and measures
- misleading advertising
- deceptive marketing practices
- quality assurance, e.g., birth control devices
- efficacy of drugs (versus harmful effects)
- efficacy of professional services

(c) Related to income level and flow

- employment insurance (was UI)
- Canada Pension Plan; Old Age Pension
- welfare payments (various income transfers)
- worker's compensation
- crop insurance
- disaster relief (*ad hoc*)

Risks related to resource exploitation

- Regulation of the utilization of renewable resources: fish, timber, water, wildlife
- Regulation of non-renewable resources:[105] petroleum (e.g., failure to recover the maximal economically recoverable amount); natural gas; minerals.

Food-related

- prevent contamination in production and distribution of food
- chemicals used in processing or in growing animals or crops for food
- pesticide residues on food
- bovine growth hormone in milk
- irradiation of food

Occupation-related [106]

- accidents
- job-related diseases, e.g., miner's lung
- job-related disabilities, e.g., carpal tunnel syndrome

New (high) Technology

- biotechnology, e.g., synthetic hormones
- genetic engineering, e.g., cloning
- new information technologies used to deliver government programs

Nuclear power-related

- reactor accidents with release of nuclear materials
- storage of spent fuel rods
- mining of uranium
- water pollution (heat)

Other Safety-related Risks

(a) *Infrastructure* (some overlap with transportation-related category)

- dams
- bridges
- electric power lines
- roadways
- natural gas lines

(b) *Exogenous risks*

- weather (hurricanes, ice storms, tornados, floods, drought)
- earthquakes
- nuclear accident in other countries
- forest fires (due to lightning)

Security-related

(a) *National security*

- defence against invasion or attack by other means (e.g., missiles)
- protection against subversion from within

(b) *Personal (physical) security of citizens*

- police, to maintain domestic order
- fire prevention and suppression

Rights-related

- human rights (including the *Charter of Rights and Freedoms*)
- collective bargaining
- humane slaughter of animals

Appendix 2   Problems in trying to improve risk communication

Here I review three factors that are likely to limit efforts to improve risk communication: (1) lack of knowledge of *how* to do it; (2) citizens' lack of trust in government; and (3) the idea that more risk communication could well be perceived as another attempt at news management by government.

1   Lack of knowledge

While there is a quickly growing literature on risk communication[107] (the term was first coined in 1984), it is fair to say that our knowledge of how to do risk communication *effectively* is still quite limited. There is no clear formula for which there is a high probability of success. Generally, see Gutteling and Wiegman 1996.

For example, one aspect of improving risk communication is helping citizens gain some perspective on risks more generally during the heat of a particular risk controversy. This means comparing various risks; but comparing risks is a difficult task.[108] The degree of acceptability to the public of various types of comparisons varies a great deal. However, this information should not be taken as creating a set of absolute constraints. Rather, the public's views about comparing risks should be treated as part of the gap between experts and the general public that is to be addressed by improved risk communication.

2   Citizens' lack of trust in government

A growing number of writers on risk management, particularly risk communication, emphasize the importance of trust in efforts to communicate with the public about situations perceived to be fraught with risk (see Slovic 1993). If this is so, it is no wonder that governments' pronouncements of risk issues may be treated with scant respect by citizens. They are affected by the significant decline in confidence in almost all of society's institutions over the past three decades.

Further, critics (and ordinary citizens) can point to plenty of examples where governments have a questionable record of dealing with risk issues (see Powell and Leiss 1997). One of the larger recent scandals is the failure of the federal government in regulating the Red Cross as administrator of the national blood system: the Krever Inquiry found that not only were top officials of the Red Cross negligent but also that Health Canada's top officials and ministers failed to supervise the Red Cross properly. The result was that Canada's blood supply became contaminated with HIV and Hepatitis C. The federal and provincial governments' latest offer of compensation (at taxpayer's expense) totals $1.1 billion but the final bill will be more.

Official government pronouncements on risk issues are usually influenced by cabinet ministers' strong desire to put a positive spin on almost all issues. In general, our political leaders abhor "bad news" because they feel that voters will punish them for "telling it like it is." They appear to have some justification—just think about the fate of candidates and parties that told voters during election campaigns that if elected they would raise taxes or cut services.[109]

It must be appreciated that ministers face an institutionalized opposition that interprets its role as doing almost everything it can to "tear the guts out of the Government" (with a view to replacing it forthwith or at the next election). Also, there is some evidence to suggest that some elements in the news media see themselves as the true opposition to the Government of the day rather than neutral purveyors of facts. It must be kept in mind at all times that the press (print or electronic) is in the competitive business of delivering audiences to advertisers. The market for "infotainment" is larger and more lucrative than that for detailed dispassionate reportage. Thus the emphasis on scandals, disasters (natural and man-made), personalities (particularly the unhealthy attributes thereof), and all manner of "bad news."

Why should citizens believe government statements about the risks of various hazards when it has become routine for federal ministers of finance to manipulate the numbers in the (tax) budget to create a certain picture or image (and hence to shape expectations). Government itself is at least partly responsible for the "credibility gap." "Spinning" by ministers and their paid helpers has become a major activity (see Fox 1999). Substance counts for little. The game (and that is the correct description) is one of "impression (or image) management."

Governments cannot routinely attempt to con the public and reasonably expect to be believed on other occasions when they deem that "it really matters." The problem for governments seeking to improve the management of risks is this: improvements in risk management depend in part on increasing citizen's trust of the experts and risk analysts employed by government,[110] but governments routinely act in ways which cause citizens to distrust them. How is the circle to be squared?

3   Is more and better risk communication just another attempt at news management by government?

For governments, the objective of the elaborate and expensive communication efforts is *management* of the news that the public relies so heavily upon for its understanding and opinions of the world. The central goal is to convey certain impressions or images rather than to convey substantive content. There is a conflict between scientific inquiry, which flourishes only when information flows are not constrained,[111] and the responsibilities of senior officials. To serve the interests of ministers, they are expected to manage the flow of information relevant to policy-making.

In Canada, the failures of government efforts to communicate with the public (usually via the news media) are more subtle than flat-out lying. Rather it is a matter of the following:

(1) Information is used in a selective fashion (namely that which supports the government's position).

(2) Great emphasis is placed on those facts that tend to make the government look good (or least bad).

(3) The whole story is not always told, at least at one time. The details are often discovered and revealed publicly and, then, reluctantly acknowledged by government spokespersons. In general, this involves papering over embarrassing information by resorting to the claim of confidentiality.

(4) "Bad news" is made public when it is least likely to obtain much visibility in the news media.

Spin is central to government's efforts to manage the news. The concept of spin by government officials and spokespersons has become so common that Howard Kurtz, in his new book, *Spin Cycle* (331 pages), nowhere defines "spin" or "spin cycle."[112]

What is spin? In general, it involves efforts by a newsmaker (or by someone on his behalf) to directly or indirectly influence how what he has said or done will be portrayed in the news media. Overall, these efforts attempt to obtain a more favourable interpretation of what has been said or done.

It appears that when the press focuses on government activities there is a "battle" over the competing messages to be sent to the public. It is frequently argued (e.g., Kurtz 1998) that in covering the government the press wants to focus on scandal, error, malfeasance, misfeasance, embarrassment to the powers that be, and inconsistency by policy makers. On the other hand, the politicians in power want to use the news media to deliver their own message and not to stray from that message despite intense pressure by reporters. They want the press to report their accomplishments and to project an image of caring and compassion as well as to project competence and being on top of breaking issues.

Acknowledgments

I am indebted to Cynthia Hendricks and Helen Ho for skilled and prompt word processing services, and to Margot Priest, Laura Jones and the copy-editor for helpful comments. The usual caveat applies, of course.

Notes

1 The literature dealing with basic ideas about risk includes Adams 1995; Bayerische 1993; Bernstein 1996; Douglas and Wildavsky 1982; Douglas 1992; Fischhoff, Watson, and Hope 1984; Rescher 1983.

2 Accidents were the leading cause of death in 1996 for persons under the age of 44. The most important categories were motor vehicle accidents (38 percent), falls (31 percent), poisoning (9 percent), drowning and suffocation (5 percent), and fires (4 percent) (McIlroy 1999: A3). In the twentieth century, the life expectancy of Americans has increased from 48 to 73 years for men and from 51 to 80 years for women (Crossen 1996: B1).

3 These include hang gliding, mountain biking, flying ultralight aircraft, some types of snow boarding, heli-skiing, and para-sailing. See Buhasz 1999 and Canadian Press 1999.

4 One might interpret a good part of government efforts to deal with risks as a response to rent-seeking behaviour.

5 For another classification that focuses on health and safety risks, see Powell and Leiss 1997: 218.

6 It must be noted that some environmentalists promote the idea of biocentrism, namely that man should not be given a higher priority than other living things. Indeed, for some environmentalists, man is seen as inherently destructive of the natural environment.

7 Risk regulation in some form goes back over a century in Canada. For example, federal health-protection regulation began in 1875 with provisions aimed at preventing the adulteration of food, beverages, and drugs (Aubuchon 1999: 1). Generally, see Priest and Wohl 1980.

8 Generally, see Anon. 1993; Brunk, Harworth, and Lee 1991; Cumming 1981; Finkel 1990; Garrick and Gekler 1991; Graham and Rhomberg 1996; Hadden 1984; Hallenback 1993; Lave 1982; Molak 1996; Morgan 1993; Morgan and Henrion 1992; Nichols and Zeckhauser 1986; Presidential/Congressional Commission on Risk Assessment and Risk Management 1997; Wilson and Crouch 1987.

9 Risk management is not, as suggested by Health Canada (1998a: 15) in its white paper for the renewal of health protection legislation, "a scientific process for identifying health hazards and deciding what to do about them." Although science dominates the risk assessment component of

risk management, other normative elements are necessarily present. The scientific paradigm is itself a normative proposition based on the norm of rationality (see Rollin 1995). Unfortunately, rationality is under siege in various areas these days.

10 See, for example, Covello and Mumpower 1985; Fischer et al. 1991; Keeney 1984, 1990; Konheim 1988; Kraus et al. 1992; Lund 1995; McDaniels et al. 1992; Mertz et al. 1998.

11 These were officially categorized in 1980 and now estimated to be the most common form of mental illness among Americans, afflicting some 23 million people.

12 Recall the grim joke to the effect that one nuclear event can ruin an entire day.

13 "And yet imagination, especially about the future, is precisely the engine that drives so many fears—fear of the unknown, fear of nuclear holocaust and in recent years—fear of contracting AIDS" (Hall 1999: 45). Greenpeace created fear about the leaching of softeners used in some children's teethers and toys. See Stanbury et al. 2000.

14 A very useful discussion of a variety of risk controversies is contained in Neal and Davies 1998 and Powell and Leiss 1997.

15 Generally, see Fischer et al. 1991; Fischhoff 1991, 1994, 1995; Gilroy 1993; Howard 1984; Jasanoff 1993; Johnson and Covello 1987; Kasperson et al. 1988; Kasperson and Kasperson 1996; Keeney 1994; Kraus et al. 1992; Powell 1998; McDaniels et al. 1992; Mertz et al. 1998; Nelkin 1985; Shrader-Frechette 1991; Slovic 1987, Slovic et al. 1985a, 1987; Slovic, Fischhoff, and Lichtenstein 1979, 1982; Slovic, Flynn, Mertz and Mullican 1993.

16 There are, however, some attributes of a hazard (risky situation) that are largely objective.

17 The federal Health Protection Branch risk-assessment framework since 1993 sets out the following criteria for the analysis of options for public policy: (1) weighing of health risk against health benefits, uncertainties in the risk estimates, or application of such principles such as ALARA ("as low as reasonably achievable") or *de minimis* (i.e., the risk is too small that most people are uninterested in giving up the risk-producing activity; (2) individual and societal perspective on the issue; (3) public's perception of the risk; (4) feasibility of the proposed options, their economic and environmental impact; and (5) societal, political and cultural implications of each option (Health Canada 1993).

18 These debates may create an ever greater degree of cognitive dissonance among the general public.

19 Generally, see Iyengar 1991; Schon and Rein 1994; Tannen 1993.

20 The way an issue is framed need not be static; it can evolve over time. Therefore, the way a risk problem is conceptualized changes.

21 See the discussion under Pathology #8, Section 3.

22 Note that an American study found that women scientists find the world to be a riskier place than do their male counterparts (Strauss 1995: A3).

23 There are some notable exceptions: (a) risks of small probability whose adverse consequences are large and irreversible (e.g., nuclear plant melt-

down), (b) the minimax rule is used where our knowledge of a risk is subject to serious uncertainty (see Fraiberg and Trebilcock 1998).

24 The most fearful risks are those that create the greatest disutility for the individual where utility incorporates all attributes relevant to the individual.

25 See Chociolko 1995: 19–20; Rollin 1995. Experts have biases, to be sure, but then so do lay persons, even if we simply label theirs as a richer characterization of risks. The real issue is which set of biases will be given more weight.

26 On the problems with comparing risks, see Slovic et al. 1990; and the discussion in Gutteling and Wiegman 1996: 135–38. The latter also discusses the use of graphic aids in making comparisons (135–42).

27 Generally, see Arrow et al. 1996; Lave 1996; Leonard and Zeckhauser 1986.

28 See Mihlar 1997. Fraiberg and Trebilcock (1998) propose that federal departments and agencies be given a set of core assumptions upon which to base the mandatory cost-benefit analysis for major new regulations. Also, they propose that the CBA be subject to a notice and comment period and a peer review, which would be published.

29 This history up to early 1997 can be found in Powell and Leiss 1997.

30 This went on sale in the United States in February 1994.

31 Health Canada itself had made this determination in 1986 (Powell and Leiss 1997: 125).

32 According to a news release from Health Canada (1999a), there is "an increased risk of mastitis of up to 25 percent, of infertility by 18 percent and of lameness by up to 50 percent. These increased risks and overall reduced body condition lead to a 20–25 percent increased risk of culling from the herd." Note that the criteria for not approving a new veterinary product in Canada include harm to animals.

33 The Expert Panel of the Canadian Veterinary Medical Association, set up at the request of Health Canada, reported that rbST increased milk yield an average of 11.3 percent in primiparous cows and 15.6 percent in multiparous cows (CVMA Expert Panel 1998).

34 Note that because the decision on rbST did not involve a new regulation, Health Canada did not have to conduct a cost-benefit analysis. See Health Canada 1999a.

35 Note, however, that discussions with senior officials who administer the policy indicates that the concept of efficiency adopted by the government is far more elastic than what economists mean by the term.

36 The Regulatory Affairs Directorate (1995) defines a new major regulation as one (a) for which the estimated present value of costs is over $50 million or (b) the present value of costs is from $100,000 to $50 million and the "degree of acceptance" is deemed to be "low." It appears that the costs in this context include income transfers (see Consulting and Audit Canada 1995).

37 It should be noted that the manual prepared by the Canada Consulting Group (1995) to assist government officials in applying CBA to new regulations has notable flaws related to the definition of true social costs and social benefits as opposed to taxes and income transfers.

38 For example, no estimate of the total benefits was made for the three sets of water-pollution regulations applied to the pulp and paper industry effective May 1992 despite an estimated social cost of almost $5 billion. See Stanbury 1992: 146.

39 A few studies for the federal government have used a specific number. For example, Abt Associates (1986) in a CBA for the federal government stated that the value of a life saved lies in the range of $1 million to $10 million. In Abt Associates 1988 a value of $5 million was used. Transport Canada (1985, 1986a, 1986b) used a value of $325,000 (in 1985 dollars) based on the "minimum cost of a road accident" involving a fatality. This number was not intended to be an estimate of the economic value of a statistical life.

40 The range reflects differences in the type of risks studied to ascertain the willingness of individuals to pay to reduce a small risk or the amount demanded to accept slightly higher risks.

41 Because so few proper cost-benefit analyses are performed in Canada, it is not possible to provide Canadian examples.

42 Tengs and Graham (1996: 172) found that 185 life-saving interventions in the United States averted about 56,700 premature deaths (592,000 life years) annually at a cost of $376,000 per life saved. They show that if the total "budget" of $21.4 billion was spent in the most cost-effective fashion, an additional 60,200 lives could be saved at an average cost of $183,000. If the analysis is done to maximize the number of years of life saved when a premature death is prevented, the same budget would save 1,230,000 years of life annually—an increase of over 100 percent.

43 Tengs and Graham (1996: 178) propose the following rule of thumb: invest in all interventions to save lives costing up to US$5 million per life saved and none in interventions costing more.

44 Graham says that American government policy toward risks is characterized by "a syndrome of paranoia and neglect" (1996: 184).

45 This is the term Tengs et al. (1995) apply to the American government's investment in life-saving interventions.

46 The Delaney Amendment passed by the United States in 1957 requires the federal government to ban from processed food any trace of synthetic substances implicated as human carcinogens. It ignores natural carcinogens that may pose vastly greater hazards. When the Amendment was passed, it was assumed that environmental exposures to synthetic chemicals accounted for up to 90 percent of all cancers. Further, instruments could only measure parts per million. Today, better information indicates that such chemicals account for a tiny fraction of cancers and instruments can detect parts per quadrillion. In 1993, the Clinton Administration proposed to amend the Delaney Amendment to incorporate the test of "negligible risk" as proposed by the National Academy of Sciences (see Easterbrook 1995: 447–48).

47 Recently, Ames and Gold have said that pollution appears to account for less than 1 per cent of human cancer (1996: 4). Tobacco accounts for about one-third of cancer (and about one-quarter of heart disease) (1996: 9).

Note, however, that in Canada the federal and most provincial governments have imposed very high taxes on cigarettes with the stated objective of reducing consumption.

48 Based on figures for the United States. The figures for Canada would be comparable. Gratt indicates that the estimated number of annual cancer cases caused by a pollutant in the United States is from 1,726 to 2,706 (1996: 253). These include some of the most strictly regulated substances, e.g., acroylonitrile (13), arsenic (68), asbestos (88), benzene (181), coke-oven emissions (7), dioxin (2 to 125), vinyl chloride (25), hydrazine (6), and trichlorethylene (7).

49 While we do not have comparable data for Canada, I note that Viscusi's (1992) summary of 33 risk-reducing regulations created between 1980 and 1989 in the United States indicated that the number of lives saved per year ranged from 0.001 to 1,850. For 25 of the regulations, the number was less than ten per year; for 11, the number was less than one per year.

50 For example, the air navigation system alone costs about $900 million per year.

51 Vancouver Sun, March 23, 1999: B2, reporting Transport Canada data.

52 Vancouver Sun, March 23, 1999: B2.

53 In 1994, all transport-related deaths amount to only 26 percent of all deaths in Canada due to "external causes." But, this category includes suicides and homicides, which account for 32 percent of all "external causes" of death. Thus, all accidental deaths (8,591 in 1994) accounted for only 4.3 percent of all deaths in 1994. Given the government's intense focus on accidental deaths, it appears that it is working on problems whose incidence is tiny to modest in the larger scheme of things.

54 On setting priorities for risk reduction activities, generally see Applegate 1992; EPA 1987; Grabowski and Vernon 1977; Lave et al. 1994; Moffet 1996.

55 Note that in parts of Africa and India, AIDS is a vastly more important cause of death. See National Post, April 14, 1999: A17.

56 One could also make the comparison between AIDS and prostate cancer. In 1996, about 18,200 men were diagnosed and about 4,000 will die from the disease (see Trevor Lautens column, Vancouver Sun, November 2, 1996: A19).

57 In 1994, Ottawa spent $43.4 million on AIDS research versus $4 million on breast cancer (see Bueckert 1995).

58 By 1998, the number was up to 11,400 (see Globe and Mail, December 2, 1998: A7). Therefore, the comparable number of deaths due to breast cancer would be 70,000.

59 1,489 men and 139 women. See Statistics Canada 1996.

60 The National Cancer Institute of Canada (1998) put the average lifetime probability of a woman developing cancer at 0.35 and the risk of dying of cancer at 0.224. For breast cancer, the figures are 0.108 and 0.04 respectively—the highest of all types of cancer. The figures for lung cancer by comparison are 0.047 and 0.042 respectively.

61 For example, an AIDS activist argues that the much higher spending per death on AIDS research is justified because AIDS is not just another disease: "it's a disease without a cure; its relatively new; there are comparatively fewer treatments available for people affected by HIV diseases." John Chenier, editor of The Lobby Monitor suggests that "the funding [of various diseases] reflects the power of those not only who have the disease, but those who fear the disease, and those who are prepared to research it. All of those groups have lobbies" (Bueckert 1995: A9).

62 It is hard to avoid the conclusion that, in the most general terms, old age is by far the most important cause of death in Canada: in 1994, three-quarters of those who died were 65 or older and almost 39 percent were over age 80.

63 Note that 56 percent of males and 38 percent of females who died in 1993 were less than 75 years of age.

64 The data for the United States can be found in Gratt 1996: 249.

65 I refer to the two efforts by or for EPA; see Science Advisory Board 1991; EPA 1987. Efforts by American states are described in Minard 1996.

66 For example, The Health Protection Branch of Health Canada employs 2,922 people (two-thirds of whom are scientists and science-support staff) and spends about $230 million annually (Aubuchon 1999: 2). Activities relating to the Food and Drugs Act account for one-third of HPB's budget. Between 1994/1995 and 1998/1999, HPB's budget was cut by only 8 percent compared to 32.9 percent for Environment Canada, 30 percent for Fisheries and Oceans, and 58.4 percent for Natural Resources.

67 Transport Canada website: tc.gc.ca, Transportation of Dangerous Goods.

68 Transport Canada, Performance Report, 1996/97 (website: tc.gc.ca).

69 The good news is that the federal government is beginning to examine the issue of risk management (see ADM Working Group on Risk Management 2000). In the United States, the EPA made an effort in 1989 to rank risks with a view to establishing priorities for further regulation. See also Science Advisory Board 1991. In general, environmental groups have been critical of these efforts.

70 Regulations are used to implement all governing instruments. Regulation consists of government-made rules backed by penalties designed to modify the economic behaviour of individuals or organizations in the private sector.

71 For the Health Protection Branch's protocol, see Health Canada, 1993. It is being updated; see Health Protection Branch 1999. See also Scoffield 2000.

72 It is possible that the benefits outweigh the costs but there is no way of knowing this at present in Canada.

73 The initial steps for a regulatory budget (easily adapted to a risk-reduction budget) for the federal government are set out in Stanbury 1992: 186–87.

74 The fear of risks is more complex than can be described by conventional measures of risk aversion. I use the phrase to refer to sum of the richer characterization of risks employed by ordinary citizens described in section 2 above.

75 See Neal 1999; Neal and Davies 1998; Stanbury et al. 2000. "Any group that's lobbying for money is going to try to maximize the number of deaths from their particular malady," according to math professor and author of A Mathematician Reads the Newspaper. He continues, "Then the numbers are often stated baldly, without context, definition or how they're arrived at" (Crossen 1996: B1). A good example is a 1996 cover story on prostate cancer in Time magazine. It stated that men have one chance in five of getting prostate cancer. But, this is the risk over a lifetime (almost 80 years). For a man aged 40, the risk of getting this form of cancer (not dying of it) in the next ten years is .001; over the next 20 years, it is .01. Even at age 70, the risk of getting prostate cancer is .05. The data show that men are far more likely to die of heart disease (Crossen 1996: B1). Greenpeace's efforts to obtain a ban on children's toys and teethers made of PVC containing phthalates by the use of fear is described in Stanbury (Stanbury et al. 2000b).

76 The archetypes are Ralph Nader and, on health issues, Jeremy Rifkin.

77 See Federal Focus Inc. 1991: table C-2; Hahn 1996.

78 The term "moral hazard" comes from the insurance industry and refers to the idea that insured persons may be able to influence the timing, frequency, or size of payment(s) by their insurance companies. In this example, hikers would not pay the full cost of their rescue and so would not have the greatest incentive to avoid getting lost.

79 I have been told that a similar policy prevails in Switzerland for hikers who need to be rescued.

80 A more extensive list can be found in VanderZwaag 1996.

81 "A zero risk policy is the functional equivalent of exorcism" (Powell and Leiss 1997: 223).

82 See Cross 1996 and Graham and Weiner 1995 on risk-risk tradeoffs.

83 They note that the federal government's few statements on dioxins raise more questions than they answer and that there are inconsistencies among them (see Powell and Leiss 1997: 73–74).

84 The subsequent near hysteria in Canada when the United States decided to permit the export of PCB-laden wastes for disposal shows that the federal government's handling of risk communication in this area has not improved.

85 In practical terms, this means that the cabinet will have to act to put new institutions and policies in place early in its mandate. This means that senior public servants (largely Privy Council Office) will have to have detailed plans drafted before a new government takes office.

86 The first three criteria were previously proposed by Rescher (1983).

87 Some differentiation in terms of details or extension of the standard components will be necessary to meet the needs of particular departments and agencies.

88 This point comes from Graham 1996.

89 See Tengs and Graham 1996.

90 There is a notable exception. The Department of Transport has done an outstanding job of conducting a CBA for proposed new regulations

relating to automobile safety, e.g., seat belts, side-door impact beams, daylight running lights, and high, rear-mounted stop lights.

91 In 1999, the responsibility for administering the Regulatory Impact Analysis Statement and other aspects of the regulations-making process was shifted to the Privy Council Office (PCO).

92 This was also proposed by Fraiberg and Trebilcock (1998).

93 For example, if the number of persons in their child-bearing years increases, government can expect more demands to ensure the safety of children.

94 The flurry of newspaper stories in 1999 on genetically modified (GM) foods is an example. See Abergel et al. 1999; Dyer 1999; Johnson 1999; Kravis 1999; Munroe 1999; Powell 1999. Further, GM foods have been the focus of a major risk scare in the United Kingdom. See Neal 1999.

95 The US Surgeon General's top six priorities for saving lives and preventing disease all involve change in the individual's lifestyle: stop smoking, reduce consumption of alcohol, eat less and eat smarter, have periodic checkups for major disorders, and use seatbelts and obey speed limit (Huber 1991: 159–60).

96 For more suggestions, see Bennett and DiLorenzo 1998; Wolf 1992; Heubner and Chilton 1998.

97 A survey of 1000 American citizens by the Harvard Center for Risk Analysis in November 1993 found that over 80 percent agreed that "the government should use risk analysis to identify the most serious environmental problems and give them the highest priority in spending decisions" (Risk in Perspective 2, 1: 1994).

98 See EPA 1987; Science Advisory Committee 1991.

99 Airbags are not mandated by Transport Canada (for good economic reasons). Yet consumer preferences are such that virtually all automobile makers sell cars in Canada with at least a driver's airbag and most models also have a passenger airbag.

100 Note that more laws and regulations in Canada are mandating some form of risk communication: these include toxics-release inventories, environmental assessments, waste-management plans, permits required under land-use planning, and the regulatory agenda (which was recently discontinued).

101 Citizens' "irrational" attitudes toward many risks constitute a problem for government only where government actions to deal with those risks generate negative externalities for other citizens. Ironically, these externalities are likely to be greatest when a group with a common set of perceptions (utility for certain risks) is able to persuade government to institute policies that coerce other citizens.

102 I note that this formulation ignores the communication conducted in the scientific community through journals, monographs, books, conferences, and teaching. Bits of this evolving body of work is reflected in public risk communications—often in a selective and biased fashion. While formally public, the scientific literature and disclosure is largely separate from the communications flows related to risk controversies and public policy making.

103 Adapted from the summary in Gratt 1996: 285–87.
104 Later, the paper states that federal decision-makers "would be required, among other things, to take stock of how a given risk or risk management strategy might affect elderly, pregnant or immigrant women" (Health Canada, 1999b: 4). Why was the further differentiation of the population limited to these three categories?
105 The main focus is on efficient exploitation.
106 Most provinces regulate at least 40 occupations by licensure or certification. The regulation of occupations focuses on both physical harms and possible economic losses.
107 See, for example, Bostrom et al. 1994; Covello 1991; Covello and Allen 1988; Flynn et al. 1993; Garreck and Gekler 1991; Gray et al. 1998; Kasperson and Stallen 1991; Konheim 1988; Lundgren 1994; National Research Council 1989; Otway 1987; Powell and Leiss 1997; Sandman 1986; Viscusi and Zeckhauser 1996.
108 Generally, see Covello 1991; Davies 1996, 1994; Finkel and Golding 1993; Morgan et al. 1996; Roth, Morgan, Fischhoff, Lane, and Bostrom 1990; Slovic et al. 1990.
109 Sacrifices may be noble but they are best made by others. Other evidence of the public's (apparent) desire for "good news" is the new interpretation by American television networks of the news as "infotainment" or "edutainment" (notably the growing number of news magazine shows pioneered by 60 Minutes). Along the same lines is the growth of television time and newspaper space devoted to news about the entertainment industry (the pioneer here was Entertainment Tonight). Yet, the news is dominated by "bad news": war, accidents, natural disasters, political conflict, and any number of harms inflicted on groups and individuals. Many environmental groups since the 1970s have emphasized "bad news" and even promoted apocalyptic scenarios. Fear, it seems, sells for environmental-groups (see Stanbury 1999).
110 Generally, see Frewer et al. 1992; Slovic 1993.
111 See Hutchings et al. 1997.
112 "In recent years the modern practice of spin has come to occupy a sort of gray zone between candor and outright falsehood" (Kurtz 1998: xviii). Spin is also very much about the visuals, which include not only the foreground but also the backdrop, as Ronald Reagan's media advisors emphasized. This is, after all, the age of television.

References

Abergel, Elizabeth et al. (1999). Genetic Food Fight: Safety Assumption Not Good Enough. *Financial Post* (July 29): C7.

Abt Associates of Canada (1986). Socio-Economic Impact Analysis of Proposed Tent Flammability Regulations. Study prepared for the Department of Consumer and Corporate Affairs, Ottawa.

————— (1988). Socio-Economic Impact Analysis (SEIA) of Proposed Regulations of Consumer Products Containing Hydrofluoric Acid. Study prepared for the Department of Consumer and Corporate Affairs, Ottawa.

Adams, John (1993). The Emperor's Old Clothes: The Curious Comeback of Cost-Benefit Analysis. *Environmental Values* 2: 247–60.

————— (1995). *Risk*. London: UCL Press.

ADM Working Group on Risk Management (2000). *Risk Management in Public Policy* (January). Ottawa: Privy Council Office.

Agence France-Presse (1999). EU Scientists Warn Hormones in Beef May Cause Cancer. *Globe and Mail* (May 7): A5A.

Ahearne, John F. (1993). Integrating Risk Analysis into Public Policymaking. *Environment* (March): 16–40.

Ames, Bruce N., and L.S. Gold (1996). The Causes and Prevention of Cancer: Gaining Perspectives in the Management of Risks. In Robert W. Hahn (ed.), *Risks, Costs, and Lives Saved* (New York: Oxford University Press; Washington: AEI Press): 4–45.

Anderson, D., and P. Mullen, eds. (1998) *Faking It: The Sentimentalisation of Modern Society* (London: SAU).

Anderson, F. R. (1996). CRA [Comparative Risk Analysis] and Its Stakeholders: Advice to the Executive Office. In J. Clarence Davies (ed.) *Comparing Environmental Risks* (Washington, DC: Resources for the Future): 63–92.

Angell, Marcia (1996). *Science on Trial: The Clash of Medical Evidence and the Law in the Breast Implant Case*. New York: W.W. Norton.

Applegate J. (1992). Worst Things First, Information, and Regulatory Structure in Toxic Substances Control. *Yale Journal on Regulation* 9, 2 (Summer).

Anon. (1993). Profiles in Risk Assessments: New Science, New Contexts. *EPA Journal* 19, 1 (Jan./Feb./Mar.).

Arrow, K.J. et al. (1996). *Benefit-Cost Analysis in Environmental, Health and Safety Regulation*. Washington, DC: American Enterprise Institute.

Aubuchon, Sylvie (1999). The Health Protection Branch and Risk Management in Canada: An Overview. Unpublished paper for BAPA 501, Faculty of Commerce, University of British Columbia, March.

Auditor General of Canada (1999). Management of Food-Borne Disease Outbreak. *Report* (September). Ottawa: Auditor General of Canada.

Baladi, J.F., D. Menon, and N. Otten (1998). Use of Economic Evaluation Guidelines: 2 Years Experience in Canada. *Health Economics* 7: 221–27.

Bate, Roger (1997). *What Risk?* Oxford: Butterworth-Heinemann.

Bauer, M., ed. (1995). *Resistance to New Technology*. Cambridge: Cambridge University Press.

Bayerische, Ruck, ed. (1993). *Risk Is a Construct*. Munich: Knesebeck.

Beck, U. (1992). *Risk Society: Towards a New Modernity*. London: Sage.

Bell, Stewart (1999). Greenpeace Serves "No Public Benefit." *National Post* (June 5): A1–A2.

Bernstein, Peter L. (1996). *Against the Gods: The Remarkable Story of Risk*. New York: John Wiley.

Bord, R.J., and R.E. O'Conner (1990). Risk Communication, Knowledge, and Attitudes: Explaining Reactions to a Technology Perceived as Risky. *Risk Analysis* 10: 499–506.

Bostrom, A. et al. (1994). Evaluating Risk Communications: Completing and Correcting Mental Models of Hazardous Processes, Part 2. *Risk Analysis*: 14: 789–99.

Breyer, Stephen (1993). *Breaking the Vicious Circle: Toward Effective Risk Regulation*. Cambridge, MA: Harvard University Press.

Brody, Stuart (1997). *Sex at Risk: Lifetime Number of Partners, Frequency of Intercourse, and the LOW AIDS Risk of Vaginal Intercourse*. New Brunswick, NJ: Transaction Publishers.

Bromley, Daniel W., and Kathleen Segerson, eds. (1992). *The Social Response to Environmental Risk: Policy Formulation in an Age of Uncertainty*. Boston, MA: Kluwer Academic Publishers.

Brunk, Conrad G., L. Harworth, and B. Lee (1991). *Value Assumptions in Risk Assessment: A Case Study of the Alachlor Controversy*. Waterloo, ON: Wilfrid Laurier University.

Bucholtz, Michelle, and Mona Pirseyedi (1999). Breast Cancer Advocacy in Canada. Unpublished paper prepared to BAPA 501, Faculty of Commerce, University of British Columbia.

Bueckert, Dennis (1995). AIDS Takes Lion's Share of Research Funding. *Vancouver Sun* (December 27): A9.

Buhasz, Laszlo (1999). Going to Extremes. *Globe and Mail* (July 31): A14–A15.

Campbell, Murray (1999). Canadians' Lives Are Improving but Many Feel Insecure: Study. *Globe and Mail* (April 26): A6.

Canadian AIDS Society (1999). *HIV Transmission: Guidelines for Assessing Risk*. (Ottawa: CAIDSS.

Canadian Press (1999). Would You Buy Those Bananas if They Were Labelled "Biotech"? *Globe and Mail* (April 24): A9.

CVMA Expert Panel (1998). *Report of the Canadian Veterinary Medical Association Expert Panel on rbST, Executive Summary*. Ottawa: Health Canada. Digital document: www.hc-sc.gc.ca.

Cheney, Peter (1999). "Thrill Tax" Proposed in BC. *Globe and Mail* (March 8): A1, A2.

Chociolko, C. (1995). The Experts Disagree: A Simple Matter of Facts versus Values? *Alternatives* 21, 3 (July/August): 18–25.

Clarke, Lee (1989). *Acceptable Risk?: Making Decisions in a Toxic Environment*. Berkeley, CA: University of California Press.

Cohrssen, John J., and V.T. Covello (1989). *Risk Analysis: A Guide to Principles and Methods for Analyzing Health and Environmental Risks*. Washington, DC: US Council on Environmental Quality.

Cole, Leonard (1993). *Element of Risk: The Politics of Radon*. Washington, DC: American Association for the Advancement of Science Press.

Collenette, David (1998). Speaking Notes for a Presentation to the 16th Enhanced Safety of Vehicles Conference, Windsor (June 1). Ottawa: Department of Transport.

Consulting and Audit Canada (1995). *Benefit Cost Analysis Guide for Regulatory Programs*. Ottawa: Minister of Supply and Services Canada.

Cooper, M.G., ed. (1985). *Risk: Man-Made Hazards to Man*. Oxford: Clarendon Press.

Corelli, Rae (1995). Highway Horror Show. *Maclean's* (November 13): 62–63.

Costanza, Robert, and Laura Cornwell (1992). The 4P Approach to Dealing with Uncertainty. *Environment* 34, 9 (November): 12–20. Digital document: www.dieoff.com/page 33.htm.

Covello, V.T. (1991). Risk Comparisons and Risk Communication: Issues and Problems in Comparing Health and Environmental Risks. In Roger Kasperson and P.J. Stallen (eds.), *Communicating Risks to the Public* (Boston, MA: Kluwer Academic Publishers.

———— (1992). Trust and Credibility in Risk Communication. *Health Environment Digest* 6: 1–5.

Covello, V.T. et al., eds. (1983). *The Analysis of Actual versus Perceived Risks*. New York: Plenum.

Covello, V.T. and F. W. Allen (1988). *Seven Cardinal Rules of Risk Communication*. Washington, DC: U.S. Environmental Protection Agency OPA–87–020.

Covello, V.T., D.B. McCallum, and M.T. Pavlova (1989). Effective Risk Communication. New York: Plenum Press.

Covello, V.T., and M.W. Merkhofer (1994). *Risk Assessment Methods*. New York: Plenum Press.

Covello, V.T., and J.L. Mumpower (1985). Risk Analysis and Risk Management: A Historical Perspective. *Risk Analysis* 5: 103–20.

Covello, V.T., D. von Winterfeldt, and P. Slovic (1987). Communicating Scientific Information about Health and Environmental Risks: Problems and Opportunities from a Social and Behavioural Perspective. In V.T. Covello et al. (eds.), *Uncertainty in Risk Assessment, Risk Management and Decision Making* (New York: Plenum): 39–61.

Cross, Frank B. (1996). Paradoxical Perils of the Precautionary Principle. *Washington and Lee Law Review* 53, 3: 851–96.

Crossen, Cynthia (1996). Fright by the Numbers: Alarming Disease Data Are Frequently Flawed. *Wall Street Journal* (April 11): B1, B8.

Cumming, R.R. (1981). Is Risk Assessment a Science? *Risk Analysis* 1: 1–15.

Davies, J. Clarence, ed. (1996) Comparative Risk Analysis in the 1990s: The State of the Art. In J. Clarence Davies (ed.) *Comparing Environmental Risks: Tools for Setting Government Priorities* (Washington, DC: Resources for the Future): 1–8.

Davies, Mike (1998). *Ecology of Fear: Los Angeles and the Imagination of Disaster*. New York: Henry Holt.

Davies, T. (1994). Ranking Risks: Some Key Choices. In T. Davies (ed.), *Comparative Risk* (Washington DC: Resources for the Future).

Dickie, Mark, and Shelby Gerking (1996). Formation of Risk Beliefs, Joint Production and Willingness to Pay to Avoid Skin Cancer. *Review of Economics and Statistics* 158, 3: 451–63.

Douglas, Mary (1992). *Risk and Blame: Essays in Cultural Theory*. London: Routledge.

———— (1997). The Depoliticization of Risk. In R. J. Ellis and Michael Thompson (eds.), *Culture Matters: Essays in Honor of Aaron Wildavsky* (Boulder, CO: Westview): 121–32.

Douglas, Mary, and Aaron Wildavsky (1982). *Risk and Culture: An Essay on the Selection of Technical and Environmental Dangers*. Berkeley, CA: University of California Press.

Driedger, S.D. (1998). Browser Beware: The Web is Plagued by Misleading Medical Data. *Maclean's* (July 27): 46.

Duke, Karl, and Aaron Wildavsky (1990). Theories of Risk Perception: Who Fears What and Why? *Daedalus* 119: 41–60.

Dunlap, R.E. (1991). Trends in Public Opinion toward Environmental Issues: 1965–1990. *Society and Natural Resources* 4: 285–312.

Dyer, Gwynne (1999). Frankenstein Foods. *Globe and Mail* (February 20): D1, D5.

Easterbrook, Gregg (1995). *A Moment on the Earth: The Coming Age of Environmental Optimism*. New York: Viking/Penguin.

Easterling, D., and H. Kunreuther (1995). *The Dilemma of Siting a High Level Nuclear Waste Depository*. Boston, MA: Kluwer Academic Publishers.

Editorial (1999). Epidemic of Fear. *National Post* (July 28) A15.

Entman, R. (1993). Framing: Toward Clarification of a Fractured Paradigm. *Journal of Communication*: 43: 51–58.

Environmental Protection Agency (1987). *Unfinished Business: A Comparative Assessment of Environmental Problems*. Washington, DC: EPA, Office of Policy Analysis.

Evans, W., and P.S. Hornig (1995). Science Content and Social Context. *Public Understanding of Science* 4: 327–40.

Evenson, Brad (1999). Children Who Smoke Tend to Take Life-Threatening Risks. *National Post* (March 17): A17.

Federal Focus Inc. (1991). *Toward Common Measures*. Washington, DC: FFI.

Finkel, Adam (1990). *Confronting Uncertainty in Risk Management: A Guide for Decision-Makers*. Washington, DC: Resources for the Future.

Finkel, Adam, and Dominic Golding (1993). Alternative Paradigms: Comparative Risk Is Not the Only Model. *Environmental Protection Agency Journal* 19.

——— eds. (1994). *Worst Things First? The Debate over Risk-Based National Environmental Priorities*. Washington, DC: Resources for the Future.

Fischer, Gregory, et al. (1991). What Risks Are People Concerned about? *Risk Analysis* 11 (April): 303–14.

Fischhoff, B. (1991). Eliciting Values: Is Anything There? *American Psychologist* 46: 835–47.

——— (1994). Acceptable Risk: A Conceptual Proposal. *Risk: Health, Safety and Environment* 5: 1–28.

——— (1995). Risk Perception and Communication Unplugged: Twenty Years of Process. *Risk Analysis* 15: 137–45.

Fischhoff, B., et al. (1981a). Lay Foibles and Expert Fables in Judgments about Risks. In T.J. O'Riordan and R.K. Turner (eds.), *Progress in Resource Management and Environmental Planning* (New York: John Wiley).

Fischhoff, B., et al. (1981b) *Acceptable Risk*. Cambridge: Cambridge University Press.

Fischhoff, B., A. Bostrom, and M.J. Quadrel (1993). Risk Perception and Communication. *Annual Review of Public Health* 14: 183–203.

Fischhoff, B., S. Watson, and C. Hope (1984). Defining Risk. *Policy Sciences* 7: 123–29.

Flynn, J., P. Slovic, and C.K. Mertz (1993). The Nevada Initiative: A Risk Communication Fiasco. *Risk Analysis* 13: 497–502.

Foss, Krista (1998). Call of Danger Finds Young Men Willing to Answer. *Globe and Mail* (October 30): A4.

Foster, K.F., et al., eds. (1994) *Phantom Risk, Scientific Inference and the Law* (Cambridge, MA: MIT Press.

Fox, Bill (1999). *Spinwars, Politics and the New Media*. Toronto: Key Porter.

Fraiberg, Jeremy, and Michael J. Trebilcock (1998). Risk Regulation: Technocratic and Democratic, Tools for Regulatory Reform. *McGill Law Review* 43, 4: 835–88.

Frewer, L.J., et al. (1996). What Determines Trust in Information about Food-Related Risks? Underlying Psychological Constructs. *Risk Analysis* 16: 473–86.

Fumento, Michael (1999). Samuel Epstein: Science Meets the X-Files. *Financial Post* (May 8): D9.

Furedi, F. (1997). *Culture of Fear: Risk-Taking and the Mortality of Low Expectations*. London: Cassell.

Garrick, B. John, and W.C. Gekler, eds. (1991). *The Analysis, Communication and Perception of Risk*. New York: Plenum.

Gilroy, J.M., ed. (1993). *Environmental Risk, Environmental Values and Political Choices: Beyond Efficiency Tradeoffs in Public Policy Analysis*. Boulder, CO: Westview.

Glassner, Barry (1999). *The Culture of Fear: Why Americans Are afraid of the Wrong Things*. New York: Basic Books.

Glickman, T.S., and M. Gough, eds. (1990) *Readings in Risk*. Washington, DC, Resources for the Future.

Glickman, Theordore, et al. (1992). Acts of God and Acts of Man. Washington, DC: Resources for the Future.

Gordon, C. (1991). Governmental Rationality: An Introduction. In G. Burchell et al., (eds.), *The Foucault Effect: Studies in Governability* (Chicago: University of Chicago Press): 1–51.

Gori, Gio B., and John C. Luik (1999). *Passive Smoke: The EPA's Betrayal of Science*. Vancouver, BC: The Fraser Institute.

Gots, Ronald E. (1993). *Toxic Risks: Science, Regulation, and Perception*. Boca Raton, FL: Lewis.

Grabowski, Henry, and John Vernon (1977). Consumer Product Safety Commission. *American Economic Review* 68, 2: 284–89.

Graham, John D. (1996) Making Sense of Risk: An Agenda for Congress. In Robert W. Hahn (ed.), *Risks, Costs and Lives Saved* (New York: Oxford University Press: 183–207.

Graham, John D., and Lorenz Rhomberg (1996). How Risks Are Identified and Assessed. *The Annals of the American Academy of Political and Social Science* 545: 15–24.

Graham, John D., and J.B. Weiner (1995). Confronting Risk Tradeoffs. In John D. Graham and J.B. Weiner (eds.), *Risk versus Risk: Tradeoffs in Protecting Health and the Environment*. Cambridge: Harvard University Press: 1–41.

Graham, John D., et al. (1994). Harvard Life Saving Study. Cambridge, MA: Harvard School of Public Health, Centre for Risk Analysis.

Gratt, Lawrence B. (1996). *Air: Toxic Risk Assessment and Management*. New York: Van Nostrand Reinhold.

Gray, John (1998). Hot-Selling [Personal Water] Craft Hits Reef of Noise, Safety Concerns. *Globe and Mail* (August 3):A1, A4.

Gray, P.C.R., et al., eds. (1998). *Communicating about Risks to Environment and Health in Europe*. Boston: Kluwer Academic Publishers.

Grima, A.P., C.D. Fowle, and R.E. Munn, eds. (1992). *Risk Perspectives on Environmental Impact Assessment*. Toronto: University of Toronto.

Gross, Paul, and Norman Levitt (1994). *Higher Superstitions: The Academic Left and Its Quarrel With Science*. Baltimore, MD: Johns Hopkins University Press.

Grudotti, T. (1994). A Process to Set Priorities in Environmental Risks to Health. Ottawa: Federal-Provincial Committee on Environmental and Occupational Health.

Gutteling, J.M., and O. Wiegman (1996). *Exploring Risk Communication*. Boston, MA: Kluwer Academic Publishers.

Hacking, I. (1990). *The Taming of Chance*. Cambridge: Cambridge University Press.

Hadden, Susan G., ed. (1984). *Risk Analysis, Institutions, and Public Policy*. Port Washington, New York: Associated Faculty Press.

Hahn, Robert W. (1994). Regulation: Past, Present and Future. *Harvard Journal of Law and Public Policy* 13: 167–229.

—— (1996). Regulatory Reform: What Do the Government's Numbers Tell Us? In Robert W. Hahn (ed.), *Risks, Costs and Lives Saved: Getting Better Results from Regulation*. (New York: Oxford University Press): 208–53.

Hahn, R.W., and R.E. Litan (1997). *Improving Regulatory Accountability*. Washington, DC: Brookings and AEI.

Hall, Stephen S. (1999). Fear Itself. *New York Times Magazine* (February 28) : 42–47, 69–72, 88–90.

Hallenback, W.H. (1993). *Quantitative Risk Assessment for Environmental and Occupational Health*. Boca Raton, FL: Lewis.

Harrison, Kathryn, and George Hoberg (1994). *Risk, Science, and Politics: Regulating Toxic Substances in Canada and the United States*. Montreal: McGill-Queen's University Press.

Harvard Group on Risk Management Reform (1995). Reform of Risk Regulation: Achieving More Protection at Less Cost. Boston, MA: Centre for Risk Analysis, Harvard School of Public Health.

Hazilla, Michael, and R.J. Kopp (1990). The Social Cost of Environmental Quality Regulations: A General Equilibrium Analysis. *Journal of Political Economy* 98: 853–73.

Health Canada (1993). *Health Risk Determination*. Ottawa: Health Canada.

—— (1998a). *Health Protection for the 21st Century: Renewing the Federal Health Protection Branch, A Discussion Paper*. Ottawa: Minister of Public Works and Government Services Canada.

—— (1998b). *Shared Responsibilities, Shared Vision: Renewing the Federal Health Protection Legislation*. Ottawa: Minister of Public Works and Government Services Canada.

—— (1999a). Health Canada Rejects Bovine Growth Hormone in Canada. *News Release* (January 14).

————— (1999b). *National Consultations: Summary Report re Renewal of the Federal Health Protection Legislation*. Ottawa: Minister of Public Works and Government Services Canada.

Health and Safety Executive (1992). *The Tolerability of Risk from Nuclear Power Stations*. London: HSE.

Health Protection Branch (1998). Terms of Reference of the Science Advisory Board. Ottawa: Health Canada.

————— (1999). *Revised Description—Risk Management Framework*. Unpublished paper (March 25). Ottawa: Health Canada.

Henderson, Michael (1987). *Living with Risk*. Chichester: John Wiley & Sons.

Heubner, Stephen, and Kenneth Chilton (1998). *Questioning the Emphasis on Environmental Contaminants as a Significant Threat to Children's Health*. Policy Study 149 (November). St. Louis, MO: Centre for the Study of American Business.

Hird, John A. (1991). The Political Economy of Pork. *American Political Science Review* 85: 529–56.

Hohenemser, Christoph, and Jeanne X. Kasperson, eds. (1982). *Risk in the Technological Society*. Boulder, CO: Westview.

Hornig, S. (1993). Reading Risk: Public Response to Print Media Accounts of Technological Risk. *Public Understanding of Science* 2: 95–109.

Howard, Ronald A. (1984). On Fates Comparable to Death. *Management Science* 30, 4 (April): 407–21.

Huber, Peter W. (1984). The Market for Risk. *Regulation* (AEI) (March/April): 33–41.

————— (1991). *Galileo's Revenge: Junk Science in the Court Room*. New York: Basic Books.

Hume, Mark (2000). Extreme Measures Need to Reach Out-of-Bounds Snowboarders. *National Post* (March 29): A3.

Hutchings, J.A., et al. (1997). Is Scientific Inquiry Incompatible with Government Information Control? *Canadian Journal of Fisheries and Aquatic Sciences* 54: 1198–2014.

Imperato, Pascal J., and Greg Mitchell (1985). *Acceptable Risks*. New York: Viking Penguin.

Iyengar, S. (1991). *Is Anyone Responsible? How Television Frames Political Issues*. Chicago: University of Chicago Press.

Jasanoff, Sheila (1986). *Risk Management and Political Culture: A Comparative Study of Science In the Policy Context*. New York: Russell Sage Foundation.

————— (1993). Bridging the Two Cultures of Risk Analysis. *Risk Analysis* 13: 123–29.

Johnson, B.B., and V.T. Covello, eds. (1987). *The Social and Cultural Construction of Risk*. New York: Reidel.

Johnson, Diane (1999). France and Frankenfoods. *Globe and Mail* (August 7): D8.

Jouhar, A.J., ed. (1984). *Risk in Society: Proceedings of the First International Risk Seminar*. London: John Libbey.

Jungerman, H. (1997). When You Can't Do It Right: Ethical Dilemmas of Informing People about Risks. *Risk Decision and Policy* 2, 2: 131–45.

Kahneman, D., P. Slovic, and A. Tversky (1982). *Judgment under Uncertainty: Heuristics and Biases*. New York: Cambridge University Press.

Kasperson, Roger E., and Jeanne X. Kasperson (1983). Determining the Acceptability of Risks: Ethical and Policy Issues. In J.T. Rogers and D.V. Bates (eds.), *Risk: A Symposium on the Assessment and Perception of Risk to Human Health in Canada*, October 18 and 19, 1982 . . . Proceedings (Ottawa: Royal Society of Canada): 135–55.

Kasperson, R., et al. (1988). The Social Amplification of Risk. *Risk Analysis 8*, 2: 177–87.

Kasperson, R., and P.J.M. Stallen, eds. (1991). *Communicating Risks to the Public*. Boston: Kluwer.

Kasperson, R.E., and J.X. Kasperson (1996). The Social Amplification of Risk. *The Annals of the American Academy of Political and Social Science 545*: 95–105.

Kates, Robert W., Christoph Hohensemser, and Jeanne X. Kasperson, eds. (1985). *Perilous Progress: Managing the Hazards of Technology*. Boulder, CO: Westview.

Kedrovsky, Paul (1999). BC's Rescue Tax Has Its Own Economic and Moral Hazards. *Financial Post* (March 9): C7.

Keeney, Ralph L. (1984). Ethics, Decision Analysis, and Public Risks. *Risk Analysis 4*: 117–29.

——— (1990). Mortality Risks Induced by Economic Expenditures. *Risk Analysis 10*, 1: 147–59.

——— (1992). *Value-Focused Thinking: A Path to Creative Decision-Making*. Cambridge, MA: Harvard University Press.

——— (1994). Decisions about Life-Threatening Risks. *New England Journal of Medicine* (July 21): 193–96.

——— (1996). The Role of Values in Risk Management. *The Annals of the American Academy of Political and Social Science 545*: 126–34.

Kennedy, Mark (1999). Ottawa Slows Health Rules Overhaul. *Vancouver Sun* (July 5): A5.

Kleck, Gary (1998). What Are the Risks and Benefits of Keeping a Gun in the Home? *Journal of the American Medical Association 280*, 5: 473–75.

Konheim, C.S. (1988). Risk Communication in the Real World. *Risk Analysis 8*: 367–73.

Kraus, N., et al. (1992). Intuitive Toxicology: Expert and Lay Judgments of Chemical Risks. *Risk Analysis 12*, 2: 83–93.

Krauthammer, Charles (1999). Why Bogus Science Is Such a Headache. *National Post* (June 28): A14.

Kravis, Marie-Josee (1999). Genetically Modified Food a Looming Threat to Trade Talks. *Financial Post* (July 16): C7.

Kunreuther, H., and P. Slovic, eds. (1996). *New Directions in Risk Management*. Special issue, *The Annals of the American Academy of Political and Social Science 545* (May).

Kurtz, Howard (1998). *Spin Cycle: How the White House and the Media Manipulate the News*. New York: Touchstone/Simon and Schuster.

Laudan, Larry (1994). *The Book of Risks: Fascinating Facts about the Chances We Take Every Day*. New York: John Wiley & Sons.

———— (1997). *Danger Ahead: The Risks You* Really *Face on Life's Highway*. New York: John Wiley & Sons.

Lave, L., G. Morgan, B. Fischhoff, and P. Fischbeck (1994). *A Procedure for Risk Rating for Federal Risk Management Agencies*. Pittsburgh, : Carnegie Mellon University.

Lave, Lester B., ed. (1982). *Quantitative Risk Assessment in Regulation*. Washington, DC: The Brookings Institution.

———— (1996). Benefit Cost Analysis: Do the Benefits Exceed the Costs? In Robert W. Hahn (ed.), *Risks, Costs, and Lives Saved* (New York: Oxford University Press): 104–34.

Lawson, J.J. (1980). The Costs of Road Accidents and their Application in Economic Evaluation of Safety Programmes. *Roads and Transportation Association of Canada* (Forum 1) 2, 4: 53–63.

Le Gault, Michael (1999). Greenpeace's Medical Scare. *Financial Post* (April 10): D7.

Leiss, William (1995). "Down and Dirty": The Use and Abuse of Public Trust in Risk Communication. *Risk Analysis* 15, 6: 685–92.

———— (2000). Between Expertise and Bureaucracy: Risk Management Trapped at the Science Policy Interface. In G. Bruce Doern and Ted Reed (eds.), *Risky Business: Canada's Changing Science Based Policy and Regulatory Regime* (Toronto: University of Toronto Press): 49–74.

Leiss, William, and Christina Chociolko (1994). *Risk and Responsibility*. Montreal: McGill-Queen's Press.

Leonard, H.B., and R.J. Zeckhauser (1986). Cost-Benefit Analysis Applied to Risks: Its Philosophy and Legitimately. In Douglas Maclean (ed.), *Values at Risk* (Toronto: Rowman & Allan).

Lewis, Marlo (1997). Precautionary Petard. Digital document: www.cei.org/update/0697-ml.html.

Lind, N.C., ed. (1982). Technological Risk. *Proceedings of a Symposium on Risk in New Technologies* (December 15, 1981). Waterloo, ON: University of Waterloo Press.

Lindblim, C.E. (1959). The Science of "Muddling Through." *Public Administration Review* 19 (Spring): 79–88.

Lindquist, Evert A. (1998). Getting Results Right: Reforming Ottawa's Estimates. In Leslie A. Pal (ed.), *How Ottawa Spends, 1998–99: Balancing Act: The Post-Deficit Mandate* (Toronto: Oxford University Press): 153–90.

Litan, Robert E., and William D. Nordhaus (1983). *Reforming Federal Regulation*. New Haven, CT: Yale University Press.

Lutter, Randall, and J.F. Morrall (1994). Health and Health Analysis: A New Way to Evaluate Health and Safety Regulation. *Journal of Risk and Uncertainty* 8: 43–66.

Lund, Niels (1995). Policy Goals for Health and Safety. *Risk Analysis* 16: 639–50.

Lundgren, Regina (1994). *Risk Communications: A Handbook for Communicating Environmental, Safety and Health Risks*. Columbus, OH: Battelle Press.

MacCrimmon, K.R., and D.A. Wehrung with W.T. Stanbury (1986). *Taking Risks: The Management of Uncertainty*. New York: The Free Press.

MacLean, Douglas, ed. (1986). *Values at Risk*. Totwa: Rowman & Allanheld.

MacQueen, Ken (1999). We're So Afraid. *Vancouver Sun* (July 31): H1–H2.

McDaniels, Timothy L., et al. (1992). Risk Perception and the Value of Safety. *Risk Analysis* 12 (August): 495–503.

McIlroy, Anne (1999a). Delays in Hep C Compensation Ongoing Heartache for Victims. *Globe and Mail* (March 25): A2.

——— (1999b). Life Expectancy for Canadians Reaches New High. *Globe and Mail* (September 17): A1, A3.

McQuaid, Jim, and J.-M. Le Guen (1998). The Use of Risk Assessment in Government. In R.E. Hester and R.M. Harrison (eds.), *Risk Assessment and Risk Management* (Cambridge: Royal Society of Chemistry): 21–36.

Mallet, Gina (1996). The Politics of Breast Cancer. *Globe and Mail* (October 26): D1, D3.

Margolis, Howard (1997). What's Special about Cancer? In R. J. Ellis and Michael Thompson (eds.), *Culture Matters: Essays in Honor of Aaron Wildavsky* (Boulder, CO: Westview): 133–48.

Menashe, C.L., and M. Siegel (1998). The Power of a Frame: An Analysis of Newspaper Coverage of Tobacco Issues—United States, 1985-1996. *Journal of Health Communication* 3: 307–25.

Menon, D., F. Schubert, and G.W. Torrance (1996). Canada's New Guidelines for the Economic Evaluation of Pharmaceuticals. *Medical Care* 34: D577–D586.

Mertz, C.K., et al. (1998). Judgments of Chemical Risks: Comparisons among Senior Managers, Toxicologists, and the Public. *Risk Analysis* 18, 4: 391–404.

Michaels, Patrick (1992), *Sound and Fury: the Science and Politics of Global Warming*. Washington, DC: Cato Institute.

Mihlar, Fazil (1997). *Federal Regulatory Reform: Rhetoric or Reality?* Public Policy Sources 6. Vancouver, BC: The Fraser Institute.

Milloy, Steven (2000). Unreasonable Precautions. *Financial Post* (February 7): C7.

Minard, R.A., Jr. (1996). CRA [Comparative Risk Assessment] and the States: History, Politics and Results. In J. Clarence Davies (ed.), *Comparing Environmental Risks* (Washington, DC: Resources for the Future): 23–61.

Moffet, John (1996). Environmental Priority Setting Based on Comparative Risk and Public Input. *Canadian Public Administration* 39, 3: 362–85.

Molak, Vlaska, ed. (1996). *Fundamentals of Risk Analysis and Risk Management*. London: Lewis.

Moore, Elizabeth, and Grace Skogstad (1998). Food for Thought: Food Inspection and Renewed Federalism. In Leslie A. Pal (ed.), *How Ottawa Spends, 1998–99: Balancing Act: The Post-Deficit Mandate* (Toronto: Oxford University Press): 127–51.

Moore, Rachel, Yang Mav, Jun Zhang, and Kathy Clarke (1998). *Economic Burden of Illness in Canada, 1993*. Ottawa: Health Canada, Laboratory Centre for Disease Control.

Morgan, M. Granger, Baruch Fischhoff, Lester Lave, and Paul Fischbeck (1996). A Proposal for Ranking Risk within Federal Agencies. In J. Clarence Davies (ed.), *Comparing Environmental Risks* (Washington, DC: Resources for the Future): 111–47.

Morgan, M.G., B. Fischhoff and A. Bostrom, L. Lave, and C.J. Altman (1992). Communicating Risk to the Public. *Environmental Science and Technology* 26: 2048–56.

Morgan, M. Granger (1993). Risk Analysis and Management. *Scientific American* 269, 1 (July): 32–36.

Morgan, M. Granger, and Max Henrion (1992). *Uncertainty: A Guide to Dealing With Uncertainty in Quantitative Risk and Policy Analysis.* New York: Cambridge University Press.

Morrison, Kate, and Lydia Miljan (1996). Cheese, Politics and Human Health: How the Media Failed to Critique Government Policy. *On Balance* 9, 5 (May): 1–5, 7. Vancouver, BC: The Fraser Institute.

Munroe, Margaret (1999). Modified Crop Debate Just Got More Confusing. *Financial Post* (August 5): A17.

National Academy of Sciences (1983). *Risk Assessment in the Federal Government: Managing the Process.* Washington, DC: National Academy Press.

National Cancer Institute of Canada (1998). *Canadian Cancer Statistics, 1998.* Toronto: NCIC.

National Research Council (1989). *Improving Risk Communication.* Washington, DC: US Government Printing Office.

Neal, Mark (1999). The Rise of Anti-Risk Activism. Unpublished paper presented to the Fraser Institute's conference, Junk Science, Junk Policy: Managing Risk and Regulation, Ottawa, April 29.

Neal, Mark, and J.C.H. Davies (1998). *The Corporation under Siege: Exposing the Devices Used by Activists and Regulators in the Non-Risk Society.* London: SAU).

Nelkin, Dorothy, ed. (1985). *The Language of Risk.* Beverly Hills, CA: Sage.

——— (1989). Communicating Technological Risk: The Social Construction of Risk Perception. *Annual Review of Public Health* 10: 95–113.

Nemetz, Peter N, W.T. Stanbury, and Fred Thompson (1986). Social Regulation in Canada: An Overview and Comparison with the American Model. *Policy Studies Journal* 14, 4 (June) 580–603.

Nephin Consulting Partners (1998). *Pest Management Regulatory Agency Benchmarking Study.* Study prepared for Health Canada (September).

Neumann, Peter J. (1999). Explaining the Reluctance to Use Cost-Effectiveness Analysis in Regulatory Decision Making. Unpublished paper presented to the Fraser Institute's conference, Junk Science, Junk Policy: Managing Risk and Regulation, Ottawa, April 29.

Nichols, A., and R.J. Zeckhauser (1986). The Perils of Prudence: How Conservative Risk Assessments Distort Regulation. *Regulation* 10, 2: 13–24.

Nielsen, Karsten D. (1999). Success or Failure? An Analysis of Greenpeace's Influence on Environmental Politics in Denmark. Unpublished paper for BAPA 501, Faculty of Commerce, University of British Columbia.

Noll, Roger (1996). Reforming Risk Regulation. *The Annals of the American Academy of Political and Social Science* 545: 167–75.

Office of Management and Budget (1992). Circular A94: Guidelines and Discount Rates for Benefit-Cost Analysis of Federal Programs (October 29). Washington, DC: OMB.

Oi, Walter (1977). Safety at Any Price? *Regulation* (AEI) (November/December): 16–23.

Omenn, G.S. (1996). Putting Environmental Risks in a Public Health Context. *Public Health Reports* 111: 514–16.

Oriellet, Eric (1995). Organizational Analysis and Environmental Sociology: The Case of Greenpeace Canada. In M.D. Mehta and C.E. Ouellet (eds.), *Environmental Sociology* (North York, ON: Captus): 321–38.

Ostry, Sylvia, and W.T. Stanbury (1999). The Economic Council on Regulatory Reform: Reprise and Retrospection. In R.M. Bird, M.J. Trebilcock, and T.A. Wilson (eds.), *Rationality in Public Policy: Retrospect and Prospect, a Tribute to Douglas G. Hartle* (Toronto: Canadian Tax Foundation): 181–231.

Otway, Harry (1987). Experts, Risk Communication and Democracy. *Risk Analysis* 7, 2: 125–29.

Otway, Harry, and Detlof von Winterfeldt (1992). Expert Judgment in Risk Analysis and Management: Process, Context, and Pitfalls. *Risk Analysis* 12, 1: 83–93.

Patton, D.E. (1994). The NAS Risk Paradigm as a Medium for Communication. *Risk Analysis* 14: 375–78.

Performance Management Network Inc. (1999). Review of Canadian Best Practices in Risk Management: Summary of Findings (April 26). Study produced for the Treasury Board of Canada Secretariat.

Perrow, Charles (1984). *Normal Accidents*. New York: Basic Books.

Peters, R.G., V.T. Covello, and D.B. McCallum (1997). The Determinants of Trust and Credibility in Environmental Risk Communication: An Empirical Study. *Risk Analysis* 17: 43–54.

Pollak, Robert A. (1996). Government Risk Regulation. *The Annals of the American Academy of Political and Social Science* 545: 25–34.

Powell, Douglas (1998). An Introduction to Risk Communication and the Perception of Risk. Digital document: www.plant.uoguelph.ca/riskcomm.

——— (1999). Sierra Club's Food Scare Ignores the Real Risks. *Financial Post* (July 14): C7.

Powell, Douglas, and William Leiss (1997). *Mad Cows and Mother's Milk: The Perils of Poor Risk Communication*. Montreal & Kingston: McGill-Queen's Press.

Presidential/Congressional Commission on Risk Assessment and Risk Management (1997). *Final Report: Framework for Environmental Health Risk Management, Vol. 1*. Washington, DC: P/CCRARM. Digital document: www.riskworld.com/Nreports.

Priest, Margot, and Aron Wohl (1980). The Growth of Federal and Provincial Regulation of Economic Activity, 1867–1978. In W.T. Stanbury (ed.), *Government Regulation: Scope, Growth, Process* (Montreal: The Institute for Research on Public Policy): 69–150.

Rees, Joseph (1994). *Hostage of Each Other: The Transformation of Nuclear Safety since Three Mile Island*. Chicago: University of Chicago Press.

Regulatory Affairs Directorate (1995). *Regulatory Policy, 1995* (November). Ottawa: RAD/Treasury Board Secretariat.

Rescher, Nicholas (1983). *Risk: A Philosophical Introduction to the Theory of Risk Evaluation and Management*. Washington, DC: University Press of America.

Rhodes, Richard (1997). *Deadly Feasts: Tracing the Secrets of a Terrifying New Plague* [Mad Cow disease]. New York: Simon & Schuster.

Ricci, P.F., L.A. Sagan, and C.G. Whipple, eds. (1984). *Technological Risk Assessment*. The Hague, Netherlands: Martinus Nijhoff Publishers.

Rice, Bonnie (1995). *Polyvinyl Chloride (PVC) Plastic: Primary Contributor to the Global Dioxin Crisis.* Distributed by Greenpeace.

Roberts, Lewis, and Albert Weale, eds. (1991). *Innovation and Environmental Risk.* London: Belhaven.

Robertson, Susan, and Chris Jones (1999). Romance and Death in the Saddle. *National Post* (September 21): A3.

Rodricks, J., and M.R. Taylor (1990). Application of Risk Assessment to Food Safety Decision Making. In Glickman, T.S., and M. Gough, eds. (1990) *Readings in Risk.* Washington, DC, Resources for the Future: 143–53.

Rodricks, J.V. (1992). *Calculated Risks.* Cambridge: Cambridge University Press.

Rollin, Bernard E. (1995). *The Frankenstein Syndrome: Ethical and Social Issues in the Genetic Engineering of Animals.* New York: Cambridge University Press.

Ross, Emma (1999). Birth-Control Pill Passes Long Term Safety Test. *Globe and Mail* (January 8): A1. [Pill introduced in 1961! Over 300 million have used the pill: 25-year study of 46,000 British women].

Roth, E., M.G. Morgan, B. Fischhoff, L. Lane, and A. Bostrom (1990). What Do We Know about Making Risk Comparisons? *Risk Analysis* 10: 375–87.

Rowland, Anthony J., and Paul Cooper (1983). *Environment and Health.* London: Edward Arnold.

Royal College of Physicians and Surgeons of Canada Expert Panel (1999). *Report of the rbST Human Safety Panel.* Ottawa: Health Canada. Digital document: www.hc-sc.gc.ca (Health Canada).

Royal Society of Canada (1998). Expert Panel on Potential Health Risks of Radio-Frequency Fields from Wireless Telecommunication Devices. Digital document: www.rsc.ca/english/aug-98-new.htm.

Ruckelshaus, W.D. (1984). Risk in a Free Society. *Risk Analysis* 4: 157–65.

Salter, Liora (1988). *Mandated Science.* Boston: Kluwer Academic Publishers.

Sandman, Peter (1986). *Explaining Environmental Risk.* Washington, DC: US Environmental Protection Agency, Office of Toxic Substances.

——— (1987). Risk Communication: Facing Public Outrage. *EPA Journal* 13: 21.

Schoffield, Heather (2000). Health Protection Branch to Upgrade Battered Reputation. *Globe and Mail* (April 18): A4.

Schon, D.A., and M. Rein (1994). *Frame Reflection: Toward the Resolution of Intractable Policy Controversies.* New York: Basic Books.

Schwing, Richard C., and Walter A. Albers, Jr., eds. (1980). *Societal Risk Assessment: How Safe is Safe Enough?* New York: Plenum.

Science Advisory Board (1991). *Reducing Risk: Setting Priorities and Strategies for Environmental Protection.* Washington, DC: Environmental Protection Agency.

Shabecoff, Philip (1993). *A Fierce Green Fire: the American Environmental Movement.* New York: Hill and Wang.

Shaw, D.L., and S.E. Martin (1992). The Function of Mass Media Agenda Setting. *Journalism Quarterly* 69, 4: 909–20.

Shrader-Frechette, K.S. (1991). *Risk and Rationality: Philosophical Foundations for Populist Reform.* Berkeley: University of California Press.

Silbergeld, E.K. (1993). Risk Assessment: The Perspective and Experience of US Environmentalists. *Environmental Health Perspectives* 101, 2: 100–04.

Singer, Eleanor, and P.M. Endreny (1993). *Reporting on Risk*. New York: Russell Sage Foundation.

Singleton, W.T., and Jan Hovden, eds. (1987). *Risk and Decisions*. Chichester: John Wiley & Sons.

Sjoberg, Lennart, ed. (1987). *Risk and Society: Studies of Risk Generation and Reactions to Risk*. London: Allen & Unwin.

Skolnick, Susan A. (1985). *Book of Risks*. Bethesda, MD: National.

Slovic, P. (1987). Perception of Risk. *Science* 238 (April 17): 280–286.

——— (1992). Perception of Risk: Reflections on the Psychometric Paradigm. In S. Krimsky and D. Golding (eds.), *Social Theories of Risk* (Westport, CT: Praeger): 117–52.

——— (1993). Perceived Risk, Trust and Democracy. *Risk Analysis* 13, 6 (December).

——— (1999). Trust, Emotion, Sex, Politics and Science: Surveying the Risk Assessment Battlefield. *Risk Analysis* 17, 4: 689–701.

Slovic, P., et al. (1985a). Characterizing Perceived Risk. In R.W. Kates et al. (eds.), *Perilous Progress: Managing the Hazards of Technology*. (Boulder, CO: Westview).

Slovic, P., et al. (1985b). Regulation of Risk: A Psychological Perspective. In R.G. Noll (ed.), *Regulatory Policy and the Social Sciences* (Los Angeles: University of California Press).

Slovic, P., B. Fischhoff, and S. Lichtenstein (1979). Rating the Risks. *Environment* 21, 3: 14–20; 36–39.

——— (1982). Why Study Risk Perception. *Risk Analysis* 2: 83–91.

Slovic, P., J. Flynn, C.K. Mertz, and L. Mullican (1993). *Health Risk Perception in Canada*. Ottawa: Health Canada.

Slovic P., N. Kraus, and V.T. Covello (1990). What *Should* We Know about Making Risk Comparisons? *Risk Analysis* 10, 3: 389–92.

SmartRisk Foundation (1998). *The Economic Burden of Unintentional Injury in Canada*. Toronto: SmartRisk Foundation.

Smith, Willie (1997). Review of Expert Panels for Provision of Scientific and Technological Advice for Development of Public Policy (May). Auckland, NZ: Ministry of Research, Science and Technology.

Sparks, P., and R. Shepherd (1994). Public Perceptions of the Potential Hazards Associated with Food Production and Food Consumption: An Empirical Study. *Risk Analysis* 14: 799–806.

Sprent, Peter (1988). *Taking Risks: The Science of Uncertainty*. London: Penguin.

Stanbury, W.T. (1992) *Reforming the Federal Regulatory Process in Canada, 1971–1992* (*Minutes of Proceedings and Evidence* of the Subcommittee on Regulations and Competitiveness of the House of Commons Standing Committee on Finance, Issue 23, November 17 – December 10): A1–A293.

Stanbury, W.T. (1999). Anticipating the Impact of Environmental Interest Groups on the Future of the BC Forest Industry. Paper presented to the Northern Forest Products Association Annual Convention, Prince George, April 9.

Stanbury, W.T. (2000a). Setting the Context for Risk Management by Government. Unpublished paper presented to the 14th BC Towboat Industry

Conference (April 15), sponsored by the Council of Marine Canners. Empress Hotel, Victoria, British Columbia.

———, with Elaine Atsalakis, Dian Choi, Vivian Lau, Tammy Lee, Sindy Li, Olivia Tsang (2000b). Much Ado about (Almost) Nothing: Greenpeace and the Allegedly Toxic Teethers. This volume.

Starr, C. (1969). Social Benefit versus Technical Risk. *Science* 165: 1232–38.

Statistics Canada (1996). *Causes of Death, 1994*. Cat. No. 84-208-XPB (June). Ottawa: Statistics Canada.

Strauss, Stephen (1995). Risk-Free World within Reach, Canadians Say. *Globe and Mail* (April 26): A1, A3.

Sub-Committee on Regulations and Competitiveness (1993). Regulations and Competitiveness, Seventeenth Report of the Standing Committee on Finance, First Report of the Sub-Committee (January). Ottawa: Supply and Services Canada.

Tannen, D., ed. (1993). *Framing in Discourse*. New York: Oxford University Press.

Tengs, Tammy O., et al. (1995). Five-hundred Life-Saving Interventions and Their Cost Effectiveness. *Risk Analysis* 15: 369–90.

Tengs, T.O., and J.D. Graham (1996). The Opportunity Costs of Haphazard Social Investments in Life Saving. In R.W. Kahn (ed.), *Risk Costs and Lives Saved* (New York: Oxford University Press): 167–82.

Thomas, Simon P., and Steve E. Hrudey (1997). *Risk of Death in Canada: What We Know and How We Know It*. Edmonton, AB: University of Alberta Press.

Transport Canada (1985). *Analysis of the Effects of Proposed Regulation: Centre High-Mounted Stop Lamps* (July). Ottawa: Transport Canada.

——— (1986a). *Analysis of a Proposed Regulation Requiring Daytime Running Lights for Motor Vehicles* (June). Ottawa: Transport Canada.

——— (1986b). *Background Paper on Motor Vehicle Occupant Protection in Canada* (November). Ottawa: Transport Canada.

——— (1994). *Guide to Benefit-Cost Analysis in Transport Canada* (September). TP11875E. Ottawa: Transport Canada.

——— (1998). *Canadian Motor Vehicle Traffic Collision Statistics 1997*. Ottawa: Transport Canada.

Treasury Board Secretariat (1998). Getting Science Right in the Public Sector (Working Draft). Ottawa: TBS, Research and Analyses, Public Affairs.

Tversky, A., and D. Kahneman (1981). The Framing of Decisions and the Psychology of Choice. *Science* 211: 453–58.

United States, National Research Council (1996). *Understanding Risk: Informing Decisions in a Democratic Society*. Washington, DC: National Academy Press.

Urquhart, John, and Klaus Heilmann (1984). *Risk Watch: The Odds of Life*. New York: Facts on File.

VanderZwaag, David (1996). CEPA and the Precautionary Principle. Ottawa: Environment Canada.

Vaughan, Elaine, and Marianne Seifert (1992). Variability in the Framing of Risk Issues. *Journal of Social Issues* 48, 4: 119–35.

Vertzberger, Y.I. (1998). *Risk Taking and Decision-Making: Foreign Military Intervention Decisions* (Stanford, CA: Stanford University Press.

Viscusi, W. Kip (1990). Sources of Inconsistency in Societal Responses to Health Risks. *American Economic Review* 80, 2: 257–61.

—— (1992). *Fatal Trade-offs: Public and Private Responsibility for Risk.* New York: Oxford University Press.

—— (1995). Second Hand Smoke: Facts and Fantasy. *Regulation* 3: 42–45.

—— (1996). Economic Foundations of the Current Regulatory Reform Efforts. *Journal of Economic Perspectives* 10: 119–30.

—— (1996). The Dangers of Unbounded Commitments to Regulate Risk. In Robert W. Hahn (ed.), *Risks, Costs, and Lives Saved* (New York/Washington: Oxford University Press/AEI Press): 135–66.

Viscusi, W. Kip, and Richard Zeckhauser (1996). Hazard Communication: Warnings and Risk. In *Annals of the American Academy of Political and Social Science* 545: 106–15.

Warner, Sir Frederick, ed. (1992). *Risk Analysis, Perception and Management.* London: Royal Society.

Weinstein, N.D., and P.M. Sandman (1993). Some Criteria for Evaluating Risk Messages. *Risk Analysis* 13: 103–14.

Whelan, Elizabeth M. (1996). Our "Stolen Future" and the Precautionary Principle. *Priorities* 8: 3–5.

Whipple, Chris, and Vincent T. Covello, eds. (1985). *Risk Analysis in the Private Sector.* New York: Plenum.

Wildavsky, Aaron (1979). No Risk Is the Highest Risk of All. *American Scientist* 67, 1: 32–37. Also in Glickman, T.S., and M. Gough, eds. (1990) *Readings in Risk* (Washington, DC, Resources for the Future): 120–27.

—— (1986). Richer Is Safer. *The Public Interest* 60: 23–39.

—— (1988). *Searching for Safety.* New Brunswick, NJ: Transaction Publishers.

—— (1995). *But Is It True?* Cambridge, MA: Harvard University Press.

Wilde, Gerald J.S. (1994). *Target Risk.* Toronto: PDE Publications.

Wilkins, Kathryn, et al. (1997). Multiple Causes of Death. *Health Reports* 9, 2 (Autumn): 19–29.

Wilkins, Kathryn (1995). Causes of Death: How the Sexes Differ. *Health Reports* 7, 2: 7–16.

Wilson, R., and E.A.C. Crouch (1987). Risk Assessment and Comparisons: An Introduction. *Science* 236: 267–70.

Wilson, Richard (1979). Analyzing the Daily Risks of Life. *Technology Review* 81, 4: 41–46.

Winston, Clifford (1993). Economic Deregulation: Days of Reckoning for Microeconomists. *Journal of Economic Literature* 31: 1263–89.

Wolf, I.D. (1992). Critical Issues in Food Safety, 1991–2001. *Food Technology* 46, 1: 64–70.

Wright, Susan (1994). *Molecular Politics: Developing American and British Regulatory Policy for Genetic Engineering, 1972–1982.* Chicago: University of Chicago Press.

Zechendorf, B. (1994). What the Public Think about Biotechnology. *Biotechnology* 12: 870–75.

Zeckhauser, R.J., and W. Kip Viscusi (1990). Risk within Reason. *Science* 238: 559–64.